Taking Back the Streets

Taking Back
the Streets

Women, Youth, and Direct Democracy

Temma Kaplan

UNIVERSITY OF CALIFORNIA PRESS
Berkeley · Los Angeles · London

Portions of the prologue and chapter 1 were previously
published in "Reversing the Shame and Gendering the
Memory," in *Signs* vol. 28, no. 1 (autumn 2003):
179–99. © 2003 by The University of Chicago. All
rights reserved.

University of California Press
Berkeley and Los Angeles, California

University of California Press, Ltd.
London, England

Library of Congress Cataloging-in-Publication Data

Kaplan, Temma, 1942–.

   Taking back the streets : women, youth, and direct
democracy / Temma Kaplan.

        p.   cm.

Includes index.

        ISBN 0-520-22671-2 (cloth : alk. paper) —
ISBN 0-520-23649-1 (pbk. : alk. paper)

   1. Women in politics—Chile.   2. Women in politics—
Argentina.   3. Women in politics—Spain.   4. Youth—
Chile—Political activity.   5. Youth—Argentina—Polit-
ical activity.   6. Youth—Spain—Political activity.
7. Protest movements—Chile.   8. Protest movements—
Argentina.   9. Protest movements—Spain.   I. Title.

HQ1236.5.C5K36   2003

303.48'4'098—dc21   2003007855

Manufactured in the United States of America

12 11   10   09   08   07   06   05   04

10 9 8 7 6 5 4 3 2 1

The paper used in this publication meets the minimum
requirements of ANSI/NISO Z39.48–1992 (R 1997)
(Permanence of Paper).

To Bennett Byron Sims

Since you one were, I never since was one.
Michael Drayton (1563–1631)

Contents

Acknowledgments

This book has absorbed the energy, knowledge, and talents of many of my friends and colleagues over many years. In Spain, Ana Aguado, Nerea Aresti, Jordi Argente, Amparo Bella, María Inmaculada Benito, Inmaculada Blasco, Cristina Borderías, Angels Carabí, Joan Casanovas, Maruja Cazcarra, Magdalena Chocano, Meli Esteban, Chris Hermann, Gloria Labarta, Esperanza Martínez, Isabel Segura, Susana Tavera, Madrona Torrents, and Mercé Vilanova have nurtured me in many ways. They have helped me find materials, accompanied me to archives and demonstrations, cajoled archivists to allow me to make copies of documents, and granted me interviews, while providing me with their insights about the past.

In Argentina, Mabel Belucci, Nora de Cortiñas, Liria Evangelista, Enrique Garguin, María Luisa Lenci, Margarita Merbilhaá, Ana Julia Ramírez, Valeria Silvina Pita, Mario Tealdi, and Alejandra Vassallo have taken me into their homes, read various chapters of this manuscript, recalled their activities, and introduced me to their friends and others who could help me with my work. Those in and from Chile have been a true inspiration. Their courage and their solidarity have changed my life for the better in countless ways. Marjorie Agosín, Nieves Ayress, Rosa Ayress, Vicky Ayress, Alejandra López, Pedro Alejandro Matta, Amalia Moreno, Margot Olvarría, Margarita Romano, Veronica Shild, Victor Toro Ramírez, and Teresa Valdés have all made the kind of commitments to democracy and justice that most of us only read about in books. It has been my good fortune to call them my friends.

Librarians are unsung heroes, and none more so than those who serve during periods of repression. Montserrat Condominas at the Institut Municipal d'Història, Casa l'Ardiaca, is one such hero. I am also grateful to Olga Gonzáles and María Paz Vergara, who guided me through the Fundación de Documentación y Archivo de la Vicaría de la Solidaridad, Arzobispado de Santiago, Chile, a monument to the struggle for human rights. For many decades, Thea Druijker and Rudolf de Jong of the International Institute for Social History in Amsterdam have provided the articles and pamphlets that taught me how decentralized social movements develop and grow. Marek Hilfer, Willeke Tijssen, and Tineke Faber maintain the tradition of intellectual generosity that makes the International Institute a haven for scholars from all over the world. In the United States, Andrew Lee of the Tamiment Library at New York University and Peter Smith in the Special Collections division of Firestone Library, Princeton University, exceeded themselves in finding the material I sought. Then there are the informal keepers of the memory: Teresa Valdés has maintained the collection of ephemeral literature produced by Mujeres por la Vida during their six-year existence, and Amalia Moreno has kept the family archives of the Ayress and Moreno families.

I have been helped along the way by various research assistants, among whom I am especially grateful to Alhelí Alvarado-Díaz, Diane Creagh, Laura Kopp, Nevada Lane, and Magda Mora. Too little is said about close relationships that develop with graduate students, who frequently become our teachers. I cannot say enough about what I owe intellectually and personally to Andrea Campetella, Juan Casanovas, Brenda Elsey, Kenia Fernández, Elizabeth Friedman, Lorgia Garcia, Enrique Garguin, Magaly Henderson, Carla McDougel, Silvana Palermo, Alejandra Ossorio, Jennifer Manion, Ana Julia Rodríguez, Greg Swedberg, and Alejandra Vassallo. Ana Aguado, Lisa Baldez, Amparo Bella, Inmaculada Blasco, Marianne Hirsch, Enrique Garguin, Thomas Miller Klubock, Robert G. Moeller, Margaret Power, Ana Julia Rodriguez, Heidi Tinsman, and Norma J. Wikler have read chapters or the entire manuscript at various stages, but none is to blame for the results. I hope that Norma would have been proud to see that her suggestions improved the manuscript in significant ways.

My books get off to quick starts, change direction, and then wander for a very long time. I am truly grateful for the patience of Robert Conner and Kent Mullikin at the National Humanities Center and Joseph F. Tulchin at the Woodrow Wilson International Center for Scholars. Were it not for the support of the American Association of University Women, the American Council of Learned Societies, the Guggenheim Foundation, the Stony Brook Research Foundation, and the Rutgers University Research Fund, I could never have talked to as many people or traveled to as many archives. Thanks too to Grey Osterud for her early editorial help and to Elizabeth Berg and Jacqueline Volin for finishing the job so elegantly and expeditiously. Dannette Davis and Sheila Levine, who championed this book, were constant allies in meeting the challenges of getting it to press.

There is no way to tell T. J. and Lois Anderson, Nieves Ayress, Danilo and Margaret Bach, Judith Bennett, Dollie Burwell, Indrani Chatterjee, Lou Charnon Deutsch, Judith Funkhauser, Erich Goode, Susan and Charles Halpern, Dolores Hayden, Cynthia Herrup, Nancy Hewitt, Christopher Kennedy, Dennis Koster, Thomas Klubock, Brooke Larson, Steven Lawson, Dusa McDuff, Amy Merrill, David and Martel Montgomery, Rosalind Petchesky, Margaret Power, Hana Rosenberg, Sheila Rowbotham, Karin Shapiro, Sandhya Shukla, Deborah Silverman, Abby, Leonard, and Mathilde Sims, Kathryn Kish Sklar, Ann Snitow, Dorothy Thompson, Heidi Tinsman, Susan Wall, or Norma Wikler what they have meant to me. Ruth Bloch, Victoria de Grazia, Marianne Hirsch, Claudia Koonz, Phoebe Lithgow, Lynn and Nora Malley, Robert Moeller, Marta Petrusewich, Ellen Ross, Leo Spitzer, Mary Yeager, and Barbara Weinstein have provided all the encouragement, support, and love that I have needed, and I count them as my family.

My greatest regret is that I cannot share this book with my life partner, Bennett Sims, who died on March 5, 2002. He loved the kind of poetry he called "blood on the page," but he liked his movies to be happy stories about happy people with happy endings. Knowing that this book would be more like the poetry than the films, he nevertheless supported me with all his heart.

Taking Back the Streets

At the end of the twentieth century in places ranging from Latin America and the Caribbean to Europe, the United States, South Africa, Nigeria, Iran, Japan, China, and South Asia, women and young people of both sexes demonstrated against injustices that they thought they could not confront in any other way. Equating democracy with social justice, they took over the streets and plazas of their countries in an effort to hold public officials accountable for committing atrocities and enforcing unjust laws. They attempted to publicize what authoritarian governments were doing in secret and to force these governments from power. In Chile, the young María Prada (pseud.) mistook her government's efforts to promote public education for a totalitarian plot to brainwash students and mobilized against it. In Argentina, Nora de Cortiñas found satisfaction as a mother and housewife until her son was abducted and she attempted to find him at army bases and prisons; then she tried to reincorporate him into public life in the central plaza of her country. Teresa Valdés resisted patriarchy in her home and in authoritarian Chile by organizing street demonstrations.

The women and youth discussed in this book stand in for others all around the world who appeal to the public in the name of democracy, sometimes using shaming techniques. Even while being tortured by the Chilean military, the young Nieves Ayress recognized how her oppressors used shame to isolate and discredit her. Refusing to be shamed, acting as a witness to what she and others suffered, and bringing history and memory to bear on the dictator Augusto Pinochet and his accomplices became a means of fighting for her own self-respect and for a more just and democratic future. Ayress, with the aid of her mother and an international women's human rights community, maintained her social identity and engaged in direct action even in prison. Keeping up a tradition of struggle, she now runs a community center in the South Bronx and continues to fight for social justice and democracy, especially on behalf of New York's impoverished immigrant community.

Ayress and others devoted to social justice have seen the term *democracy* turned on its head and used to promote, for example, an army coup. Right-wing women, aided by young people, colluded with those planning a military coup against Chilean president Salvador Allende and argued that as mothers and housewives, they were "the people" whom Allende claimed to represent. Blurring populism with democracy sparked an antidemocratic movement that skewed perceptions of what was happening in Chile until it was far too late to save its democratic system of government.

Within a decade of the military coup that overthrew Allende and installed the dictatorship of Augusto Pinochet, another group of women, whose slogan was "Democracy in the country and in the home," attempted to discredit the dictatorship for its violence and extend the realm of freedom to the so-called domestic sphere. Criticizing repression wherever it occurred, these women attempted to shame the dictatorship and the military through more than 170 street demonstrations in six years.

In neighboring Argentina, a group of women who became known as the Madres de Plaza de Mayo, first led by Azucena Villaflor, moved from portraying themselves as victims whose children had been abducted to actively becoming spokespeople for political justice. From 1977 to 1983, under a military dictatorship that referred to its own actions as a Dirty War, and then for nearly three decades afterward, when representative democracy failed to meet their aspirations, the Madres attempted to redefine justice. After Argentina's return to a civilian government, Hebe de Bonafini kept her group of the Madres de Plaza de Mayo in the spotlight by becoming a thorn in the side of those who wanted to forget. But she antagonized many of her former allies, among them many of the original Madres, who thought her behavior crude and authoritarian. They split off and formed an organization called Las Madres de Plaza de Mayo–Línea Fundadora—the Founding-Line Mothers of the Plaza de Mayo—and ran it according to strict democratic principles. Two separate and often antagonistic groups of Madres still struggle for their own versions of justice in Argentina.

In the mid-1990s, just when many thought the saga of democratic struggles in the streets was over, and others feared that the younger generation would tire of hearing about the bloody history that had engulfed many of their parents, young people in Argentina who called themselves HIJOS (Hijos por la Identidad y la Justicia contra el Olvido y el Silencio, Children for Identity and Justice against Oblivion and Silence) began to carry out *escraches*—rowdy and theatrical street demonstrations—to shame former torturers and their superiors. Followed by the same sort of direct action in Chile (there the demonstrations were called *funas*), the *escraches* were intended to bring debates about democracy and justice out of hiding and into the public arena. By turning the tables on those who punished and shamed their victims, young people, sometimes supported by former political prisoners and survivors of the torture centers of Chile and Argentina, publicly ridiculed the criminals who had run their countries and then lived with impunity beyond the reach of the legal system. In Spain, recalling the long years of fascist repression in prison and then fighting against injustices such as the adultery law that was used to take children from their mothers under the Spanish dictator Francisco Franco, young women such as María Inmaculada Benito and María Angeles Muñoz risked their own reputation and custody of their children in order to extend the meaning of democracy to include decriminalizing women's sexuality.

All over the globe, ordinary women and youthful demonstrators frequently have mobilized, even under authoritarian governments, but Chile, Argentina, and Spain provide especially good examples of the patterns of resistance that emerged in the last third of the twentieth century. Spain had an unbroken history of authoritarian government from the end of the Spanish Civil War in 1939 until the elections of 1977. Yet women and young people of both sexes engaged in sporadic resistance movements for democracy during that entire period. Spain was one of the first countries to undergo what became known as a "transition to democracy," in which a parliamentary system followed an authoritarian regime without a protracted military struggle and without punishing the perpetrators of atrocities. From 1970 to 1990, Chile went from a democratic government with a Socialist president, to a dictatorship, and then to what became known as a "protected democracy." Mobilizations of women and youth played a significant role in each of these shifts. Argentina saw the establishment of a particularly brutal military government between 1976 and 1982 that seemed intent on obliterating an entire generation of people whom it considered tainted by their commitment to social justice. Turning *disappeared* into a transitive verb, the military kidnapped thirty thousand people, a majority of whom were young men and women, whose mothers went looking for them. The transition to democracy in 1983 resulted in the trials of Argentina's leading generals. But blanket amnesties following a series of attempted military coups led women and young people to protest. Refusing government exhortations to forget, women such as the Madres de Plaza de Mayo insist that there can be no democracy without a full accounting of atrocities. Similar movements took place around the world to right wrongs perpetrators hoped would be forgotten.

When seemingly repressed or politically inactive people mobilize, certain discernible patterns emerge. By placing their bodies on the line and by engaging in political spectacle, women and youth can sometimes reverse the shame that repressive governments impose. Demonstrators transform the streets and plazas into liberated territory where they can express their own ideas about democracy and justice by calling individuals, and indeed whole social systems, to account. Popular mobilizations help shape how the public thinks about politics. With props, costumes, and silhouettes painted on walls, women and youth have employed their own bodies to represent the dead and missing and to make visual arguments in support of their own versions of history. Countering "the diffuse and anonymous power" of dictators, those who engage in street demonstrations often make inchoate terror visible.[1]

According to the French sociologist Maurice Halbwach, who launched the study of historical memory, ideas contain images, which are more than mere illustrations. "There are no ideas without images," Halbwach has written. "Or, to put it more precisely, ideas and images do not designate two elements, one social and the other individual, of our states of consciousness, but rather two points of view from which society can simultaneously consider the same objects that it situates in the totality of its notions or in its life and history."[2] Along with words, which are severely constrained under authoritarian regimes, people can display their own images of the truth using their own bodies. Carefully shaping the meaning of the imagery they project, they can paint grotesque portraits of those they oppose.

Direct action is a tactic those promoting democracy frequently use to exercise power nonviolently. But direct action can also be violent. For example, in the name of justice, vigilantes in the American South and

Midwest lynched African American men for allegedly engaging in sexual relations with white women, or for standing up for their own rights. In South Africa, people presumed guilty of conspiring with the apartheid government were sometimes set on fire with tires around their neck. Yet direct action also provides a means by which people can persuade authoritarian governments to stop their violent practices or to give an accounting of what they have done.

Most of the groups whose stories appear in this book promoted participatory democracy through direct action. Participatory democracy entails people forming committees and holding public meetings to govern themselves. It includes speaking out and perhaps suffering the consequences. The opposite of the secret ballot, participatory democracy incorporates people into the body politic in very public ways. In one case considered here, a reactionary group of women organized for the express purpose of overthrowing a democratically elected Socialist government in Chile. Yet even they made their arguments in public and used the term *democracy* to justify their mobilizations.

Most of the women and young people of both sexes who appear here presumed that democracy involves commitments to social justice, equality, and ethical behavior carried out through popular initiatives and verbal arguments. In mass mobilizations and performances geared toward attracting public attention, activists pitted their bodies against dictators and authoritarian regimes. Whether fighting against Augusto Pinochet in Chile, the military junta in Argentina, or the dictatorship of Francisco Franco in Spain, demonstrators used the terms *democracy* and *justice* to indicate inequities ranging from military repression and torture to domestic violence. In the course of resisting unjust authorities and their successors, activists often forged entirely new communities.

During a crisis, politics is everybody's business, and the sense of community many of us immediately felt after 9/11 in New York intensified my longstanding interest in collective life. I learned to grieve in public in front of shrines made up of candles, jewelry, teddy bears, and children's drawings. I had seen photographs of the disappeared in Chile and Argentina, and I saw them again in the subways and bus kiosks of New York. Parks, street corners, squares, fire stations, and sites around the World Trade Center became public forums in which people discussed what was happening. Most of the graffiti and the writing on scrolls of paper that covered walls all over the city spoke of solidarity. And people filled the streets. On Sunday, 16 September, as I sat in my living room, I heard a marching band. Following the music to the nearest fire station, I joined firefighters and sixty other neighbors for an impromptu civic revival meeting organized by students from a small college in Alabama. The band members had gathered their instruments, traveled twenty hours by car, and marched from firehouse to firehouse on the West Side of Manhattan. They played "America the Beautiful" and "Battle Hymn of the Republic" for neighborhood people in New York. Then, late Sunday afternoon, they packed up their instruments and drove home. Such experiences gave me a renewed appreciation for the pleasure of solidarity. I understood again why people I interviewed for this book risked everything to establish their ties to one another while undergoing torture in prison; and why their friends, relatives, and compatriots dared to march or hold hunger strikes when the forces of the Argentine, Chilean, or Spanish dictatorships could crush them. I shared with my neighbors and friends a desire to talk, take photographs, and otherwise record what was happening.

Whether they called themselves feminists or activists, all of the women and young people in this book used their gender and generational identities strategically. They acted out their versions of the truth in highly specific ways. Suppressing references to the differences among them, some of these groups homogenized their identities and presented themselves simply as "women" who spoke for all the people; others did so as "mothers" who had extralegal rights to defend their children. The right-wing women of Poder Femenino (Feminine Power) in Chile purposely conflated gender with populism. The liberal and left-wing Mujeres por la Vida (Women for Life) sometimes spoke for liberty, justice, and democracy as if they were feminine virtues, explicitly arguing in one of their slogans that "freedom has a woman's name" (la libertad is a feminine noun). Yet respect for motherhood did not save Azucena de Villaflor, the founder of the Madres de Plaza de Mayo, when the Argentine military detained, tortured, and murdered her during the Dirty War. Before and after her death, her colleagues tried to shame the government through their marches in the Plaza de Mayo. Risking death and torture, the women and young people described in this book turned shaming into a public act to project their own assessment of what was happening around them.

SHAMING RITUALS

A frequently overlooked form of direct action, shaming rituals are a means of fighting back and nonviolently undermining the legitimacy of authorities. Feeling humiliated, being made ashamed, and shaming one's opponents are largely unrecognized as attempts to establish the authority of one's views. Shame, by which children learn self-discipline at the same time as they learn about gender and their place in society, often intensifies when people suffer maltreatment such as torture. Shame fragments sexual identity and inhibits solidarity. Under authoritarian regimes that used a combination of state terror and shame to keep people quiet, it took special courage to divulge publicly one's opposition to the government. Yet many women and young people did precisely that. They overcame their fears, including fear of being shamed, in hopes of ending government atrocities and restoring public life. They used shared cultural values to cast aspersion on officials in sexual ways that exposed the depths of their depravity. By revealing what governments would rather keep hidden and forcing the military and the police to participate in dialogues even when they preferred to remain silent about their actions, opponents promoted their own interpretations of the structure of power.[3]

Shaming is a profoundly political act in which gender plays an important part. Working in different milieus, philosophers, social psychologists, anthropologists, psychoanalysts, and sociologists have written a great deal about how individuals and groups balance shame and solidarity. Hungarian philosopher Agnes Heller considers shame to be the way individuals are socialized to obey the rules of their culture.[4] She writes:

> When the child learns of *what* he or she should be ashamed, he or she learns thereby the legitimation of a system of domination. The more shame is internalized, the less brutal force is needed in order to integrate a social structure.... [T]he political system of domination is legitimized by the internalization of shame.[5]

Heller's arguments help explain how shame connects those who use brutal force and activists who survive it. Violence and feelings of helplessness trigger shame. Since children learn shame at the same time as they learn their gender and cultural identity, the use of physical force, as in torture, can put both these identities into question. Shame undercuts solidarity by weakening the personal identity that ties people to their family and community.

Having succumbed to violence, especially when one provides the torturers with information—and, according to survivor Victor Toro,[6] everyone reveals something under torture—a person feels sullied and unworthy of rejoining his or her group or association. In many cultures, suffering, especially sexual abuse or violence that seems to target one's gender, makes the person believe that he or she has intentionally violated taboos and is responsible for his or her own humiliation. Survivors therefore feel ashamed and enter a conspiracy of silence with their torturers, blaming themselves for their individual suffering and, even more, for their own survival when so many others have died. One way to overcome shame is to admit what happened, rejoin the group, and place the blame on the perpetrators, a process some political activists were able to achieve.

Heller's theory offers a way to understand how shame functions under authoritarian regimes and in movements to overthrow them. No system of authority can work without people trained—often to their own detriment—to enforce the shared values of the culture. The enforcers who socialize children are disproportionately women. As the caretakers of children, mothers, grandmothers, and other women teach children both gender and shame. As shame replaces force in creating loyalty to a group, and presumably in promoting collective identities, sexuality and power merge. The content of masculinity and femininity may vary enormously, but masculinity and femininity in any particular culture and historical period appear "natural" and fundamental. Gender identity shapes the categories in which other identities develop, and mothers and grandmothers have the ultimate power of defining both gender and shame. This gives older women enormous moral power and provides young people of both sexes with the authority to hold their governments accountable for the values they proclaim.

According to social psychologists June Price Tangney and Ronda L Dearing, shame can also isolate people and intensify self-involvement.[7] Many victims of violence, as well as many of those who stood by the sidelines as others were kidnapped from homes, cafés, and streets in Argentina, were ashamed. Feelings of shame, Tangney and Dearing argue, often drive people to lash out against those they have hurt, whom they blame for their feelings of inadequacy. Tangney and Dearing contrast shame with guilt, which, they claim, makes people feel empathy for their victims.

Therapist and activist Inger Agger also deals with shame, but she is specifically concerned with its place in collective behavior. In Denmark, she treated women refugees from Latin America and the Middle East. As fighters for social justice, they had frequently suffered sexual assaults when they were political prisoners. They had psychological problems that inhibited them from regaining their sense of identity. Agger realized that they were not the women they had been brought up to be: many had violated their ascribed roles as good daughters and mothers by engaging in politics. Then the sense of purpose they felt as activists had deserted them, replaced by the shameful sense that they had contributed to their own suffering through their political engagement.[8]

Agger investigated how gender made male and female political prisoners suffer shame differently. Being stripped and brutalized made male prisoners focus on their own bodies. Physical pain broke down their sense of masculinity and robbed them of their ability to identify with others. Anal rape transformed these men into their images of a battered woman and, Agger claims, effectively feminized them in their own mind. Derogatory comments about their bodies isolated these men from others and made it difficult to resist authority. Male prisoners frequently felt emasculated by their sense of helplessness. Unless they could confide in others what they might have disclosed under torture, they became isolated. By confessing, they could reintegrate into the group and reestablish their sense of solidarity.

Women suffered psychological torture in the form of comments about their bodies and failure to measure up to the female ideal that the torturers held. According to sociologist Pilar Calveiro, who was imprisoned in several Argentine concentration camps, torturers told women prisoners that they were bad mothers, domineering women, prostitutes, unattractive fanatics, and sex-hungry monsters who had engaged in politics to find a man.[9] From this perspective, the men with whom they joined must also be inadequate, for what other kind of man would associate with such a woman? The torturers exaggerated what may have been familiar warnings. Their mothers and grandmothers, charged with inculcating shame as a means of protecting them from physical attacks, used shared cultural values to tie the girls to their families and communities.[10] But in the mouths of the torturers, these psychological attacks undermined the women's political and personal identities. One thin woman recalled how her torturers made fun of her body for being too flat, and another talked about how her tormentors told her that a fat woman like her only engaged in politics to get a man.[11] The torturers implied that she merited punishment because she was a bad woman, not because she was a political adversary.

Although the goals of torture were the same whether employed on women or men—to get information, destroy the person, wipe out his or her ability to identify with others, and thus reduce potential opposition—sexual torture affected men and women differently.[12] In the concentration camps of Latin America, many women experienced a form of gender distortion that exaggerated the sexuality they had been socialized to hide. According to Inger Agger, women are made to feel guilty because the torture they suffer "is the activation of sexuality to induce shame and guilt."[13] Almost all the women survivors remember how their torturers showed disgust for their smelly, dirty, blood-smeared bodies, unable as the women were to bathe or mop up menstrual blood.[14] By reducing women to their bodies, presenting the female body as contemptible and sexualizing the violence against them, the torturers attempted to transform women from political activists to pathetic victims. Reestablishing ties of solidarity in prison—that is, recalling a public connection—became an essential part of resisting, as political prisoners such as Matilde Landa found out on death row in Franco's Spain, Pilar Calveiro learned in Argentina, and Nieves Ayress discovered in Chile. In fact, Ayress recalls that when she was with other women, they frequently caressed each other, trying to reclaim their bodies from the torturers' hands.[15] Telling stories, giving testimony, and engaging in collective action provided a means by which to regain power. Both in their own stories and in popular mobilizations against the government, women survivors needed to redress the balance. They strove to put the shame where it belonged—on the consciences of the torturers.

All the women considered here risked shame because of their political activities. But they also used shame as a form of direct action against their adversaries. For example, when police tried to break up fights during a 1971 demonstration of right-wing women in Chile, the right accused the government of "moral castration." Those same women, joining with other right-wing activists to provoke a military coup, gave feathers and threw chicken feed at the soldiers, claiming that the military lacked the virility to confront the Socialists who ran the government. A decade later, women opposing the dictatorship plastered Santiago with silhouettes labeled with the names of people who had disappeared. When police and soldiers destroyed the images, they were forced to symbolically do in public what they had previously done in secret. By calling attention to actions the government wanted to keep hidden, by casting those other activities in a suspicious light, and most of all, by characterizing the sexuality of the authorities in derogatory ways, direct action through shaming rituals helped discredit those in power and set the stage for participatory democracy.

VARIETIES OF DEMOCRACY

Participatory democracy, which entails equal decision-making by all demonstrators, appeared at one time or another in most of the movements against authoritarian regimes of the latter third of the twentieth century. Many of the women and young people considered here hoped to institute a social system they called "democracy," a word they frequently used interchangeably with "justice." The rhetoric of "democracy" was all too familiar to me and to others reared in schools obsessed with democracy. Most of my early education taught me to situate the history of the United States in the struggles of various groups to achieve a place in a democratic society. Even if blacks, immigrants, and Native Americans did not always enjoy the benefits of democracy, the pursuit of democracy, we learned, was a goal worth fighting for.

In school, democracy was synonymous with representative democracy, which depends on constitutions, laws, and legislative, judicial, and executive bodies. But I developed my own commitment to participatory or direct democracy as a foot soldier in the Civil Rights, antiwar, and New Left student movements of the 1960s and in later feminist struggles. This form of democracy includes forming committees to write and distribute flyers and pamphlets and backing up opinions in public debates, demonstrations, sit-ins, and hunger strikes. It sometimes means wearing distinctive costumes, chanting slogans, painting signs and murals, and otherwise performing in public in the hope of enhancing the common good. It entails the transformation of public spaces, such as streets, plazas, courtrooms, and media outlets, into democratic spaces where people can express themselves and invite others to respond. Direct or participatory democracy is a political theory in motion, worked out in the practices of the social movements that promote them.

The contradictory uses of the term *democracy* owe a great deal to Cold War terminology.[16] According to the National Security Doctrine of the United States, partially institutionalized in the School of the Americas in 1946 and the Truman Doctrine of 1947, the United States and its allies were locked in a struggle to the death with the Soviet Union. Dividing the world between "communism" and "democracy," the United States in the postwar period sought to prevent communists or even reformers from coming to power in Greece, Guatemala, and Iraq and from sharing power in Italy. As part of the war on communism, the United States launched the School of the Americas in 1946. first in Panama and then in Fort Benning, Georgia, the School of the Americas (renamed the Western Hemisphere Institute for Security Cooperation in October 2001) indoctrinated sixty thousand police and soldiers, including many of Latin America's future dictators.[17] At the school, students learned to define democracy to mean everything the So-

viet Union opposed. Since the Soviets spoke about the triumph of workers and peasants, any aspiration to land reform, improved conditions of
rural or urban workers, or greater resources for the poor, including milk
for their children, could be denigrated as "communist."[18] From the
1960s to the 1980s, priests and nuns, who made a commitment to the
poor by teaching peasants to read or by providing medical care to land-
less workers, could be murdered as "communists."

The alternative to communism, according to the National Security
Doctrine, was "democracy." People on the right and the left both used
the term. Democracy could stand for their own candidates gaining
power. It could mean the institution or reinstitution of legislatures and
elected presidents. Democracy could mean justice or the redistribution
of power in any direction. The word could situate people vis-à-vis their
political opponents, including the government in power.

For many of us in the New Left and the women's movement from the
late 1960s on, democracy referred both to a process of resolving differences and to political goals for the future. It implied, according to political scientist Jean Cohen, "expand[ing] and democratiz[ing] public
spaces from the university to the polity."[19] Democracy meant working
out differences by talking and trying to institute vast social changes
through militant but peaceful means. Among the goals of democracy
was a near-universal right to participate in the allocation of social and
economic resources. Democracy included decision-making about personal life, from domestic relations to sexual preferences. Democracy
consisted of negotiating for power and deciding how power would be
constructed and reconstructed in normal interactions between people.
Democracy also involved civil disobedience to reveal the violence inher-
ent in the social system.[20]

STREET SPECTACLES

The five groups of women and young people from Chile, Argentina, and
Spain who appear here chose to make their arguments for democracy
and justice by spectacular acts in front of an audience. Similar stories
could be told about their cohort elsewhere. Although we may relegate
street spectacles to faraway times and places, they are a more important
part of contemporary intellectual and political life than one might ordinarily imagine. Spectacles function as ritualized performances, in which
what is seen is far more important than anything said or written. In fact,
spectacles work as visual metaphors, substituting a series of acts for ar-

guments. By following appropriate sequences and incorporating gestures and images, spectacles can bring new meanings to the symbols they manipulate.[21] Using sights and movements carried on in sacred religious or secular spaces, spectacles appeal to the emotions in order to promote ideas by visual means. Furthermore, they employ gestures and props to demonstrate political goals through visual metaphors. This kind of ritualized behavior in the form of spectacles provides a useful form of action for women trying to emphasize their similarities.

Because spectacles are so variable, they can be used to enhance the existing political order, challenge the dominant system, or empower new social groups by playing on established meanings. Opposition to established authorities can take the form of raucous parades by dissidents, secular pilgrimages, ridicule of administrative practices, demonstrations to express outrage against a state of affairs that has gone too far, or organized marches that appropriate the practices of powerful institutions—the Catholic Church or the British monarchy, for example. Because it is hard to control the visual elements in spectacles, they sometimes display more than their organizers intend. The patterns of street rituals frequently conjure up religious and political pageants, visually evoking a sense of legitimacy. Thus the repetition of certain rituals, such as mass demonstrations and secular pilgrimages, the use of objects of devotion, like photographs, to harness great sentiment, and the transformation of public spaces to express new meaning frequently bestow on participants the authority they otherwise lack.

Movements such as those described here are not limited to traditional arenas of political action. Instead the actors plant their bodies in the streets, plazas, and public spaces, as well as in front of television cameras, where their presence will be most noticeable. Their activities have been denigrated as the work of crazy women, "locas" or "hysterical housewives," but they are certainly much more. Women emphasizing their position as mothers and housewives have frequently followed the practice of making spectacles of themselves in order to state their argument for a system of rights organized according to those particular roles. And young people of both sexes throw decorum to the wind in order to act out their opposition to what authorities are doing. Making themselves into objects of curiosity and contempt, these women and youth force others to see what they may not want to see. By using their own bodies to ridicule authorities, they function as distorting mirrors, bending the images of those in power to shame and deform them.

Theorists unfamiliar with the way young people—male and female—

and women are shut out of political processes that directly affect their lives often ignore the dynamics of their grassroots efforts to win justice and democracy and the ways in which they redefine where politics will take place. Most critics misjudge the seditious performances of young people, who win a hearing by acting as if they were unreasonable and out of control. Without considering a generation as a category, it is easy to overlook and underestimate young people's strategic arguments for alternative visions of society. And those theorists who group together all forms of maternalism frequently disregard the way that some women, manipulating their society's multivalent notions of motherhood, can exploit that role to reveal the contradictions in what authorities are saying. In an age that places a premium on writing, it is easy to undervalue the way spectacles can be used to express political and social goals. Extending the sphere of politics to include actual and symbolic public representations of women may instigate serious investigation of the roles gender and generational differences play in the public realm.

Consideration of the way women and young people make spectacles of themselves reveals how gender and generational identities contribute to demonstrators' cultural repertoire and shape their political performances. The view of political culture from the perspective of women and young people taking to the streets offers an opportunity to reverse the trend to divide gender and political studies and use the achievements of nearly thirty years of feminist research to help change the terms of debate about political movements.

CHAPTER I

Staying Alive through Struggle

I got off the phone and began to cry. My friend Luz de las Nieves Ayress Moreno, known as Nieves Ayress, a human rights activist in the Latino community of the South Bronx, had gone for a biopsy following a questionable mammogram, but the hospital had sent her home: they had lost her records for the third time. Her job tutoring a child in Brooklyn, an hour's subway ride away from her home, nets about a thousand dollars too much annually for her to qualify for Medicaid. Her employers pay her decently and contribute to Social Security, but she has no health insurance, so she must seek care at public hospitals, which routinely lose her records. She finally had the biopsy, but the clinic made her wait a month to get the results. Only when she agreed to lose a half day's work and return to the Bronx to see the doctor in person did she learn that the tests were negative.

I cried from frustration and rage about the way Ayress must keep fighting. For months she had felt excruciating pain in her breasts, not a sign of cancer but worrisome nonetheless. Her breasts are riddled with scar tissue from the torture she suffered in Chilean prisons between 1973 and 1976, during the dictatorship of Augusto Pinochet. She first told her story from prison, and after her release publicized her own ordeal and the plight of others by speaking publicly and privately about the regime's campaign of torture and repression. In October 1998—when Pinochet, who had ruled Chile for seventeen years, was detained in London for human rights abuses—Ayress told her story again. Unwilling to collaborate with her former oppressors by remaining silent, she has always insisted on speaking the truth when faced with authority. In a life devoted to social justice and gender equity, she bears witness to the past in order to bring about a more just future.

The story of the Chilean government's use of sexual torture to humiliate and silence its adversaries includes graphic descriptions of the brutality Ayress and so many others were forced to endure in Chile. Unlike many victims of torture, Ayress refused to be ashamed or to keep the violence secret. In fact, she wrote a testimony, and Inés Antúnez, a woman friend who was going into exile, hid it in her vagina and then passed it on to international human rights advocates, publicizing Ayress's ordeal while it was still happening. This clever stratagem made the vagina into an instrument of publicity to shame the torturers. Ayress and her mother attacked the Chilean dictatorship at the height of its power. By speaking out, even in prison, Ayress resisted the military's authority to demean her and define the meaning of her life. She found witnesses: first her mother and Antúnez, later foreign journalists and members of international women's organizations. Ayress continues to publicize her memories of past atrocities, not out of a desire for vengeance, but out of a commitment to liberating contemporary victims of injustice. She encourages other women to speak out, and she urges local women, members of human rights organizations, and scholar-activists like me to engage in direct action by spreading her story, thus promoting freedom for a host of people who suffer now as she did then.

Ayress's narrative, first told orally to Antúnez and to her mother, was written down for the prisoner to take into exile. The account initially appeared in her mother's letters to officials and a petition to a Chilean court for a writ of habeas corpus for her daughter. The *Washington Post* reported the story in May 1974. A communiqué from the Women's International Democratic Federation publicized her story eight months later. When Ayress was expelled from Chile at the end of 1976, she took her testimony to Germany, Italy, Morocco, Cuba, and Mexico—wherever there were Chilean relief organizations fighting to remove Pinochet and restore Chilean democracy.

In Cuba, Nieves Ayress met Victor Toro Ramírez, a Chilean exile who became her companion. Like most political activists, Ayress knew Toro by reputation as one of the founders of the Movimiento de Izquierda Revolucionaria (Movement of the Revolutionary Left, MIR) and as the leader responsible for mobilizing the poorest and most oppressed workers and peasants in Chile. Following the coup, he became one of the dictatorship's most hunted enemies. Captured in April 1974, he survived the torture and extermination camps at the Villa Grimaldi and Tres Alamos, where he befriended Ayress's brother. Ayress and Toro had a daughter while in Cuba, but after Ayress was sexually attacked by a common criminal, they left for Mexico. Stranded in the United States when an earthquake destroyed their home, they settled in New York City's South Bronx, one of the poorest areas of the United States. In 1987, these consummate political organizers founded Vamos a la Peña del Bronx, a community center that defends the cultural and political rights of poor black and Latino immigrants. The organization feeds five thousand people a year, promotes environmental justice, organizes rent strikes, and educates about AIDS. It helps publicize police brutality and supports women who are resisting domestic violence—for Ayress, one of its most important services.

I first met Nieves Ayress in early 1999, when I was doing research on Latin American women immigrants. I had read the articles about her in the Spanish-language press after Pinochet was detained, and I wondered whether she connected her present activities in the South Bronx with her previous life.[1] As we spoke about her life before, during, and after her traumatic imprisonment, I discovered that she had grown up in a family of political activists and had participated in the heady, hopeful period of the Allende government, when a socialist democracy seemed within the grasp of Chilean society. Her deep sense of connection to other political activists had sustained her in prison, and political commitments had rewoven the fabric of her life despite the rent that Pinochet and the torturers had made.

Ayress had clearly inherited a socialist commitment from her grandparents, who were founders of workers' cooperatives around the nitrate mines of northern Chile; from her aunt, a seamstress and labor organizer; and from her parents, who had met in union struggles and supported the Cuban revolution in its earliest stages.[2] In the late 1960s, when she was in her early twenties, Ayress became a fervent advocate of fundamental social change in Latin America. She believed not only in an equal distribution of resources to enable everyone to live with dignity, but also, unlike most sixties radicals in the region, in equal rights for women. Eager to take part in the international movement for social justice, she hitchhiked through Chile, Perú, and Bolivia, making contact with young radicals all over the continent. She joined Ché Guevara's Ejército de Liberación Nacional de Bolivia (Bolivian National Liberation Army) after his death, working with the guerrillas while criticizing their treatment of women. Without dishonoring the dead or blaming the victims, she recalls that her association in the early 1970s of democracy with the liberation of women made her comrades suggest that she was an infiltrator trying to sow havoc among the revolutionaries. Ché Guevara himself suffered from the gender biases of the time. For example, in his book on guerrilla warfare, he recommended that guerrilla bands include some women, since "it is very pleasing to a soldier subjected to the extremely hard conditions of this life to be able to look forward to a seasoned meal which tastes like something. One of the great tortures of the [Cuban] war was eating a cold, sticky, tasteless mess. Furthermore, it is easier to keep [women] in these domestic tasks; one of the problems in guerrilla bands is that the [men] are constantly trying to get out of these tasks."[3] Although the main book of testimonies that has appeared on women in guerrilla movements of that period focuses on Argentina, the testimonies confirm Ayress's description of the serious difficulties encountered by a single woman who was not a partner of one of the male leaders.[4]

Returning to Chile in 1970, Ayress supported the Popular Unity government of Salvador Allende. In 1971 she won a scholarship to study film and television production in Cuba. She left for a year, but returned to Chile when her beloved grandmother died. She took up graduate studies in early child development and, at the same time, began organizing in La Legua, a working-class enclave on the south side of Santiago.

STATE TERRORISM

Like many revolutionaries in the 1960s, Ayress was optimistic about changing international and local priorities by defeating governments and corporations that valued profits over human needs. The election of Socialist leader Salvador Allende as president of Chile and his pursuit of a democratic road to socialism—the "Vía Chilena," or Chilean way—promised to link social and economic justice with democracy, a combination that Ayress and her family had always espoused. But social reformers, elated by the possibilities for change, underestimated the violence that those with vested interests were willing to use to maintain their own wealth and power. In 1973, a few weeks after the military coup of 11 September, a neighbor denounced Ayress as a student activist, and she found herself at the National Soccer Stadium along with about twenty-five thousand other prisoners. While the Chilean air force converted some of its bases into torture chambers, and the navy used a ship, the *Esmeralda,* to incarcerate and interrogate people, the army set up interrogation centers in private buildings and public arenas, such as the Chilean and National stadiums. The military and armed police held and tortured workers, students, labor lawyers, health care profession-als, and members of liberal and leftist political groups. Ayress and countless others were given electric shocks from cattle prods placed on sensitive areas of their bodies. Some died under torture.

The thirty-one-year-old American journalist Charles Horman Jr., me-morialized in the film *Missing* (1982), was at the beach resort of Viñas del Mar when the coup d'état took place. Returning to Santiago, he re-ported to his wife, Joyce Horman, that he was surprised by the unusu-ally large number of U.S. military attachés he had seen near the naval base. He suspected that the presence of so many Americans indicated complicity in planning the coup. Shortly after Horman's return to San-tiago, he was abducted and murdered by the Chilean military, perhaps with the knowledge of its American advisors.[5] The Chilean folksinger Victor Jara, who was taken to the Chilean Stadium in downtown Santi-ago, was forced to play protest songs as his captors cut off his fingers. His crime was having tried to lead the prisoners in singing the anthem of the Popular Unity coalition, whose election the right wing and the military never forgave. Ayress and countless others—perhaps up to 150,000 people—were arrested and tortured, with another 40,000 peo-ple sent to concentration camps and some 10,000 people killed. All told, some 200,000 Chileans suffered violent repression, out of a popu-lation of under eleven million.[6]

While at the stadium, Ayress was questioned about where guns and ammunition were held. Her tormentors also asked about the positions of Soviet submarines along the Chilean coasts and where the Russian air force planned to drop bombs, "as if Moscow were going to tell me all its plans," she now says sarcastically.[7] Somewhat cavalierly, she says she got off easy with just electric shocks the first time. According to Ayress, the army, navy, air force, and police went wild after the coup, killing and maiming anyone they believed had supported Allende or in-ternational leftist causes. After being released from the stadium, Ayress moved to her own apartment, returned to the university, and tried to al-leviate suffering in the working-class neighborhood of La Legua.

In mid-June 1974, Augusto Pinochet officially launched the Directo-rio de Inteligencia Nacional (National Information Center, DINA), which was widely known as the Chilean gestapo. A secret intelligence unit that used torture as its main investigative tool, the DINA had begun its activities as early as November 1973.[8] It focused especially on men and women, like Ayress, who were involved in working-class districts such as La Legua, where the Ayress family had close friends. That neighborhood, with its preponderance of militant factory workers and community activists, had been to Allende's Popular Unity government what Montgomery, Alabama, was to Martin Luther King's early Civil Rights movement. Gallows humor circulating among activists predicted that after the army attacked the presidential palace of La Moneda, they would march on La Legua.[9] The joke proved to be tragically prophetic.

Suppressing La Legua and anyone connected with it played an especially important role in the mythology Pinochet used to justify the coup. Along with the neighborhoods of La Victoria, El 4 de Septiembre (Fourth of September), and San Miguel, La Legua represented everything the right wing and the military detested: La Victoria and El 4 de Septiembre were squatter communities taken in land seizures. San Miguel, where Nieves Ayress grew up, and La Legua, where she organized after the coup, were solid working-class districts whose residents were highly organized in unions and leftist parties. In Santiago, progressives took their political and personal identities from their neighborhoods.

Pinochet and the right-wing militants, who had spent three years destabilizing the Popular Unity government, claimed that political chaos and the threat of a preemptive left-wing coup made getting rid of Allende imperative. Although in 1970 Allende had been elected by a plurality of only 36.2 percent, his Popular Unity coalition had increased its margin of victory in the provincial and then the congressional elections of March 1973, winning a 47 percent plurality. Pinochet and the army, with supporters ranging from Christian Democrats to the neofascist organization Patria y Libertad (Fatherland and Freedom), with its swastika-like emblem of a lighting bolt, promoted the view that working-class leaders in neighborhoods like La Legua had been stockpiling arms to overthrow the government and establish a dictatorship of the proletariat. Charging that the March 1973 elections had been rigged, Pinochet and his apologists claimed in retrospect that "the best defense is a well-planned offense."[10]

Having taken the lead in overturning Chilean democracy, the armed forces and police under Augusto Pinochet attempted to destroy all opposition. In fact, despite the militant rhetoric immediately preceding the coup, there was very little armed resistance to the military except in La Legua. Margarita del Carmen Durán Gajardo, a childhood friend of

Nieves Ayress, was a witness to that armed struggle. Durán, a member of the Communist Youth and the daughter of Communist Party leaders, had gone to class that morning at the University of Chile.[11] At 11:30 A.M., she realized that a coup was under way and fled home to La Legua. In the heart of the district, at calle Riesele near calle Santa Rosa, she saw a group she recognized as belonging to the local Socialist Party. Expecting to meet other workers' groups coming from the north side of the city of Santiago, the group waited for reinforcements at Sumar polyester factory.

Soon a busload of armed national police, or carabineros, appeared, and they began shooting at the workers. For the first time that day, a group of citizens shot back. The police raised a white flag, the shooting stopped, and the police bus sped to a nearby hospital with their wounded. Later the police and soldiers returned and laid siege to the district. Members of the original column filtered out in small groups, hiding their small cache of arms in an abandoned house. Then the army invaded La Legua, seizing four hundred people. Among them were Margarita Durán, her father, her sister, and a fifteen-year-old neighbor. Their captors took them first to the Chilean air force barracks in El Bosque on the outskirts of the city, then to National Stadium. Margarita Durán was released almost immediately. Others were released within twenty-five days. Her father, a member of the Central Committee of the Communist Party, was kept in prison for two months, undergoing extensive torture.[12]

One of the other participants in the shooting on the day of the coup, a man called Antonio who claimed to be from a district on the other side of town, kept in contact with the people in La Legua. When some local men got out of prison in October, Antonio introduced them to an Argentine he called Comandante Alberto Esteban. Nieves Ayress, working underground as "Valeria," also met Esteban, whom she deeply distrusted. Little has been said about how provocateurs exploited left-wing men's fears about their masculinity, but Ayress now thinks that machismo made her comrades take unnecessary risks.[13] Thirty years later, Ayress still doesn't know who Esteban really was, but she regrets his power over her group.

UNDERGROUND

Unwilling to hide and do nothing, Ayress and her remaining group decided to engage in their own intelligence activities. They suspected that

the refrigerated trucks that appeared in the streets with increasing fre-
quency bore some connection to the disappearance of people from their
community. By following the trucks, they tried to locate the buildings
where their friends were being taken and presumably tortured. Ayress's
group traced the trucks to a fashionable street near Santiago's oldest religious building, the church of San Francisco. Just off the main boule-
vard of Santiago, avenida Bernardo O'Higgins, known popularly as the
Alameda, there was a beaux-arts building with wrought-iron balconies.
Known by its address, Londrés 38, the building had previously housed
a Socialist Party center. The amateur sleuths did not know that the
armed forces had seized the building and converted it into the headquarters of military intelligence.

Ayress located the precise address of the prison and torture center
only when she herself was incarcerated there after being betrayed by Esteban.[14] He had described himself as a member of the Argentine Ejército
Revolucionario del Pueblo (People's Revolutionary Army, ERP), and
had claimed that he was helping to set up a similar group in Chile. According to Durán's account, he wanted to use the arms stashes from La
Legua to train Chilean guerrillas. Margarita Durán insisted twenty
years later that Luis Orellana, her Socialist boyfriend, had strongly opposed the plan. When a local activist disappeared in mid-December
1973, Durán and Orellana fled from La Legua to her aunt's house in another district. In the middle of the night of 20 December 1973, the police arrested them. Among their captors was a tall, dark-haired, dark-
eyed official named Marcelo Morén Brito, who a few months later
became the commander of the Villa Grimaldi, Santiago's most notorious concentration camp. What happened next illustrates the practices
typical of government terrorists. The officers blindfolded Margarita
Durán, Luis Orellana, and Luis's brother Sigfrido and threw them into
the back of a refrigerated truck. The truck stopped at Londrés 38, and
the guards took the Orellana brothers, along with local Communist
Party members, to the second floor, where they were severely tortured
during interrogation about the hidden arms.

In retrospect, one of the most controversial aspects of the history of
this period concerns those who broke under torture. Part of the strategy
of the authorities was to humiliate their victims, making it difficult to
maintain solidarity. The subjects of torture, who were cut off from af-
fective or social ties, were encouraged to betray their friends to end their
own suffering. Among those who collaborated were two women: Marcia Alejandra Merino Vega, called Skinny Alejandra (La Flaca Alejan-

dra), a member of the MIR; and Luz Arce Sandoval, who belonged to the Socialist Party. These two women not only survived by identifying people with whom they had worked politically, but even became employees of DINA.[15] Some people who broke under torture—as well as some who continued to resist—recognized their torturers as agents who had infiltrated their political groups. When Marcia Merino was first tortured, she recognized Osvaldo Romo Mena, "El Guatón Romo," with whom she had organized in a working-class neighborhood of Santiago.[16] The confusion and mistrust sown by agents provocateurs who appeared first as comrades and then as torturers may have prompted some prisoners to betray their comrades. Yet some who changed sides under torture carried out their new tasks with little reluctance. According to survivors and to El Guatón Romo, Merino engaged in her work with rare enthusiasm, although she twice later tried to commit suicide.[17] On the other hand, Lumi Videla, a charismatic student leader and organizer of the MIR, pretended to collaborate but tried to help her comrades. When the authorities discovered what she was doing, they murdered her and threw her body over the garden wall of the Italian Embassy, where refugees seeking asylum had found a safe haven.[18]

Both heroes, such as Ayress and Videla, and collaborators, such as Arce and Merino, faced sexual degradation in the concentration camps. Psychologist Inger Agger has made us aware of how torturers reduce prisoners' sense of agency and authority by carrying out violent acts that appear sexual.[19] Shame diminishes female prisoners' capacity to show solidarity, which is vital to continued resistance. Merino, Arce, and Ayress all speak and write about the humiliation of being kept naked, suffering from vaginal infections, and being unable to wipe away menstrual blood, as well as about the pain of their wounds. Disgust at their own dirty and smelly bodies appears frequently in these women's accounts. Male prisoners' thoughts also focused on their bodies, although in a somewhat different way. Men who were forced into sexual intercourse, suffered anal rape, were subject to constant beatings, and heard unremitting, insulting comments about their bodies felt increasingly ashamed. To intensify men's sense of impotence, they were sometimes forced to stand by powerlessly and watch as their loved ones were raped and tortured. For example, the torturers raped Margarita Durán in front of Luis Orellana and the other men from La Legua. Viewing themselves as victims froze both men and women in time and inhibited their capacity to remember or imagine alternatives. Physical pain impaired their sense of self and interfered with their mental ability to resist. Isolated from others, some submitted to the overwhelming authority of the military, while others continued to resist.

The security forces underestimated Durán and unwittingly turned her into a witness to their brutality. On 21 December 1973, they took Durán and Sigfrido Orellana to the outskirts of Santiago and dumped them on the road. Alive despite the torture, the two sought refuge with friends. The next day, the radio announced that five "extremists," including Luis Orellana, had been killed in an armed confrontation with the army. When Durán claimed her friends' bodies at the morgue, she noted bruises, burn marks, and other signs of torture.[20] The bodies of the eleven comrades who had followed Comandante Esteban also turned up in December 1973, their corpses marked by extensive torture. Haunted by horrific images of their friends' last hours, survivors such as Durán and Ayress record their own memories, bear witness to the suffering and death of others, and publicize these testimonies in order to complete the historical record and hold the torturers up to public scrutiny. Taking action entails making visible what has been hidden.

In late 1973, hiding still seemed a possible survival strategy. Margarita Durán's family, in the hope of saving their daughter, moved to a different working-class section of Santiago, but Margarita was constantly followed. In the early hours of 29 January 1974, just a day before Nieves Ayress was captured, Margarita Durán again came face to face with Alberto Esteban, who appeared in bloodstained shirt and pants at the head of a posse. He grabbed Margarita Durán, her father, a cousin, and Sigfrido Orellana. Blindfolded but able to catch a glimpse of her surroundings from under the cloth mask, Durán realized that they were returning to Londrés 38. Esteban, with the mixture of vanity and cruelty that characterized many of the torturers, explained why he was in Chile and why he was intent on wiping out "subversives." His brother had been abducted in Argentina and murdered by members of ERP, he claimed, and since he believed that Chilean radicals had aided ERP, he wanted vengeance.

Esteban, like other Pinochet supporters, held a special animus toward women who were considered radicals, and treated them with deliberate and extreme brutality. Esteban tried to obtain information from Durán that he had been unable to obtain from Luis Orellana: an outline of how the underground Socialist Party planned to resist the regime. Later, at a concentration camp, Durán faced another torturer, a man known as Quintana, who wanted her to reveal the Socialists' plan for overthrowing the military dictatorship and to tell him where the arms from La Legua were stockpiled.[21] Although Margarita Durán and Luis Orellana had been romantically involved, she was a Communist, not a Socialist, and even twenty years later she insisted that she had no information to give.[22] Unfortunately, she had a photo of her girlhood friend, Nieves Ayress, among her belongings. Under torture, she identified Ayress as the person in the picture.

This identification seems to have been the beginning of the military's effort to target Nieves Ayress. Ayress only learned in July 2000 that her friend had identified her, when I returned from doing research in the Chilean archives and told her about the statement Durán had made in 1990. Ayress was quick to explain that there is a difference between Durán, who was unable to withstand the pain and linked Ayress's name to a photograph that the torturers already had, and women like Marcia Merino and Luz Arce, who were collaborators.[23]

Confident even now about the righteousness of her political mission, Ayress must have been even more assured when she was younger, before the coup, her imprisonment and torture, and her emigration from Chile. Because Nieves Ayress came from a leftist family, had aligned herself with progressive movements in other Latin American countries, and had resisted the Pinochet regime, she fit the security forces' stereotype of the committed revolutionary. She must have struck DINA as a possible resistance leader. How else can we explain why this twenty-five-year-old woman, who was not a high-ranking party leader, became the focus of so much government attention?[24]

Pinochet, who knew that the Popular Unity government had attracted liberals and leftists from all over the world, feared those he oppressed. Pilar Calveiro, a sociologist who survived Argentina's concentration and extermination camps, has argued that the paranoid vision of authoritarian dictators required killing their presumed enemies before those enemies got them.[25] Projecting plans for the total extermination of everyone who opposed the Chilean dictatorship—that is, anyone who had supported Allende's Popular Unity government or any other movement for social change—Pinochet's agents attempted to crush people like Ayress, Durán, and Orellana. His forces spied on all known leftist groups, captured and tortured whomever they could, and tried to silence those who remained "free." In addition to crushing indigenous social movements and severing Chileans' links with international movements for social change, Pinochet attempted to coordinate the repressive activities of authoritarian governments throughout Latin America.

Within a year of the coup, Chile led Paraguay, Uruguay, Argentina, Bolivia, and Brazil in creating an international ring called Operation Condor to scoop up, torture, and murder presumed enemies of their regime
all over the world.[26]

TRYING TO CRUSH A REVOLUTIONARY FAMILY

On 30 January 1974, Nieves Ayress was captured when she went to see
her family, whom she visited periodically while remaining underground.
In addition to Nieves's activism, the authorities had other reasons to
suspect her family. DINA worried especially about people who had
both leftist sympathies and technical skills; Nieves's father, Carlos Orlando Ayress Soto, made specialized measuring instruments for hospitals and laboratories and had long been associated with movements for
social change. DINA may have believed that the Ayress family could
build triggering devices for bombs. At about 10:30 in the morning,
when Nieves arrived at her family's factory at Valdovinos 1403, virtually next door to the family home on calle Enrique Matte, in the San
Miguel district on the south side of Santiago, she found her father, her
youngest brother, Tato, and a group of employees being held captive by
Comandante Esteban and twelve carabineros.[27] Carlos Ayress, hoping
against hope that the men without warrants were thieves rather than
soldiers, took his life in his hands and ran to the police station a block
away, where he reported the assault. The local police chief denied any
responsibility and charged security forces with the raid. Startled but
courageous, Ayress returned to the factory to be with his children and
his employees. The national police, surprised to see him back, loaded
the family into two unmarked yellow Chevrolet trucks. The rest of the
posse went to the family home.

The next part of the story is pieced together from letters that Virginia
Moreno, Nieves's mother, wrote to various officials while searching for
her husband, son, and daughter. Like her compatriots in the Agrupación de Familiares de Detenidos Desaparecidos (Association of Families of the Detained and Disappeared), Moreno immediately began
looking for her loved ones. On the day her family was abducted from
the factory, Moreno was rinsing clothes on the patio of their home. Comandante Esteban and some men who wore civilian dress but carried
guns entered the house at about 11:30 in the morning. Esteban, whom
she described as a dirty blond with a moustache and beard, led a group
of men who treated Moreno roughly, telling her to shut up and never

explaining who they were or what they wanted. They certainly did not provide any warrant. In her letters, Moreno portrayed the men as marauders who carried off cameras, the stereo, some cassettes, and a stereo cleaner, after holding her, her two younger daughters, and one of her sons prisoner in their home until about 3 P.M.[28]

When the men left, Moreno sent the children to stay with family friends. Learning that Nieves, Tato, and Carlos had all been carried off, Moreno went to the factory, supposedly to organize the books so that the factory could continue to fulfill its orders. She remained there until late in the evening. When she returned to the house, she encountered a young man with a gun. Seeing the battered back door, she realized that the police had broken in after she left. The upholstered furniture and appliances were ripped open, the bedrooms ransacked, a set of precision tools lay broken on the floor, and some jewelry was missing.[29]

In the first of many letters, Moreno effectively created an official record about her missing husband, daughter, and son. When most people in Chile were understandably too terrified to acknowledge what was going on around them, she acted as a witness to what was happening to her country and her family. Now that her memory has fallen victim to Alzheimer's Disease, that written record has enabled her daughter to make her story part of the collective memory.

Interviews conducted with Nieves Ayress, with Virginia Moreno's younger sister Amalia, and with Nieves's younger sister Rosita, about DINA's attack on the family reveal Virginia Moreno's determination to continue fighting. Realizing, as Ayress did before her arrest, that the time was not propitious for open resistance to the military, members of the Ayress-Moreno family seemed to believe that history would play its part in restoring justice once mobilization was again possible. Thus Virginia Moreno created a family portrait, half romantic fiction, half the truth from her vantage point. She portrayed a hard-working family engaged in a specialized industry, rather than a left-wing family with a long tradition of labor and political activism. Throughout her letters, Moreno pretended to believe that a gang of hoodlums, rather than the authorities, had wrecked her home and kidnapped her family.[30] Picturing herself as an outraged citizen, she focused on the material goods the marauders took. She carefully omitted the names of her other daughters, Rosita and Vicky, aged nineteen and sixteen. Amalia Moreno remembers that Virginia immediately sent Rosita and Vicky to stay with friends elsewhere in Chile and then, within the year, to Argentina. When attacks on the left intensified there, Moreno arranged for them to go to Cuba. The two older sons, Alex and Carlos José, escaped to Europe.

THE USE OF SEXUAL TORTURE

For Nieves Ayress, her father Carlos, and her youngest brother, Tato, years of suffering began on 30 January 1974. Nieves's father and brother were held until late May 1976; Nieves remained a prisoner even longer. Initially the kidnapers blindfolded all three and took them downtown to Londrés 38. This stage of her captivity is documented in detail because Ayress wrote it down while she was still in prison and Inés Antúnez, a former political ally whom Ayress encountered in the Women's Correctional Facility, took it out of the prison when she was released into exile.[31]

According to a practice that became routinized in Chile and Argentina, Nieves Ayress was immediately stripped. Forced to stand blindfolded and nude, she faced at least six torturers at each session. Among them she recognized the distinctive accents of Alberto Esteban, the Argentine, and of a Brazilian, a Peruvian, and three Chileans.[32] She has periodically testified about what came next. This version is Virginia Moreno's contemporary account of what happened to her daughter. "They began with insults, beatings, and punches," to her stomach, head, and ears. Esteban yelled at her, "Speak, red dog, or we will shoot your father and little brother right in front of you." The Argentine then pulled out a gun and made a noise as if a cannon was shooting, but no bullet came out. The next day they used cattle prods on her genitals. They also employed an appliance they called the "parilla" or "barbecue grill," a metal table on which she was forced to lie, naked and wet, with her arms and legs splayed, as the torturers applied electric current to every orifice of her body.[33] According to Ayress, "One is no longer more than a body, a sack of flesh, a side of meat."[34] The second day, they brought in an eighteen-year-old man Nieves knew from La Legua and threatened to shoot him too. This time, instead of imitating the sound of a shooting, they actually murdered the young man as she stood by helplessly. As he died, he murmured to her, "Talk, Nieves, save your own life."[35] The torturers were trying to show their prisoners that resistance was impossible and choice meaningless. Like men who were forced to watch loved ones being tortured and raped, Ayress was subjected to cruel demonstrations of her own powerlessness.

Next the torturers cut deep gashes all over Nieves's body, putting lit cigarettes and then electric prods in the wounds. They hung her from the ceiling, stuffed sticks and bottles in her anus and vagina, and raped her. Repeatedly, she passed out. Once, when she regained consciousness, the five men who were tormenting her brought in her father and her teenage brother and threatened to force them to rape her. She lost consciousness again.[36] Nieves claims to have been raped more than forty times, and asserts that she was tortured by General Manuel Contreras Sepúlveda, the head of DINA.[37]

On 1 February 1974, after three days that must have seemed like a lifetime of torture, all three members of the Ayress family were taken, along with Margarita Durán and her father, brother, and cousins, to the concentration camp at Tejas Verdes near the barracks of the School of Army Engineers, located on the road between Santiago and Valparaiso. The refrigerated trucks in which they were transported added to their discomfort, making their battered bodies seem like carcasses of meat. Tejas Verdes had once been a summer camp, and the prisoners were housed in cabins. At 7 A.M. they were routinely taken to be tortured, and they were returned to the cabins at 10 P.M. Between torture sessions, they were kept in closets that lacked any ventilation, even in February, the height of Chile's hot summer.[38]

According to Ayress's later account, Tejas Verdes deserves to be called an extermination camp: "They sent the hopeless cases to Tejas Verdes, activists who were close to death. They threw them on one cot or another and left them there [to die]. Then the torture continued, but with more variety."[39] Nieves Ayress, about whom the international community was to learn in detail, spent most of February 1974 serving as an experimental subject for DINA, as her torturers sought to learn about possible armed resistance at La Legua and to amuse themselves by experimenting on the body and mind of an attractive twenty-five-year-old woman.

Medical professionals played an important role in these experiments. Like Nazi doctors in German concentration camps, many Chilean physicians and nurses collaborated with the torturers. During several torture sessions at Londrés 38, when Nieves Ayress had blacked out and her heart seemed to have stopped, a doctor came in to revive her. After Ayress's first torture session at Tejas Verdes, when she appeared close to death, a nurse examined her. Her menstrual periods stopped after multiple rapes, and she began experiencing nausea along with excruciating pain. At first, she tried to disguise her fears of pregnancy: "I was pregnant, but I tried to keep the news secret since a doctor at Tejas Verdes wanted to [experiment] to discover the limits of the pain a pregnant woman could endure."[40] When Ayress later reached the Women's Correctional Facility in Santiago, a Dr. Mery, who taught gynecology at the Catholic University Medical School, quickly realized that Ayress was pregnant and congratulated her for the honor she would gain by "being able to bear a child for the fatherland."[41] But he didn't stop the torture, which caused her to suffer a miscarriage. In Argentina, certain doctors were more careful. In one of those paradoxes highlighted by Pilar Calveiro, the same doctor who was studying methods of torturing pregnant women would interrupt torture sessions to monitor the heartbeat of the fetus, about whose potential life he was deeply concerned.[42] Doctors in Chile and Argentina did not limit themselves to experimenting with the reproductive lives of their prisoners. Pedro Alejandro Matta, another survivor of Pinochet's camps, explains that many of Chile's leading cardiologists perfected their craft by keeping torture victims alive. Torturers were trained to break ribs in order to massage a heart that gave out as a result of electric shocks.[43] Of course, broken ribs only intensified the suffering of victims, who were frequently brought back to life when their pain made death preferable.

Nieves Ayress, who is as determined now as she was then not to become a martyr, keeps these painful memories alive because she continues to resist what the Pinochet regime tried to do to her and thousands of others. Conditions at the camp were designed to break down any human relations or solidarity that prisoners might develop. Ayress was frequently kept in isolation during the first year of her imprisonment. At such times, she was held in a cell about four feet by four feet. Food came once a day and was thrown on the floor, forcing her to eat like an animal on all fours. Most days a guard took her to a latrine at 6 A.M. Since she had no soap and no way to heal the burns and cuts that left open wounds all over and inside her body, she had massive infections. The shackling, electric shocks, and rapes were standard fare, but the torturers outdid themselves with bestiality. Ingrid Olderock, a member of the national police, trained Dobermans to rape women.[44] With Nieves Ayress and other women prisoners, they introduced starving rats into the vagina, where the terrified rodents ripped and bit in their attempts to get out.

Nieves Ayress, her brother, and her father, along with many others from La Legua who had survived Tejas Verdes, were shipped back to Santiago on 26 February 1974. While Carlos and Tato Ayress were dropped off at the National Stadium, Margarita Durán and Nieves Ayress were taken to the Women's Correctional Facility at 8 avenida

Vicuña McKenna, in the southern part of Santiago. Durán remained there for four months. She was moved briefly to another concentration camp, Tres Alamos, on the outskirts of Santiago, and then was freed on 26 July 1974. Fearing future abductions, she left for Argentina on 4 September 1974. Afterward, she fled to Canada. When representative democracy returned to Chile, Durán returned to her parents' home in La Legua after sixteen years of exile.

After 26 February 1974, Ayress took advantage of the limited contact with other prisoners that was allowed in the Women's Correctional Facility. Still a consummate political organizer, Nieves told the story of her month-long ordeal to Inés Antúnez, with whom she had previously worked in various political movements. Although Ayress was weak and suffered from infections all over her body, the two women decided that Ayress should write out her testimony so that Antúnez, who was about to be sent into exile, could secretly carry it with her. Antúnez went to Argentina, where she passed the note to Fanny Edelman, the secretary general of the Women's International Democratic Federation, founded by French survivors of Nazi concentration camps and former members of the Resistance. Inés Antúnez bore witness to Nieves Ayress's suffering and brought international attention to her case.

In early March 1974, Virginia Moreno, having heard nothing about her family for twenty-seven days, received an anonymous telephone call telling her that her daughter was being held in the Women's Correctional Facility and that her husband and son were in concentration camps. Since the abduction, Moreno had combed the city of Santiago, seeking information about her family. Other parents in Chile, looking for their missing relatives, formed the Agrupación de Familiares de Detenidos Desaparecidos. The phone call, coupled with the fact that Ayress was temporarily housed in a regular prison rather than a secret detention center, provided Moreno with an opportunity all families of the missing craved: the possibility of interceding on behalf of their children. Armed with specific information about her daughter, Moreno demanded to see her. Shortly before 8 March 1974, Virginia Moreno received word that she could come to the prison. Ayress confided in her mother about the ordeal she had endured, and Moreno immediately turned to publicity to save her family. The letters to officials that followed that meeting map out the case Virginia Moreno pursued for three years to help liberate her family.[45]

On 11 March, Moreno went to the Criminal Court of San Miguel and filed for a writ of habeas corpus for her daughter, who had never been formally arrested or charged. Moreno described her daughter's torture and rape. She also entered into the court record a clipping that had appeared in the government's official newspaper, *La Tercera de la Hora,* alleging that the government was searching for an Argentine radical, whose picture they provided. Realizing that authorities were trying to help Esteban infiltrate other resistance groups, Moreno exposed him. Although Virginia Moreno's direct action made her a formidable opponent of the regime, her major achievement was publicizing the story of her daughter's ordeal in foreign newspapers. Reversing the generational order by which parents customarily relay their memories to their children, Virginia Moreno recorded and bore public witness to her daughter's account of torture and imprisonment. Although she received threatening anonymous phone calls, she herself was never detained. Largely through her efforts, her husband and son were released from prison in May 1976, and her daughter was freed in December 1976.

In shaping their family's tragedy into a national epic, Nieves Ayress and her mother proclaimed the gendered nature of political repression. Moreno's petition for a writ of habeas corpus provided a detailed account of the sexual dimension of her daughter's torture.[46] The *Washington Post* correspondent in Chile, Joseph Novitski, found the writ, which had been denied but remained on file. He featured Ayress's testimony in a lead article, published in the *Washington Post* on 27 May 1974, outlining some of the horrors for which the Chilean government was responsible.[47] Apparently taking special care not to offend the dictatorship, Novitski said that repression seemed to be diminishing in Chile, eight months after the coup. But he commented that "the new government has behaved most often like an occupying army establishing rules for civilians to live by." According to Novitski, "Chile's twenty-eight Catholic bishops claim that prisoners are regularly tortured." In order to protect his sources, Novitski described Chile as a small country where news travels quickly. The reports about torture, he claimed, circulated widely, even though prisoners were not charged with crimes and people did not usually know where the secret prisons were located. Novitski reminded his readers that "charges of torture are hard to prove, and the junta's rebuttals are hard to evaluate because the victims have almost all remained nameless."[48]

The complaint Moreno made to the First Criminal Court of San Miguel about the abduction and torture of her husband and two children was devastating to the regime because it provided detailed evidence of the military rulers' brutality. Novitski summarized Moreno's case, saying that "her daughter had been tortured in four ways before being turned over to an army regiment where she was unharmed, and later confined in Santiago's women's jail," and providing specific descriptions of the torture. In a well-researched piece of investigative journalism, he followed the petition for habeas corpus through the courts. Novitski reported that after the criminal court judge claimed that he did not have jurisdiction, the case passed to the army prosecutor's office, and then to the air force prosecutor, who was supposedly drawing up charges against Ayress.[49] Novitski implied that there was a separate agency, more powerful than the army or the air force, which was carrying out the protection of the regime and the repression of dissidents. That organization began its work around November 1973 and was formally organized as DINA on 14 June 1974. Although DINA was secret, it operated with the highest powers, seemingly separate from and superior to those of the military and armed police.

Rafael Otero, the Chilean columnist for *La Segunda,* a Spanish-language newspaper published in Santiago, who wrote "Charquican" (Gossip) about Washington, D.C. under the pen name of Paz Alegría, rushed to defend Pinochet's reputation. He wrote two quick rebuttals to Novitski's *Washington Post* article: a piece entitled "A Perfect State of Health," which appeared as a gossip column on 4 June 1974 but was dated 27 May 1974, and "The Rivals of 'Playboy,'" which appeared as a signed article under his own name on 4 June 1974. In both articles, he sought to humiliate Nieves Ayress in much the same way as the torturers had.[50] Attempting to control the damage to the Pinochet regime's public image, Paz Alegría disputed Novitski's conclusions and his evidence. Alegría claimed that Novitski based his arguments about Ayress's torture on *"rumores"* or *"capuchas"* that were circulating in Chile. Alegría's use of the term *capuchas,* while theoretically correct as a synonym for *rumores,* revealed more than it intended: torture victims were usually masked and frequently hooded with capuchas so that victims could not identify their torturers, who in turn were spared seeing the pain on their victims' faces. The term evoked what it was intended to deny.

Paz Alegría claimed that Nieves Ayress was in perfect health in the Women's Correctional Prison.[51] What particularly aroused Alegría's ire was that Virginia Moreno's statement about what happened to her daughter was not just hearsay but rather part of a sworn statement to the court, and that Joseph Novitski could cite a case number for the statement. Alegría contended that the charges that Moreno made and

Novitski repeated were outrageous. Yet Novitski had cited the original claim made to the First Criminal Court of San Miguel at 4 P.M. on 11 March 1974.[52] He quoted from Moreno's statement that her daughter

> was raped ferociously by three or four men. She was handcuffed and blind-folded. . . . Also they introduced sticks into her vagina. They tied her up and separated her legs and made rats walk over her, making them enter her vagina. They did the same thing with spiders. They applied electric current to her tongue, ears, and vagina. They hit her head, especially behind the ears. They hit her in the stomach. They hung her up, sometimes by the legs and sometimes by the arms. They terrorized her because she had traveled to Cuba on a scholarship to study cinema in 1971.[53]

Alegría asked ingenuously why, if Ayress was in such bad shape, she had been sent to the prison rather than the hospital. He assured readers that the government would never permit torture and argued that the whole case might well be a fabrication. Alegría undercut his case by overstating it. The gossip columnist made especially unfortunate comparisons between the Ayress allegations and situations in the United States at the time. He asked whether the Nixon administration, which was then riddled with scandal about Vice President Spiro T. Agnew's conviction for corruption and the Watergate break-in and cover-up, was filled with criminals just because they had uncovered one, and whether the governor of Maryland and the police permitted the rape of young black women just because two police officers had been charged with murdering one of them.[54] Such comparisons did not enhance the columnist's credibility with readers of the *Washington Post*.

Rafael Otero's second article, which purported to be a serious opinion piece, took up the charges of sexual torture, which must have especially embarrassed the Pinochet regime.[55] Otero ridiculed the charges: "I confess that among the many statements I've read that hover between truth and fiction, the thing that [is] most confusing is the case of the obstetrical rats and the gynecological spiders." Venturing another comparison with American society, he criticized the United States for having the greatest number of rapes of any country and aligned himself with feminists, who claimed that victims of rape hated to report the crimes committed against them because "they suffer more from police interrogations and in the [cross-examinations of the defense] lawyers than from the attacks of those degenerates who raped them." Positioning himself among proponents of justice for women, Otero contended that Novitski's article about the rats' "excursion through the genitals of Luz de las Nieves is destined to provoke a horrific impact in this country [the United States]." The rest of the article drips with sarcasm, suggesting, "Miss Luz de las Nieves [leaving out her surname] did not travel to Cuba to study film, but theater and science fiction." He accused her of repeating an ancient superstition that rats climb up women's legs and into their genitals. Referring to Freud, whose psychological theories the dictatorship detested as much as it did the communist theories of Marx, Otero suggested that such irrational fears accounted for women's terror of rats. Thus he dismissed Ayress's testimony.

Virginia Moreno responded with outrage to these articles on 5 June, the day after Otero's second article appeared. In a letter to the editor of *La Segunda* that she clearly hoped would be printed but never was, she assumed the mantle of the suffering spouse and parent, claiming that "no one has the right to ridicule [*hacer mofa*] the pain of a wife and mother." Denying any selfish motivation, she asserted: "I am a dignified and honest woman and I have never sought to publicize my pain."[56] Amalia Moreno recalls how her sister summoned all her energy to combat this ideological attack on her daughter.[57] Virginia Moreno had taken a calculated risk in publicizing her daughter's case. She must have worried that the publicity might provoke the secret police to torture Nieves even more, even if it also might prevent them from murdering her. In fact, although Ayress knew nothing about the exchange published in American newspapers, she was repeatedly interrogated about the "conspiracy" in which she and her mother were allegedly engaged.[58]

Nieves Ayress was kept in the Women's Correctional Prison longer than had at first been announced, but by late spring of 1974 she was taken to Tres Alamos, the secret detention site that stood on the army base of Cuatro Alamos on the outskirts of Santiago. Between that time and her release into exile on 8 December 1976, she was moved among a variety of concentration camps.

INTERNATIONALIZING THE CAMPAIGN
AGAINST HUMAN RIGHTS ABUSES

International human rights groups first heard about what had been happening to Nieves Ayress from a communiqué dated 18–21 February 1975, to the Third Session of the International Commission on Crimes of the Military Junta in Chile distributed by Fanny Edelman, the secretary general of the Women's International Democratic Federation. They distributed a press release that included Ayress's full testimony.[59] Entitled "The Situation of Women" and based on the testimony that Inés

Antúnez had given to Edelman in Argentina, the communiqué explained Nieves Ayress's abduction, her incarceration in various concentration camps, and her mother's attempt to file formal charges in order to publicize the sexual torture Ayress had suffered.[60] Edelman, who became Ayress's chief advocate, included additional evidence about the Pinochet regime's torture of women to substantiate Ayress's statement. For example, a doctor from the International Association of Women who had examined women prisoners at Buen Pastor Prison in Santiago indicated that they too had scars and sores showing that they had been tortured.[61] The ad hoc working group of the United Nations Commission on Human Rights, the Organization of American States, and the Women's International Democratic Federation provided detailed evidence about state terror in Chile. By bearing witness, Edelman helped keep Ayress's story alive as a gendered historical account of the Pinochet dictatorship and a call to action against it.

What makes Ayress's story so remarkable, given its shocking, excruciatingly detailed descriptions of sexual torture, is its focus upon what happened to the speaker. In most places where the torturers have done their worst, in countries such as Argentina, Chile, and South Africa, women have generally been the majority of those testifying to atrocities against comrades and family members, but very few women have been willing to speak about suffering they themselves endured.[62] Since many cultures share the torturers' and rapists' confusion of violence with sex, women who have withstood torture that seems to sully them sexually are often reluctant to discuss any part of their own suffering. For Ayress, telling her story was a political statement, a form of direct action linking her to her community, both in prison and after she had gone into exile.

Once Nieves Ayress was released from prison, she took over the story-telling from Inés Antúnez and Virginia Moreno. Seeking refuge temporarily in Germany, she immediately joined the MIR, which struggled in exile and sought to expose the continuing brutality of the regime. Ayress, who had been in prison for three years with little or no expectation of release, promoted the cause of other prisoners, including those who were still hidden in concentration camps and those who had been murdered. Why she did so, and how she found the strength to tell and retell the appalling story of her suffering, is a question worthy of careful consideration. Understanding Nieves Ayress as a witness to her own torture requires us to understand how political prisoners resist and recover from trauma.

During her captivity, Nieves had forced herself to remain conscious of the prison and the people around her in order to stay alive and keep her sanity. If she let down her guard, there was no guarantee of her sanity, even if she survived. As Pilar Calveiro has pointed out, many prisoners who were alone, chained, and awaiting the next torture session tried to wipe their memories clean, fearing that they would not be able to withstand the pain and would blurt out the names of those closest to them. "When a militant is captured he not only pretends not to know, he authentically forgets: he forgets the information that may put other people in danger; he forgets names, houses, and even faces. He has lost the capacity to remember precise information, especially that having to do with names and addresses. This is a recurring pattern among survivors."[63]

Comparing Nieves Ayress with other torture survivors underscores the force of will it took for her to remember her comrades and speak publicly about her ordeal. Ayress needed to remember as a way of maintaining connection. She had enough confidence in her ability to withstand torture without betraying her friends that she dared to keep a historical record, registering not only particular incidents, but also their meanings. In an interview that appeared in the *Sunday Times* of London just eleven days after her release from prison, Nieves Ayress challenged the Chilean government's argument that because 304 prisoners were released on 8 December 1976, all political prisoners in Chile were now free. Bearing witness, as others would do for almost thirty years after her, Ayress counted almost two thousand people who had disappeared after she had seen them in the concentration camps.[64] The words of a survivor carried special weight, a fact that Pinochet must have realized. Ayress's memories were not mere expressions of political opinion, but provided detailed evidence about the way in which DINA had employed torture. The *Sunday Times* article refers to her as "Chile junta's top victim," and claims that she was "the only Chilean political prisoner subject to a decree putting her in close custody 'forever.'"[65] Dismissing the importance that the newspaper accorded her, the Chilean government tried to disparage her, just as they had ridiculed her mother. The Pinochet regime referred to her as a "poor unreliable demented creature on whose evidence no reliance could be placed." Antony Terry, the *Sunday Times* reporter who interviewed her right after her arrival in Berlin, countered by saying that she was "a lively and highly intelligent woman and still attractive despite her appalling suffering."[66]

That "appalling suffering" was the central focus of many of the articles about Nieves Ayress, both those published at the time and those that have appeared since Pinochet's detention in London. Virginia Moreno had to get world attention in order to save her daughter's life, and the methods of torture were part of the story. In recalling the details of the torture, Virginia Moreno, Nieves Ayress, and most historians are forced to make the same unpleasant choices. Even this chapter speaks of Ayress's torture in the passive voice, as if she were an object on which powerful others acted, and describes forms of suffering that most victims find unspeakable. Yet associating a specific person with specific forms of suffering provides evidence of human rights abuses. The details of torture experienced by women like Nieves Ayress transform general charges against authoritarian governments into specific indictments of officials in the Pinochet regime that can be pursued in court. Insofar as those interested in justice associate it with public exposure, those responsible for torturing others must appear, not as part of the machinery of power, but as specific people who committed particular crimes.

Ayress asserts that she learned a different kind of politics in prison than she had understood before the coup. Although Ayress was regarded as a dangerous enemy of Chilean sovereignty, she spent her final year in prison in Sequimich, near the little town of Pirque in the mountains above Santiago, where she finally enjoyed the company of other women. At that time, she came to understand the centrality of feminism to democratic struggles. She remembers that "there were doctors, professors and other professionals along with humble people and together we created a clothes factory in which we each earned something; we organized a child care center because many of the women gave birth in the concentration camps. Within the prison we created a communal society."[67] Ayress's distaste for machismo also intensified because of what she and other women prisoners suffered. In a marked departure from her customary calm and reflective demeanor, Ayress fulminates against the men who chastised wives who had "dishonored them" by being raped in prison. If nostalgia enters into any of Ayress's memories of her imprisonment, it appears in the stories she remembers about these women. One of them embroidered a poem with a needle and some of her own hair, while another, who was dying of untreated cancer, kept herself alive until she succeeded in seeing her partner, who was also a political prisoner.[68]

In all these women, especially her mother and Inés Antúnez, Ayress found personal as well as political supporters. Moreno and Antúnez were entirely selfless. Either of them could have denied the truth of what Ayress told them, or simply remained silent out of fear. Either of them could have shared Ayress's fate if the extent of their support had become known to the authorities. Yet these two women risked their own lives out of love and solidarity. Their commitments must have helped Nieves Ayress maintain her sense of belonging to a community. At the beginning of her ordeal, when the only men she saw were the torturers, the guards, and the doctors who supported the regime, she may have associated Antúnez and her mother with a community of women. But it is important to remember that not all women were supportive. When Ayress was in the Women's Correctional Prison in Santiago, she was under the strict control of Chilean nuns who never challenged the authority of the government or the torturers. Through the support of her family and friends, by maintaining her connections to the community from which she had been taken, and even by creating a community in prison, Ayress survived with her sense of solidarity intact.

Being unvanquished is what Nieves Ayress treasures most. She began her political life as a young activist committed to social justice, and she has never wavered from that course. Finding strength in solidarity, her work with women living with AIDS and survivors of domestic violence provides her with her greatest sense of accomplishment. One achievement she counts as a special triumph is powerfully gendered: her ability to have a child. Survivors of the kind of torture Ayress underwent are often physically as well as mentally damaged, and many never make a full recovery. The tearing of her cervix and the toxoplasmosis transmitted by rats made bearing a child almost impossible for Ayress. Reconstructive surgery provided her with a miraculous recovery. "My daughter is my triumph over the military," Nieves Ayress says with great pleasure.[69]

In their efforts to seek justice and record what happened, survivors and their supporters have worked out different strategies to give voice to their experiences and perspectives. Those who have interviewed Nieves Ayress or heard her speak in person or on film about her experiences remark that she discusses the torture as if in a trance, or as if she were reading her own testimony from a book. Words fail her, as they do most victims of torture. Many survivors, like Pilar Calveiro, write about their torture in the third person. Some prisoners in the concentration camps relinquished any hopes for the future and tried, even after their liberation, to suppress their memories in order to overcome their yearning and grief for all they had lost. Always an activist, Nieves Ayress risked personal exposure and continues to insist on remembering.

CHAPTER 2

Pots and Pans Will Break My Bones

Nieves Ayress was not the only one determined to remember. Among Salvador Allende's advisors, Valencian Joan Garcés had already written about some of the political crises the government endured, and he continued to act as a witness after he escaped from Chile.[1] But few wrote about daily life under the Popular Unity (Unidad Popular, UP) government. Two exceptions, María Correa Morandé and Teresa Donoso Loero, wrote from their perspective as right-wing women leaders who proudly boasted about helping to overthrow the UP.[2] On the other side, just after the coup, trying to keep alive the memory of what Allende had tried to achieve, American activist Carol Andreas reflected on her life in Chile.[3] But many people who dedicated themselves to getting people out of the country and publicizing the continued repression had no time to reminisce about how they fit into the movement to democratize Chile. Writers Ariel Dorfman and Marc Cooper had to wait almost thirty years to recall the heady days of the UP and the growing crisis that engulfed it.[4]

The Chile I encountered in the 1990s was a far cry from the country from which Nieves Ayress was expelled in 1977. A plebiscite in 1988, designed to keep dictator Augusto Pinochet in power for another decade, accomplished the impossible: he was voted out of office and replaced by a moderate democracy. It was difficult to reconstruct the history of actions that are shrouded in silence born of regret and shame. Rather than remember their own fears and the ways they acted on them, many decent people who abhorred the violence that followed the military coup wanted to focus on their resistance to the dictatorship or even on their dissatisfaction with the so-called transition to democracy. Remembering one facet of the past served to overcome another.

As I interviewed women in Chile who had opposed the dictatorship of Augusto Pinochet during the 1980s, I also tried to talk with women about the final days of the UP, especially the last three months, when women from all walks of life turned against the government in massive demonstrations. But it seemed impossible for women to speak of that period. If they said anything about 1973, they focused on the coup of 11 September as a traumatic event that had happened *to* them, not as the culmination of a political process in which they might have played some small part. When I asked women who had not been members of the well-organized right-wing women's movement about the long lines at grocery stores, the sense of disorder that the American embargo caused, or the sense of chaos that the right wing promoted and exploited, I was surprised to find that almost all of them changed the subject. Instead of talking about their memories of those final months and days, they told me what they were doing on the day of the coup in which Allende died. After my 1994 research trip, I returned to the United States, where a new student, María Prada (pseud.), inadvertently provided me with many explanations for the resistance I had encountered.[5] María, who was at the center of a group of smart and sophisticated Latin American graduate students, asked me to work with her in a tutorial. We had long and intense discussions about how to interpret what people meant by their actions and how symbols and rituals might figure in resistance. We constantly examined the kinds of public spectacles organized by those seeking power. Dissatisfied with how limited our methods were, we grappled with how to free the past from the censorship of contemporary insights.

By chance, María and I found ourselves on a long train ride together. Chatting personally for the first time, I learned that her soft Spanish accent was Chilean, not Colombian, as I had at first presumed. She told me that her family had come to the United States a few months after the coup. As a sixteen-year-old student leader in high school, she had vivid memories of Allende's last days. Unlike many of her fellow Chileans, she recalled her activities during the six months preceding the coup. Most Chileans remember the violent overthrow of their government in much the same way that Americans remember the assassination of President John F. Kennedy or the attacks on the World Trade Center and the

Pentagon: the coup ripped people from their past and created a new view of their place in the world. History was reassembled in light of what happened after. The death of Chilean democracy cauterized the feelings of some who had been critical of the Popular Unity government. Many people abandoned hopes that the removal of Allende by a military coup would eliminate the strikes, shortages, and social disorder that the right wing promoted during Allende's last years. Shameful that demonstrating against Allende may have contributed to his downfall, people were reluctant to talk about what they had felt and done before the coup.

A guilty conscience frequently leads to the suppression of memory. After all, memory is always selective. Why dwell on those memories that cause grief and pain? A generation of historians has tried to explain how extraordinary events are integrated into people's everyday life. Alessandro Portelli and Luisa Passerini, writing about Italy, have tried to understand resistance and accommodation under Fascism through interviews with ordinary people, while Claudia Koonz, writing about Germany, and Lisa Baldez and Margaret Power, in their work on right-wing women leaders in Chile, have focused on ways women leaders tried to make what they were doing appear apolitical.[6]

When I told María about my frustrating attempts to interview women in Chile about their memories of the final days before the coup, she dropped a bombshell. Although her father was a socialist doctor and her mother an open-minded woman from a landowning family, María had been sent to the Italian school in Chile, an institution with ultraconservative views. During the last year of Allende's presidency, when María was sixteen, she was president of the student body. María remembers being among the conservative students who threw rocks (from the subway under construction in Santiago) at government supporters. She recalls the feelings of outrage and self-righteousness she and the other students felt that led them to street fighting. Her group entertained the wives of the striking copper miners, whose poignant marches to Santiago in April and June 1973 discredited the government, seeming to show that Allende could not even serve the workers in whose name the government was carrying out massive reforms. Along with other youth largely from private Catholic schools, María organized to oppose Allende's attempts to extend public education. This program was presented as a part of a socialist plot to indoctrinate children and remove them—perhaps even physically—from their families. María followed her family to the United States a year after the coup and gradually recognized what Pinochet was doing. She became active in solidarity campaigns with people suffering from the violence in Chile and other Latin American countries, and slowly became a critic of U.S. foreign policy.

María Prada was not my only informant. One of the few people in Chile who had been willing to speak candidly about how her daily life drew her into activities that undermined Allende was a woman in her late seventies. Alicia Cabrini (pseud.) was the retired director of a private girls' school. I had gone to Rancagua, near El Teniente mine, to meet her daughter, Violeta Rosas (pseud.), a journalist said to have information about the mine workers' strikes against Allende. We enjoyed each other's company, and she invited me to lunch at her parents' home. Her mother, Alicia, knew exactly what I was asking when I inquired about the difficult time before the coup. She responded without rancor: "With five kids in school, all I did was worry about how to put food on the table. If it weren't for Pepa Blanca's [pseud.] father [the local store-keeper], we would have starved. He hid milk, sugar, and rice for his old customers. He sold them to us for a fair price. But we would have paid anything just to get the food we needed."[7] A woman whose grown children ran the gamut of political opinions, Alicia Cabrini was not ashamed to admit that she did what she had to do to feed and clothe her family during hard times in the early 1970s. While liberals and leftists emphasized their hatred of the dictatorship that had overthrown Allende, Alicia recalled how, as a mother, she had been desperate. Along with women who did not have her contacts, she stood in long lines, waiting for provisions that never appeared on the shelves. She was grateful to the storekeeper who had favored her family for helping them get through this terrible time. In Alicia I had found someone old enough and in María I had found someone young enough not to suffer guilty amnesia about even the minimal role they had played in undermining Allende.

Women even younger than María remember women's demonstrations in Chile. A few years ago, at a prominent university in the southern United States, a group of women students was looking for resonant symbols for a demonstration about welfare rights. They vaguely recalled that in some other country, in the not-too-distant past, large groups of women, banging pots and pans and complaining that the authorities were not providing necessary food and medicine, had helped overthrow their government. Since the American students had only known Chile under the authoritarian dictatorship of Augusto Pinochet,

they presumed that Pinochet's government was the object of these
women's wrath, so they adopted the symbol of the empty pots and pans,
entirely unconscious that in using it for a progressive purpose, they
were turning its meaning around. Certain symbols, such as the Confed-
erate flag or the swastika, are so powerfully associated with one group
that they can never be redeemed. Other symbols, such as pots and pans,
can take on different meanings in other political and social contexts.
That most women in Chile, like those at this university, may have been
unaware of those long, deep cultural traditions of symbolic action
around consumer issues does not make those traditions less important;
the most powerful symbols are carried on in just this way, as part of the
cultural repertoire on which ordinary people draw at moments of crisis.
In fact, such noisy and raucous women's demonstrations had erupted in
Europe, North America, and South America at least back to seven-
teenth century to censure speculators and attack the government for
failing to ensure a sufficient supply of food.[8]

Vivid images of Chilean women banging empty pots with lids and
spoons, shouting for increased food supplies, claiming that the government was undemocratic, and urging the military to take power to end
the "chaos" came to haunt Allende's regime in Chile. These protests
grew in size and attracted women from the working class as well as
from the middle class. The most dramatic demonstration, which took
place in Santiago on 5 September 1973, six days before the military
stepped in, involved approximately fifty to a hundred thousand women.
Such demonstrations, in which women denied their political character
under the cover of gender and called into question the masculinity of
men who opposed them, engaged massive numbers of ordinary women.
They protested shortages of basic necessities and contributed to the
sense that Allende's Popular Unity government was undemocratic and
could not maintain order. The very words *order* and *chaos* became
justifications for the military coup.

In fact, massive demonstrations, like vociferous arguments, are signs
of democracy so long as antagonists do not resort to the use of violence.
Hundreds of thousands of people marched in support of the Popular
Unity government on 4 September, marking the third anniversary of Allende's election.[9] The day before the UP demonstration, a right-wing
women's coalition called El Poder Femenino (Feminine Power) led a call
for Allende to restore order or resign and let a plebiscite determine
Chile's fate.[10] On the afternoon of 5 September, El Poder Femenino,
along with the right-wing National Party, a group of women profes-

sionals, members of the conservative Christian Democratic Party, and hundreds of thousands of supporters marched, calling for Allende to step down.[11] Taking place only six days before the military coup that resulted in a seventeen-year dictatorship, the massive women's march has been engraved on people's memories inside and outside of Chile.[12] From San Borja Hospital to Santa Rosa along the Alameda, or avenida Bernardo O'Higgins, hundreds of thousands of women and their supporters took over downtown Santiago.

In Santiago, the crowd chanted, "Allende, escucha, mujeres somos muchas" (Listen, Allende, of us women there are many); "¡Que se vaya!" (Get going!); and "La única solución, que se tome el avión" (The only way to end the pain is that you take an airplane). The crowd listened to Euviges Cuéllar Zamora, the wife of a striking truck driver, as she denounced the government.[13]

Those familiar with the levels of repression that soon followed can only marvel at—and perhaps also shiver at—the freedom of these right-wing women and their supporters to spread out across public spaces and act out their rituals of protest. Even in comparison to many self-proclaimed democratic governments, Popular Unity exercised an extraordinary degree of forbearance in its treatment of opponents. Yet the government—prisoner of its preoccupation with the obvious organizational strength of male adversaries in the conservative Christian Democrat and right-wing Fatherland and Freedom political parties—was helpless before groups claiming to act only in their capacity as women and mothers. Allende and his supporters failed to recognize that street politics could be as much a forum for public debate as were pronouncements from intellectuals and critics.[14] The Popular Unity government, refusing to recognize the panic that motivated working-class and poor women to mobilize along with women who would usually be their class enemies, also lacked verbal weapons to confront opponents presenting themselves as apolitical women.

SPEAKING AND ACTING "AS WOMEN"

Frequently, groups of women speak out "as women" about public issues, legitimating their activities by denying that they want to promote any overtly political goals. Despite their unconventional political behavior—which in Chile between 1971 and 1973 included parading en masse in public places, confronting government officials, and calling on men to use violence to restore "order,"—they say they are only doing what they were raised to do as "good women." They are, they proclaim, acting as mothers, wives, and household managers, roles that are not usually understood in political terms. When they demonstrate in the streets, these women say that they are doing so because they are struggling to fulfill their responsibility to provide for their families, and necessity has compelled them to seek relief from those who have made their task impossible. These groups insist that they are not challenging the prevailing gender system, but acting within its dictates and striving to uphold their womanly role. Indeed, in Chile by 1973, they went so far as to shame men into fulfilling what they saw as their manly responsibilities. Acting in the name of womanhood, allegedly to preserve their families and communities, women's groups justify actions that are overtly political, take them well outside their usual domain of the home, the neighborhood, and the marketplace, and directly challenge state power.

The rhetoric of acting in public "as women" is not the exclusive property of either the right or the left. The right wing mobilized women on this basis in Chile before the coup, but at other times and in other places, left-wing movements have used the same approach. Indeed, this type of appeal can enhance women's support of almost any kind of political movement. In the early twentieth century, across Europe and the Americas, both progressive and reactionary groups appealed to women with such language, as did some organized women's groups.

One especially clear example comes from Spain, where during certain crises women mobilized "as women." In my research on women's political activism in Barcelona, which became a center of anarchism and other left-wing political movements, I gave the term *female consciousness* to the condition by which some women and men come to believe that a whole category of people calling themselves "women" or claiming to act in pursuit of widely accepted "feminine" goals have privileges to act under certain conditions.[15] That belief, which contrasts clearly with feminist assertions of women's rights, has been a galvanizing force for movements on both the right and the left. It gives women license to act politically without requiring them to question the fundamental social order, and it enables women to act independently of men, even to defy and confront them, without appearing to challenge them at all. This stance, then, can serve as an effective cover for more controversial political positions, as well as for unconventional public actions. Proclaiming that they are seeking only to preserve their families and communities in the face of material hardship and social disorder, women can justify their political activism to themselves and to others.

Nowhere was this more striking than in the role Chilean women played in undermining support for the Popular Unity government in Chile between 1970 and 1973. From the moment Allende was elected, right-wing women speaking and acting "as women" participated in increasingly violent public events that led up to the overthrow of the Popular Unity government. Posing as passive victims while seeking the violent overthrow of the government certainly seems like a paradoxical act; that women did this in the name of womanhood is even more puzzling. Moving the confrontation from the political to the civic realm, the women set the stage for massive use of violence against those who had been elected to power. The women could never have instigated the army coup by themselves, but they discredited Allende and provided moral cover for the plotters.

A minority government, Allende's Popular Unity Party was elected in 1970 by a plurality rather than a majority; Allende received only 36.2 percent of the popular vote. The electoral returns revealed a substantial gender gap: Allende won 30.5 percent of the votes cast by women and 42 percent of those cast by men.[16] In fact, 69.5 percent of women's votes went to candidates who ran against Allende.[17] The Popular Unity government roused the hopes of the left and the fears of the right, while the center became more and more fluid.

Women who opposed the Popular Unity program began to speak and act "as women" even before Allende took office. Just after the election on 4 September 1970, a group of women wearing black dresses held a mock funeral outside the presidential palace, theatrically mourning the death of democracy in Chile. A group with no name had gathered twenty thousand signatures from women, which a small group presented to the outgoing Christian Democratic president, asking him to refuse to confirm Allende the "Communist," because he had won a plurality rather than a majority. Gathering so many signatures so quickly showed a high degree of organization. On 9 September 1970, approximately twenty women held a silent protest march, warning "el poder público" (public power or public opinion) about their fears for the country's future. In flyers bearing the headline "El poder femenino es la fuerza unida de la nación" (Woman power is the united force of the country), the organizers explained their actions: "We don't wish to see our country subjected to foreign ideologies. We repudiate the insolent minority that is trying to impose upon us an alien tyranny, which claims to speak in the name of the people but whose only objective is to crush us and reduce us to the slavery of countries within the clutches of international communism."[18] From that day on, every afternoon, a group of well-dressed women kept silent vigil in front of the presidential palace, carrying signs with the slogan, "Chile is and will be a free country" (Chile es y será un país libre).[19]

Between the election and Allende's inauguration on 24 October 1970, forces within Chile, aided by the U.S. State Department and the Central Intelligence Agency (CIA), attempted to prevent Allende from coming to power. The United States supplied arms through the CIA that may or may not have been used to kidnap and murder General René Schneider, commander-in-chief of the armed forces, who was committed to obeying the constitution.[20] Despite well-organized opposition, the constitutional succession took place. However, tightly coordinated actions by the Chilean right and the United States continued to destabilize the government. Despite these early activities, during the first year Allende was in office, right-wing women were relatively quiescent. Chilean businessmen such as Augustín Edwards, scion of a vast media empire that included the newspaper El Mercurio, allegedly met on 14 or 15 September with Richard Helms, the director of the CIA, to discuss how to destabilize Allende and force him from power.[21] And the United States embarked on an economic embargo of Chile, making it harder for Chileans to receive spare parts and supplies. Ultimately, the embargo, combined with declining copper prices on the world market, reduced Chile's foreign currency supplies and led to increasing shortages of basic necessities.

The first massive demonstration of women against the Popular Unity government took place on 1 December 1971, a year after the Popular Unity government came to power and just as Fidel Castro was preparing to leave Chile after a three-and-a-half-week visit. Because the last women's mobilization led almost immediately to the coup, it converged with the memory of the first "March of the Empty Pots" two years earlier. At the first march, a mass of women, estimated at between 10,000 and 100,000, marched through the downtown area, beating pots and pans with lids and spoons and waving empty shopping bags.[22] Disparaging the government's ability to supply basic necessities and demanding that Allende step down, the march was a triumph for a group of women drawn from the right-wing and conservative parties. Organized covertly but with a permit to march, the women wended their way from the Plaza Baquedano through the fashionable Forestal Park near the art museum and then to the Plaza Vicuña Mackenna. "Women from the shantytowns, housewives, professionals, working-class women, employees, members of political groups, and women who were unaffiliated" sang songs too witty to have been improvised along the way. They carried objects symbolizing their views, such as a plastic baby wearing a sign saying that it had no diapers because of cloth shortages. A sign ridiculing Fidel Castro, who had just visited Chile, proclaimed, "¡No hay carne, fúmate un habano!" (There is no meat, let them smoke Havanas), an explicit allusion to Marie Antoinette's infamous "Let them eat cake." The women's chants parodied those of the leftist Popular Unity: "El pueblo unido jamas será vencido" (The people united will never be defeated) became "La izquierda unida nos tiene sin comida" (The united left has left us without food).[23]

Only now, a generation later, when democracy has been restored to Chile and a women's movement has transformed the consciousness of many women in Chile and the United States, has it become possible to tell a more fully developed story of women's organized opposition to the Allende government. Margaret Power, an American historian, and Lisa Baldez, an American political scientist, have each conducted extensive research on the individuals and groups that organized these women's demonstrations. Power tried through the Freedom of Information Act to secure documents that might show whether and how the CIA aided women who were mobilizing against the Popular Unity government, but her efforts proved unsuccessful when the government refused to release the documents. Power and Baldez carried out judicious interviews with many of the women who organized the March of the Empty Pots. On the basis of their research, Power and Baldez argue compellingly that sophisticated political operatives on the right were able to undermine the legitimacy of a government committed to social change by organizing such demonstrations.[24] The marches were carefully organized in advance by right-wing leaders, yet deliberately presented to the public as gatherings of women who were moved by simple material needs rather than political convictions.

The March of the Empty Pots was, in fact, organized by the Democratic Women's Front, made up of women from the National Party and Christian Democrats. Although the Christian Democrats, National Party, Radical Democrats, and neofascist Patria y Libertad (Fatherland and Freedom) Party all applauded the women's action, the conservative newspaper *El Mercurio* referred to the women as "unaffiliated" and to their march as "spontaneous." This seems an odd designation, since the article appeared the morning before the march took place. In using this phrase, the organizers and journalists probably meant that women who

never belonged to political parties or unions could act on their sentiments. Articles in *El Mercurio* and other conservative journals helped to
spread the word about the demonstration, calling on women to bring
pots, shopping bags, and Chilean flags.[25] According to Tila Castillo,
whom the paper called a neighborhood leader, participants would not
carry rocks, chains, or sticks, but only empty shopping bags and pots.
The women would not use symbols that evoked aggression or violence,
but only those that evoked their abject condition.[26]

According to Michèle Mattelart, a progressive Belgian sociologist
who lived in Chile during the UP period and wrote within months of the
coup, most women's demonstrations were led by privileged, upper-class
women. "The women's demonstrations always followed the same pattern. Assembled around a central group of bourgeois women of all ages,
who arrived in automobiles and were often accompanied by their maids,
were women from the petite bourgeoisie (always in the majority), together with a lesser number of women from the 'poblaciones' (shantytowns) and the Lumpenproletariat. All of these were encircled by the
militants, helmeted and armed with chains."[27] Her disparaging remarks
about the "Lumpenproletariat" referred to poor people who might support anyone who promised them food. The women's armed guards generally were young neofascists who sought out confrontations with the
police. Although other critics on the left tried to argue that the crowd
was limited exclusively to wealthy women, that was not the case.[28]

Immediately after the December march, most people on the left denigrated the organizers as rich women and their maids. Margaret Power
cites a newspaper editorial arguing that the women undertook "the
supreme sacrifice of giving up their afternoon teas or their appointments at the beauty parlor to protest in the name of their class."[29] But
Power also quotes a woman who had served on the Central Committee
of the Communist Party at the time. She admits that no one on the left,
and certainly not in the Communist Party, "ever carried out any serious
or profound studies of the right's capacity to organize women."[30]

Mobilizations became the order of the day. They provided a chance to
demonstrate the growing power of the right wing and discredit the government. Frequent mobilizations gave government opponents a chance
to let off steam through action rather than words; these "peaceful"
demonstrations were often surrounded by violent incidents in which
groups of young right-wing and left-wing men fought one another and
the police. These women's demonstrations were hardly as spontaneous
and apolitical as the right claimed, but rather were carefully orchestrated

as part of a comprehensive strategy to demonstrate that the regime was unable to guarantee either plenty or peace. Even the March of the Empty Pots concluded with a violent conflict among armed youths. When the march converged on the corner of calles Alameda and Miraflores in front of the Santa Lucía Theater, near the park of the same name and not far from the National Library, a melee broke out. Armed right-wing young men jumped to the conservative women's aid: the right-wing youths charged leftist youths whom they claimed had attacked them with clubs and rocks.[31] Later in the evening, as remnants of the march demonstrated in Las Condes, one of Santiago's wealthiest neighborhoods, the police released tear gas, causing eye irritations and wounding several people with canisters. The conservative *El Mercurio* claimed that leftwing demonstrators and the police injured one hundred rightists and arrested seventy-three, and that the left-wing demonstrators who attacked them were in league with the police.[32]

Following the March of the Empty Pots, the right-wing Nationalist Party issued a press release emphasizing the gendered nature of the emerging conflict: "Once again, the courage and civic responsibility of Chilean women has been demonstrated.... They have shown how they value freedom and how they defend it.... The armed bands of Marxism...demonstrate the moral castration that communism imposes through its executors and instruments to attack in the most treacherous manner women who are upholding their legitimate rights.... Chilean women demonstrated yesterday...that they treasure freedom." And speaking on behalf of the Mujeres Nacionales (Nationalist Women), Carmen Sáenz de Phillips claimed, "Yesterday's massive women's demonstration showed that the Chilean woman is engaging in a decisive and valiant fight.... The fear the sectarian elements hoped to inspire in us did not have the effect they desired."[33] The Nationalists applauded the women's direct political action against Allende. No longer were they passive victims of male aggression to be defended by other men. Now they were freedom fighters battling against impotent leftist men. Rather than depoliticize the women, the right wing cast them in an allegory as triumphant citizens and argued that leftist men were no match for them in their civic struggle.

The term *moral castration,* which the National Party's press release applied to left-wing men, seems strange in this context, but the theme of failed masculinity is like a coda that was repeated again and again in the struggle against Allende, until it, like the material hardships suffered by women, became a justification for the coup. Political ideologies frequently presume a close, even necessary relationship between authority and masculinity. Although each culture defines masculinity in its own way, in many cultures women—especially women as mothers, although not often as wives—exercise extraordinary authority in judging what is masculine. In most cultures, for example, attacking women, especially if they are with children, diminishes a man's masculinity, casting him in the role of a bully or, worse still, revealing him as not a "real man." The main exception to the rule that manly men must not attack women seems to be when the women are not deemed womanly: if the women can be portrayed as "unnatural"; if they fail to fulfill the traditional obligations of traditional heterosexual women in that particular culture; if they seem unconcerned about their children; or if they seem to be overtly sexual or too openly political—if, in other words, they seem to be insufficiently feminine or overtly masculine, according to the prevailing definitions of their time and place. The phrase *moral castration* implies symbolic dismemberment; by failing to fulfill the obligations of masculinity, men lose their moral standing as men. The newspaper thus suggested that the Popular Unity men attacked women because they were afraid to confront the men who opposed them and instead turned their cowardly anger on otherwise "helpless" women. Since the women, although they were acting collectively and in public, claimed to be expressing social need rather than any particular political position, the women demonstrators maintained their feminine role. That is, they were "politically marginal, but socially legitimate."[34] By referring to the crowd simply as "women" and not as political adversaries, *El Mercurio* cast the government in an especially bad light.

Numerous smaller demonstrations followed the March of the Empty Pots. Almost every evening between 8 and 10 P.M., housewives who opposed the government beat pots on their balconies in the wealthy neighborhoods of Santiago and most other Chilean cities. Chilean activist Teresa Valdés remembers with horror the violent din of those pots, as if people were beating on her head.[35] Within three months of the march, the right-wing women's coordinating group El Poder Femenino had been formed. Its members were upper-class housewives, female journalists for right-wing papers, and women professionals.[36] This well-organized group couched its attacks on Allende in the language of democracy, as if merely being a socialist made him undemocratic.

There were certainly serious shortages in Allende's Chile. These shortages were caused by capital flight, black markets, and speculation and hoarding, all of which were more or less consciously orchestrated by the Chilean upper class. Dramatic declines in copper prices and the consequent loss of foreign exchange weakened the country's position within the international economy. These problems were exacerbated by declines in foreign credit, aid, and supplies, as the United States deliberately attempted to destabilize the Allende government.[37] Within the Popular Unity government, inexperienced and inadequately trained administrators and bad planning in major sectors of production and distribution contributed to the difficulty of keeping the economy stable. Taking advantage of agrarian reform legislation that the Christian Democrats had promulgated in 1965, the Popular Unity government expropriated 1,000 agricultural properties during its first year, in contrast to the 1,400 properties its predecessor had nationalized between 1965 and 1970.[38] The accelerated pace of land reform impressed people of all classes that fundamental social and economic change was occurring in Chile.[39] Moreover, honest attempts to enable poorer groups to improve their standard of living by raising wages, freezing prices, and distributing milk to poor children led the rich to believe that they no longer had control over the economy. The upper class had previously enjoyed this privilege at the expense of the poor, and many believed that if they lost this monopoly they would be deprived of basic necessities.[40]

Lines at stores and markets lengthened as shortages worsened. Wealthy women's servants returned home empty-handed. María Prada remembers that her family's maid stood in line for days to get basic necessities for the household. However, her family was better off than most because Prada's father, a doctor, had many grateful clients who gave him goods in return for his medical services. Barter became more common among those who had something to trade.

When conservatives hammered away at the issue of irregular supplies, they deliberately aroused fear in women of all classes. Women who bore the responsibility of providing food, clothing, and medicine for their families were afraid of shortages. Speaking almost twenty years later in a documentary about Chilean women from the PBS *Americas* series, Alicia Romo, an opponent of Allende who became one of the few high-ranking women in the Chilean government after the military coup, recalled that when the UP government was in power she could only knit for her baby by unraveling wool from other sweaters. Because of shortages of cloth, she claims, friends had to supply her with old diapers for her child.[41] The Popular Unity government guaranteed a half-liter of milk to all Chilean children, so some children had milk for the first time in their lives. They and their families even tasted meat occasionally. Wider distribution of food may have symbolized the disappearance of class distinctions, sowing fears among the upper and middle classes that went well beyond the scarcity of food. Few changes in everyday material life are more disturbing than the loss of privileges to people who believe, perhaps correctly, that their lives depend on enjoying what others lack.

The final word from the ostensible organizers of the March of the Empty Pots came in a full-page statement entitled "We As Women Protest," published in *El Mercurio* and signed by Nina Donoso, who described herself as the secretary general of Unidad Nacional Femenina (National Feminine Unity, or UNAFE, a group that may have been a false front). She claimed that women and mothers, without distinctions of age, class, or political affiliation, had organized to protest "the shortages of articles necessary to the life of a civilized people: food, transportation, cloth, clothing, thread, medicines and other goods."[42] Donoso characterizes the demonstrators simply as "women" and explicitly rejects in advance the idea that they were acting as members of a class or a political group.

As conflict in Chile escalated during the early 1970s, the organized presence of large numbers of women on the right became a powerful threat to political authority. Women from all classes who demonstrated against the Popular Unity government did so as housewives, asserting or even assuming a traditional womanly role and challenging the army to fulfill the traditionally masculine role of protecting women and children. Some committed political adversaries even hid their political identity behind the mask of suffering homemaker. At a time when an embargo by the United States, a strike by transport workers, and deliberate withholding of supplies from the market by merchants were making it difficult for women to buy food for their families, women who led rightwing political parties attempted to overthrow the government by proclaiming themselves victims and by inducing large numbers of other women, who did not share either their middle-class status or their reactionary political ideology, to join the protests they organized.[43]

MOBILIZING HOUSEWIVES

Women like Alicia Romo showed their genius in the way they structured their appeal to other women. Soon after the coup, Michèle Mattelart asked how wealthy right-wing women had created a populist movement that seemed to mute class differences. The notion of mothers and housewives as a single group regardless of class was a compelling public image used in the assault on Allende, even though it denied the material inequalities that structured women's lives.[44] María de los Angeles Crummet, a young American activist who interviewed ten leaders of the right-wing women's movement in 1974, claims that "by defining women on the basis of natural rather than historical attributes, by proclaiming the universality of the condition of womanhood, EPF [El Poder Femenino] attempted to establish a fundamental unity of interests between all women, over and beyond any social, economic or ideological differences. This category of 'women' implicitly presented the women's opposition movement as a democratic movement acting in the name of 'the women of Chile that constitute more than half of the population of this country.' "[45]

The Popular Unity government did not conduct a concerted campaign to mobilize housewives in support of the shift toward a more equal distribution of resources, or present its program to housewives as requiring a temporary, perhaps painful, transitional period of economic readjustment. Government officials were themselves unprepared for the severity of the shortages, and most were utterly unaware of the potential power that groups of discontented, even desperate women might wield. The right wing was therefore able to capture this issue, and conservative women began to speak to and for all housewives, regardless of class.

The government made only one successful effort to engage ordinary women in discussion about how social change would affect their lives as housewives. Pedro Vuskovic, the minister of economy, development, and reconstruction, met with thousands of women on 29 July 1971 in National Stadium in Santiago to discuss shortages and what the government planned to do about them. In a model attempt to carry on a popular discussion of government strategy, Vuskovic admitted that growth in the purchasing power of the working classes had put stress on consumption; a 20 to 30 percent increase in production was required to meet the demand, but the government had been unable to achieve that target. Not all the problems were the government's fault, however; Vuskovic contended that the upper-class opposition was hoarding supplies in a deliberate attempt to destabilize the government.[46] Advising UP supporters to organize their neighborhoods through Mothers Centers (Centros de Madres), Neighborhood Committees (Juntas de Vecinos), and other groups, he urged women to negotiate with small shopkeepers and to monitor supplies to see what they could achieve through citizen action. Vuskovic promised to assign government officials to help neighborhood women, laying out a plan that actually functioned to some degree in working-class and poor neighborhoods.[47] However, because the government never controlled more than 30 percent of all food supplies, hoarding continued and the black market operated with impunity during the three years of the Popular Unity government.[48]

Had the government held regularly scheduled mass meetings of women similar to this one, there would have been a public arena where the government could focus attention on those women who thought of themselves principally as their family's providers. Without such meetings, the government could be made to appear oblivious to the problems of everyday life that concerned Chilean women of all classes. According to Edy Kaufman, a scrupulous and generally balanced historian, "The rightist camp took a more role-oriented approach. . . . The conservatives, who could no longer allow women to remain passively at home, required that they mobilize in defense of 'democracy,' relying on traditional images and values regarding the behavior of women. Arguments about food scarcity and the destruction of the family were used to mobilize the female consumer . . . driven by 'survival instinct.' "[49] His analysis raises questions about how, when, and which women mobilize, but it does not fully explain why conservatives "could no longer permit women to wait passively at home," how they "required women to mobilize," why they portrayed their struggle as a defense of democracy, or how they promoted women's public political activity. In fact, by speaking of women's "survival instinct," Kaufman echoes the dominant gender system's assumption that women are not political actors, an assumption that the movement's right-wing women leaders certainly did not share, even if they used such rhetoric in their propaganda.

One explanation for the relative ease with which ordinary Chilean women were mobilized to participate in politics during this critical period lies in their relatively high degree of organization. Although comparatively few married and single women worked for wages in the formal economy, and therefore relatively few women belonged to the trade unions that supported the Popular Unity coalition, women were well organized in their neighborhoods. By 1971, Mothers Centers were established both in Santiago and in smaller cities and rural communities across the country.

These Mothers Centers had grown out of a long series of government efforts to serve women in their families and mobilize them politically. As early as 1947, the Chilean government attempted to provide public assistance, including help in managing increases in the cost of living. The government reinforced the idea of motherhood as the mainstay of the family and inaugurated a Housewives Association (Asociación de Dueñas de Casa). From 1954 on, the organizations, founded separately, that became known as Mothers Centers counseled women on how to qualify for state benefits. They also brought ordinary women into the political process to a much greater degree than in most other countries. The proportion of eligible women voters who participated in elections rose from 27.2 percent in 1958 to 62.7 percent in 1964, undoubtedly reflecting the influence of the Mothers Centers.[50] In fact, women's votes provided the margin of victory or defeat in both presidential elections.

Under the Christian Democratic administration that governed Chile between 1964 and 1970, attracting peasant and working-class women into the Mothers Centers became a priority. Middle-class women trained poor women to be more skilled mothers and housewives through classes on cooking, health care, and sewing. The women who participated in these lessons frequently formed patronage relationships with their richer teachers and friendships with their sister students. When election time rolled around, women who frequented the Mothers Centers could readily be persuaded to vote for conservative candidates.[51]

Allende knew that women were an electoral force he had to reckon with. Chilean women's votes frequently determined the outcome of hotly contested elections. When Allende first ran for president in 1958, he lost even though he had 18,000 more male votes than his opponent, Jorge Alessandri. Alessandri won by 33,000 votes because the overwhelming majority of women cast their votes for him.[52] In late July 1971, in a speech to the Radical Party, part of the coalition that made up Popular Unity, Allende argued: "Our great task, our great obligation is to make it possible for the Chilean woman—our sister, daughter, mother and friend—to understand that we need her and will fight for her because she is the seed of our future."[53] The fact that Allende referred to the universal woman rather than to the Chilean citizen who might happen to be a woman suggests that he felt awkward about his political relationship to women. His statement also implies that the UP was fighting *for* that woman rather than counting her as a political actor.

By the time Allende made this speech, the Popular Unity government had already instituted some programs to improve women's status. One of the early reforms carried out by the Popular Unity Party permitted unmarried women to receive family assistance allotments, which had previously been denied them. The Christian Democrats had insisted that only married women who met the highest moral standards should be eligible for benefits. Attentive to the broad social issues that affected the poorest women, the Popular Unity government was less astute about the actual work that housewives performed as distributors of life's necessities. The Women's Front of Popular Unity and the National Secretariat of Women created public laundries, soup kitchens, nurseries, and childcare centers, as well as workshops where women learned to produce crafts they could sell to increase their family's income. But the government underestimated women's growing concern about the scarcity of food, clothing, and medicine.[54]

By placing distribution of basic goods in the hands of the Juntas de Abastecimiento y Control de Precios (Committees to Control Prices and Supplies) to monitor hoarding, price gauging, and the black market, the government accomplished a great deal.[55] To counter this effort, right-wing women from El Poder Femenino practiced dirty tricks and set up mock distribution and price control committees to harass people.[56] As shortages increased and the opposing parties traded charges and countercharges about hoarding and mismanagement, fear spiraled out of control. The rapid reappearance of food and medicine following the coup lends credence to Popular Unity's argument that supplies were deliberately being withheld in order to disrupt the economy, but that was not clear until after the overthrow of Allende. During the critical months of 1973, many women feared that the economy was shrinking and that they would soon want for the barest essentials.

Women's anxiety found expression in Mothers Centers. At the time of the coup in 1973, over a million women participated in twenty thousand Mothers Centers.[57] The Comisión de Centros de Madres (Coordinating Commission of the Mothers Centers, COCEMA) was a powerful network linking local centers and allying women from different neighborhood. Elite women among the Christian Democrats volunteered at the centers, giving speeches about current events and teaching domestic skills. They also created a public space in which significant numbers of lower-middle-class and working-class women learned to participate in public life. Rather than take over the leadership of the centers through COCEMA, the left remained suspicious of the centers, viewing them as fundamentally religious, authoritarian, and uncontrollable, according to a Brazilian feminist in exile in Chile.[58] Treating the Mothers Centers and their constituents as a right-wing force to be ignored or opposed rather than as a way to reach and politicize ordinary women may have been a self-fulfilling prophecy and a fatal error for the Popular Unity coalition.

THE GROWING CRISIS: APRIL TO JUNE 1973

María Prada remembers the right-wing agitation that followed the surprising strength shown by the Popular Unity coalition in the congressional elections of March 1973. In the face of political defeat, the right attempted to overthrow Allende by force. It bears repeating that the UP had increased its plurality from a little over 36 percent in the presidential elections of 1970 to 44 percent in the parliamentary elections of 1973. There was still a gender gap in the returns: Allende received only 39 percent of the women's vote as compared with 48 percent of the men's, although the percentage of votes gained was greater among women than among men. Allende seemed aware that women's votes might play an important role in the election, for when he discussed rationing liquor, he joked that it would undoubtedly lose him some men's votes but might increase his support among women.[59]

Inflation reached new heights in April 1973, spiraling to 238 percent, about 1 percent a day, through September. Wages failed to keep pace; the highest paid workers saw wage increases of no more than 112 percent. The increasing gap between wages and the cost of living put serious pressure on most Chileans. Many organized groups, notably miners, truck owners, and students, began to demonstrate and strike.[60] We now know that the CIA prompted the rebellion of the truckers, whose confederation consisted of 169 associations that controlled transportation along the 2,800 miles of roads that ran the length of Chile. Most raw materials, fuel, and food traveled by truck. In October 1972, the country had been nearly paralyzed by a two-week national truckers' strike that opposed the government's attempts to establish a state-owned trucking company. In 1973, owner-operators feared the creation of a national agency to regulate trucking, and were outraged by the difficulty of securing spare parts and by declines in real income as inflation grew. The Chilean Truck Owners Association won higher rates and assurances about parts, but the truckers' rebellion induced the government to arrest their leader—thus making him into a martyr— admit the military into the cabinet, and declare a state of emergency in Santiago.[61]

At the end of April 1973, many of the copper miners of El Teniente and their wives turned against the government, an even more serious development in both economic and political terms. Up to that time, copper was Chile's main source of foreign exchange. When between one-third and one-half of the nation's twelve thousand miners went out on strike on 18 April 1973, their action cost the Chilean economy up to one million dollars a day in lost revenues.[62] The miners and their wives had expected to increase their earnings through nationalization of the mines, and their wrath fell upon the government. The miners earned between five and eleven times what other blue-collar workers earned, but inflation and shortages of food and medicine had reduced their standard of living. In 1972, when hyperinflation set in, the miners demanded a 41 percent wage increase. The government, which had boosted salaries across the board and even provided the miners with a cost-of-living increase, refused further wage hikes.

While miners acted through their labor unions, women in the mining communities played an active political role in developing strong bonds of solidarity and mobilizing popular support for their cause. In the closed world around the mines, men do the tough work of extracting metals from caves or open pits, cut like coliseums into the earth. Women hold the community together by linking solidarity in the mines to the needs of the community.[63] One of the many struggles that took place during the last months of the Popular Unity government involved how women around the mines portrayed their situation. While the government tried to avoid a mining strike, and Socialist and Communist newspapers applauded the women who persuaded men not to strike, those women who supported the work stoppage staked a claim to positions as victims and heroines. Once again, the showdown took place around questions of women's place as consumers, not around their rights as workers or citizens.

In order to win attention for the El Teniente strike, Carmen Miranda Rodríguez, the daughter and wife of copper miners, led two other miners' wives, Hilda Zárate and Lita Rojas, in seizing Radio Rancagua. Control over the radio gave privileged access to public opinion. Nearly 95 percent of Chileans owned a radio, making it the most important means of communication in the country. For women with no other ties to the world beyond their neighborhood, the radio was a constant companion. These women formed their views in response to what they heard on the airwaves. The CIA realized that control of the airwaves was crucial to controlling public opinion, and "more than half the $8 million expended in Chile by the CIA between 1963 and 1973 went to the conservative media."[64] During the three years of the Popular Unity government, only seven of the twenty-nine radio stations in Santiago sided with the government.[65] The two major radio stations, which were in the hands of the extreme right-wing National Party and the Christian Democrats, received U.S. subsidies. The right also controlled 115 of Chile's 155 long-wave radio stations and two of the four television channels."[66] Among the few franchises favorable to the UP were those around the mines. Between April and July 1973, women from the mining communities seized many of these stations, broadcasting disparaging remarks about the government's failure to fulfill its promise to raise their standard of living or even to guarantee a subsistence wage.[67]

Carmen Miranda Rodríguez, who led the first takeover, was a twenty-nine-year-old housewife and mother who had been raised in El Teniente. She was inspired to work for the cause when she went to a rally at the mine workers' union hall in the city of Rancagua. Carmen Miranda, who always claimed to be apolitical, became a heroine of antigovernment forces. She and the other women from the mining community began broadcasting their side of the story, telling listeners about how difficult it was for them to get food for their families. Holding the station for five days and five nights, they stayed awake on the coffee and cigarettes supporters brought them. When they vacated the studio, others among the seventy miners' wives committed to their cause took over, using the radio to promote their message to a larger public. The radio station became the center of local women's activities, with a soup kitchen, or *olla común*, in the courtyard. When Miranda left the studio, she addressed a large crowd of miners and their families assembled in Balthazar Castro Gymnasium. Overcome by nervousness, she began to cry. Proclaiming that she and the seventy women who had taken turns at the radio station had been forced by circumstances to take action, Miranda explained that the women were defending the right to unionize in Chile.[68]

Portraying themselves as mediators, the women decided to stage a women's march to Santiago, accompanied only by female members of their own families. Their announced intention was to meet with President Allende in order to persuade him to intercede. Obviously, if all they wanted was to express their views, they could have sent Allende a petition. But hoping to attract favorable publicity, the group gathered on 26 June at 5:35 A.M. at the radio station. Traveling the sixty-four kilometers by car to the outskirts of Santiago, they gathered at Maipo Bridge, which they renamed Bridge of the Miners. Conservative women who had gathered there in the middle of the night cheered the arrivals. Inés Villalobos de Silva, chair of the Women's Committee of the Strike, a mother of three and the wife of a miner from the Caletones section of the El Teniente Mine, addressed the crowd.[69] She claimed that two thousand miners' wives were marching for the first time to persuade the government to pay attention to their loss of buying power and to end shortages. Their signs proclaimed: "Por una pronta solución, las mujeres en acción" (Women take action for a quick solution); "Con las uñas y los dientes defendemos El Teniente" (With nails and teeth [aligned], we will defend El Teniente mine).[70]

Before setting out from Rancagua, the women organizing the march issued a statement proclaiming that they were marching to demand a "quick solution to the strike, which had already lasted more than sixty-eight days." They also registered their complaints about how they thought their relatives and male coworkers in the mines were being treated "by the Government of Workers." The women asked Allende to come to the mines and reinstate the sixty-seven miners who had been fired; they also "demanded that threats of charging workers with breaking contracts" be stopped. At eight in the morning, when the women set out by car for the bridge, one of the women called to the journalists: "They would need a thousand *carabineros* and a hundred tanks [to stop us], and still we [would] cross the bridge."[71] Recognizing how much soldiers hate to tarnish their masculinity by attacking women claiming to be housewives and mothers, the miners' wives shielded themselves by donning that role.

The president, casting himself as a champion of women, said he was eager to consult with the women marching from the mines. He asked local army officers responsible for the province from which they were coming to protect them and announced his readiness to meet with a delegation representing the women. Yet he also cautioned the women that they did not need to demonstrate to get an audience with him and warned that the government would use any means necessary to maintain public order.[72] Although after 11 September conservatives and the military would defend their coup by claiming that chaos made them intervene, at this time they regarded Allende's concern for order as evidence of his authoritarianism.

From 1 to 2 P.M., while most of the travelers and their supporters—numbering in the thousands and including students like María Prada—marched in the streets near the presidential palace of La Moneda, a delegation of women met with Allende. The women from the mines were represented by two who had originally seized the radio station, Hilda de Zárate and Carmen Miranda, and the speaker at the bridge, Inés Villalobos. When Allende promised he would try to solve the strike within the week, they claimed they were awaiting his decision.[73] Two months later, as the strike continued without a settlement, the women returned to Santiago, this time as the guests of students at the Catholic University and their high school supporters, including María Prada. While the women remained indoors, outside La Moneda gangs from the neofascist Fatherland and Freedom Party attacked leftists, and the two groups challenged one another with stones until the police used tear gas to disperse them.[74] The Student Federation of the Catholic University in Santiago, having taken up the cause of the women, had its president proclaim: "The wives of the miners, assuming a valiant and decisive attitude, have taken an unshakable vanguard position during the whole conflict. They have decided to come to Santiago to protest by their presence against the perfidious and unjust repression and government procedures."[75]

On 26 June, three days before an unsuccessful army coup against Allende, the wives and daughters of the miners came back to Santiago, this time to an even more enthusiastic welcome. As a delegation of women met with the president, a crowd of about two thousand, including the women who had come from the mines, marched in front of Congress. The supportive crowds sang the national anthem, honoring the miners as "defenders of the right to organize," thereby associating miners, democracy, and nationalism. The crowd of demonstrators moved along calles Compañia, Estado, and Alameda toward the Catholic University, which was again hosting the miners and their wives. According to one account, the crowd was so large that when the first marchers entered the university the end of the march was still at Augustinas. A rally organized by the students took place at about 6 P.M. to cheer the miners' wives on their way home. The demonstration featured speeches by miners' wives as well as representatives of the university, students, and faculty. After receiving gold medals from the rector of the university, the people from the mines returned to Rancagua to await the president's deliberations.[76] The next day, a small number of government supporters, including wives and mothers from El Teniente and a group calling themselves the Frente Patriótico de Mujeres (Women's Patriotic Front) came to see Allende, singing Popular Unity songs.[77] Although neither the left nor the right welcomed the other's mobilization, these peaceful opposing marches suggest that Chilean society was stable enough to countenance collective activity in the streets.

In the spirit of demonstrations and counterdemonstrations, women from around the Antofagasta copper mines in the north organized their own women's march to Santiago at the end of June. Determined to increase the flow of food, they sought a strategy for overcoming shortages. They suggested marching with empty pots and pans and other household utensils to highlight their need for basic goods. Together with various unions, professional associations, and neighborhood organizations, they constituted what they called a Consejo del Hambre (Council of Hunger), which planned to hold a march on 28 June 1973. They also commemorated a 1958 law that had been designed to ensure that the northern mining provinces could always satisfy their food needs. Portraying themselves as victims, these women implied that the government's economic policies were responsible for hunger and food shortages.[78]

On 28 June 1973, an ominous article appeared in the conservative *El Mercurio* warning that bakeries in Santiago might soon run out of bread because of shortages of wheat and flour. The article claimed that each day the lines to buy bread were longer.[79] On 29 June, an unsuccessful army coup was put down by a weakened government.[80] Clearly food prices and distribution failures were the government's Achilles' heel. Why the government did not organize public meetings all over Chile to discuss these shortages, as Vuskovic had in 1971, will never be clear. In retrospect, the government might well have benefited from collaborating with petitioners and holding public discussions about what the government could do to alleviate hunger.

WOMEN AND THE COUP AGAINST ALLENDE

María Prada and Alicia Cabrini remember that by the end of August 1973, social services and food supplies in Chile had declined to such a degree that many groups spoke about being overcome by chaos. A million workers were on strike. When three hundred wives of truck owners demanded another audience with Allende on 11 August, he refused. Although it was clear that these women opposed the government, the president lost more by rejecting them than he would have by seeing them. Within two days, two Christian Democratic congresswomen joined several hundred well-dressed women in demonstrations at the presidential palace in support of the truckers.[81] Following the lead of the miners' wives, women related to truck owners took over radio stations on 15 August and held it for two days. With the help of El Poder

Femenino, they broadcast their patriotic views and their analysis of the events that were unfolding.[82] Then three hundred wives of air force officers mobilized in support of the former air force chief who was defying Allende. On 23 August, one hundred officers' wives, buttressed by three hundred members of El Poder Femenino, demanded the resignation of General Carlos Prats, making the assault on authority seem like a women's matter and appropriating the identity of "woman" for the right wing. They called for the voluntary removal of the commander-in-chief of the armed forces, Allende's chief supporter, in a letter presented to General Prats's wife, Sofia Cuthbert, at the family home. The demonstration surrounding the presentation grew violent, and the police wounded several women in the process of trying to subdue them, making those who opposed the government into martyrs.[83] Shooting at unarmed demonstrators was portrayed as callous and authoritarian.

The right wing presented Allende as a would-be tyrant, taking out on defenseless women his inability to ensure food supplies and maintain public order. In fact, Chile's economy had come to a halt since June, when the 150,000 trucks needed to transport agricultural products, copper, food, and other supplies stopped running. Without the trucks, there was no fuel during Chile's winter months of June, July, and August.[84] People on both sides wondered anxiously what would happen next. Those who supported Allende took to the streets by the hundreds of thousands on 4 September 1970 to commemorate the third anniversary of his election. The Christian Democrats had originally supported Allende's election by contributing their votes to his plurality. Once they withdrew from the coalition in June 1973, the political crisis deepened.

On 6 September, the day after the women's march, female government employees from ten provinces called on senators from the opposition parties and urged them to unseat President Allende. The senators, including their leader, Patricio Aylwin, listened while the women described how they spent their lives standing in food lines. They insisted on a treasonous scenario: "If, within a week, Congress has not used the last legal act that remains [that is, calling for a referendum], we will find it necessary to bang on the doors of the barracks of the armed forces to persuade them to save the country, restoring order and tranquility and winning peace for the people and security for property, as our constitution demands."[85] This statement was published in El Mercurio.

Allende seemed powerless to respond. Although Popular Unity had legislated numerous social reforms that would have transformed the lives of ordinary women had the economic crisis not intervened, Allende and his government simply did not understand that women claiming rights as housewives and consumers required symbolic as well as concrete responses. Doing the right thing in terms of public policy was not enough; to be successful politically, the government would have had to highlight its achievements in providing for social need. The same day that right-wing women met with the senators, Allende, celebrating the first anniversary of the creation of the National Secretariat of Women, announced that he would veto the legislation before him that dealt with women's health and abortion because Congress had eviscerated the bill he sent them. *El Mercurio* claimed that Allende also told his audience that Chile needed close to 1.5 million tons of wheat immediately, since Chile's reserves of flour would last only three or four days.[86] Fanning the flames of panic, the right wing was preparing Chile for Allende's fall.

By September 1973, food shortages were severe and universal. Although these shortages and their political consequences were almost certainly manipulated by the right, the situation was becoming desperate. Breadlines were forming at 2 A.M., and each family was rationed only one kilo of bread a day. Bread had become the principal, if not the only, food of the poor and the working class. *El Mercurio* reported that of 537 bakeries in the capital, supposedly only 167 had sufficient flour to make bread.[87] Food riots immediately followed. In the Santiago squatters' community of Guerrillero Manuel Rodríguez, fury about shortages led a crowd of over three hundred women to seize Quilin Bakery on 9 September.[88] The next day, near the working-class neighborhood known as 4 September, about five hundred working-class *men and women,* including Ester Jerez and Graciela Ahumada, forced open Olba Bakery, took 1,880 kilograms of bread and a barrel of flour, and proceeded to break windows and furniture in the shop.[89] By 9 September, half of all bakeries in Valparaiso were reported to have closed down, and elsewhere a majority of the population had no bread supplies at all over the weekend.[90] Immediately after 11 September, when the military junta overthrew Allende, bread suddenly became plentiful, making clear that many bakers and suppliers had been hoarding supplies. María Prada remembers that the day after the coup food appeared in all the shops as if by a miracle.[91]

Six days before the coup, some women had passed out flyers claiming that "Mr. Allende does not deserve to be president of the Republic. Mr. Allende has led the country into a catastrophe. We don't have bread for our children! We don't have medicine for those who are sick! We don't have clothes to wear! We don't have a roof to put over our heads!"[92] While El Poder Femenino seems the likely source of this material, many politically unaffiliated mothers echoed the sentiments it expressed.

As strikes spread all over Chile and transportation to work became difficult if not impossible, women in the mining communities of the north began to ask the government for milk for their children. One woman *El Mercurio* claimed to quote said that if the government could not help her feed her child, she would call on international relief agencies to come to Chile's aid. She explained, "I am a mother, like many Chilean women. I don't belong to any Mothers Centers or Neighborhood Councils nor to any political party. I am a mother who represents her daughter and who has the right to rebel when anxiety and powerlessness corrodes my soul, when I see my baby crying because she has no milk....I know that thousands of Chilean mothers who share my plight...suffer as I do."[93] Her "right to rebel," which all women presumably shared, entailed a certain view of motherhood and femininity that could call masculinity into question. Appearing as it did in the conservative *El Mercurio,* the authenticity of the statement might reasonably be questioned. But women who were standing on endless lines could easily identify with these sentiments, even if this particular statement might have been made by a fictional character.

El Poder Femenino promoted such opinions and actively sought military intervention to overthrow Allende. In August 1973, the group marched on the army barracks and threw grain at the soldiers, calling them "chicken" for not seizing power.[94] General Gustavo Leigh later complained self-righteously, "They said that we were chickens. They left corn at the doors of our houses. They said we were cowards. Whoever had been in my position on that day would have acted. There was no other way out."[95] As if saying "our mothers made us do it," the army justified its coup by hiding behind the aprons of Chilean women. Even more ominously, El Poder Femenino painted the word *Djakarta* on the walls and mailed letters with that word as the only message. According to Margaret Power, the word "referred to the capital of Indonesia where, following the 1965 coup, the military murdered between 300,000 and 400,000 members of the Indonesian Communist Party."[96] Say what they will now, the women of El Poder Femenino and their accomplices were anything but naive about what a military coup might accomplish.

On 10 September in Santiago, the day before the coup, a demonstration of women waving their hands and white handkerchiefs paraded in front of the Defense Ministry, demanding that the armed forces seize power. Calling "Fuerzas Armadas al poder" (Armed forces to power) and "Ejercito, marina, y aviación, salva la nación" (Army, air force, and the navy, [rise up now and] save the nation), El Poder Femenino and its followers again urged the armed forces to step in.[97]

HOW IMPORTANT WERE WOMEN
TO ALLENDE'S DOWNFALL?

On 11 September, Augusto Pinochet and a junta of military leaders from all branches of the armed forces bombed La Moneda presidential palace, seized the government, and began roundups of anyone thought to support Popular Unity. Women in the opposition proudly proclaimed the important role they had played in the ouster of Allende. "Make no mistake," said María Armanet Izquierdo, "we organized for the express purpose of helping to overthrow Allende." María Eugenia Oyarzun boasted that, if not for El Poder Femenino and its supporters, "the Popular Unity would probably still be in power today, pushing Chile toward Marxism-Leninism."[98] After the coup, according to historian Francesca Miller, conservative women donated valuables to the Pinochet government to aid the junta in reconstructing the country.[99] In fictionalized versions that conservative women wrote, and in interviews conducted both right after the coup and twenty years later, the leaders of the conservative women's organizations claimed responsibility for their achievement in overthrowing a government dedicated to improving conditions for the vast majority of the Chilean people.

How important were right-wing women in orchestrating the overthrow of Allende? Middle-class professionals, journalists, and wives of men in the conservative political parties led the wives of businessmen, small proprietors, shopkeepers, and skilled workers in a movement designed to call attention to the shortages, long lines, and government failures to stabilize the economy. The demonstrators certainly drew on women of the upper and middle classes.[100] Writing after Allende's overthrow, María Correa Morande claimed that through El Poder Femenino's contacts with people in the Radical and Christian Democratic Parties and through their connection to the Mothers Centers and Neighborhood Centers, right-wing women generated long lists of telephone numbers.[101]

This explanation accounts for Solidaridad, Orden, Libertad (Solidarity, Order, Liberty, SOL), a civic and family-oriented movement of husbands and wives that came together in April 1972, shortly after El Poder Femenino took shape.[102] The woman María Crummet calls Mrs. D. became its president. She had spent many years working with the Mothers Centers and the Neighborhood Committees, though she did not consider herself to be a political activist. Mrs. D. recalled that she and her husband, an upper-class professional, were worried about the decline of the family under a socialist administration. Working from phone numbers of people involved in parent-teacher associations, clinics, and offices, they claimed to have developed a network that they organized into a telephone tree. They masterminded some of the mobilizations and organized dirty tricks. Later, when SOL sent representatives to El Poder Femenino, which was regarded as a political organization, SOL's contacts became part of a larger right-wing network.

Together, El Poder Femenino and SOL accounted for no more than a few thousand people. Who, then, formed the marches of tens of thousands that finally overtook the government, and how did they come to believe that without their intervention, the country would whirl out of control? Analyses of right-wing women's role in Allende's downfall all contain an odd contradiction. On the one hand, critics argue that women had the power to propel the military toward a coup; on the other hand, they view these same women as pawns of the conservative and right-wing parties. No doubt many of the members of El Poder Femenino were right-wing political leaders, but that does not explain how the conservatives convinced women who were ordinarily apolitical not only to share the opposition's opinions but also to act on these ideas in street demonstrations. By mobilizing students like María Prada, who were led to believe that Allende's plan to institute widespread public education was really a communist plot to undermine the private schools, the right played to middle-class fears that giving more to the working class would mean real sacrifices and scarcity for them.[103]

Michèle Mattelart was one of a few Chilean leftists who took seriously the way the destabilization of everyday life prompted some women to take action against their government. While acknowledging the importance of the Mothers Centers and Neighborhood Associations, which were controlled by the National Party and the Christian Democrats, to the mobilization of women, she also tried to move beyond the idea that women were manipulated by the right. She called attention to women's solidarity with male relatives employed as truck drivers and miners. Mattelart tried "to take into sufficient consideration the specific problems of the women's struggle."[104]

I think that any analysis of the gendered nature of the attack on the Popular Unity government should explain how the women who were undermining a government that had come to power through the ballot box were able to present themselves as spokespeople for democracy. According to Mattelart, "The women became a 'democratic' sector of society, having been 'naturally' inspired to defend that universe of traditions, those values of 'justice' and 'liberty,' that serve to mask the oppressive fatality of the bourgeois order."[105] She also explained that the image of the mother came to be substituted for the working class. She quoted women who said: "Mr. Allende has said he would resign if working-class people demanded it. We are the people! Every child of this land has come from our womb!"[106] This equation of "the people" with democracy and the nation was made by the Popular Unity government as well. Pedro Vuskovic, speaking with women concerned about shortages in July 1971, five months before the first March of the Empty Pots, claimed that the government was trying to "improve the living standard of the workers." He described his government as a "government of the people," using the terms *workers* and *people* interchangeably.[107] Populist rhetoric could go either way politically.

Conservative women, by positioning themselves as spokespeople for a community devoid of class differences, presented themselves as helpless victims who were merely trying to reestablish social order. Assuming an identity as housewives and mothers, the right-wing leaders feigned innocence about the power struggles in which they were engaging. Of course, the dissident women found support in parties of the right. And many of their leaders were members of right-wing parties and were associated with men plotting to overturn the government. But the right-wing women leaders were able to promote and then express the fears of a large number of people.

When I first asked María Prada if her mother ever joined these mobilizations, she said she didn't think so. Then, about a year after her mother died, she called me and apologetically recalled that when she asked her father directly whether he and her mother had ever marched against Allende, he admitted that they had. They were both so frustrated by constant social strife that they thought the country would benefit from a change of government. Prada's parents left Chile immediately after the coup, returning thirty years later, at the end of their lives. Dr. Prada, who had served in the *poblaciones* (shantytowns), retired to Chile to once again use his skills to help the poor.

Within three weeks of seizing power, Pinochet reorganized the Mothers Centers. He appointed his wife, Lucía Hiriart de Pinochet, as director of them and the newly created Secretaría Nacional de la Mujer (National Secretariat of Women).[108] Democratic rhetoric was no longer necessary. Torture and murder took its place. Right-wing women did not gain in political power as a result of their leadership in the popular mobilization against Allende. After the coup, women opposition supporters were immediately demobilized, and only a few right-wing women activists found even temporary positions in the government. Having unleashed a whirlwind, Pinochet and the junta may have feared the combined power of the right-wing women, who had asserted their right to control the distribution of socially necessary resources. In the months that followed, right-wing women made no apologies. Instead, they attempted to show that mothers and housewives, regardless of class, had acted in unison.[109]

Compared to the murder and disappearances of those Pinochet viewed as enemies of the Chilean state, the demise of the rhetoric of democracy was a small casualty. Yet something precious had been lost. The Popular Unity government had captured the interest of social reformers all over the world when Allende promised that his revolution would bring "moral achievement, generosity, a spirit of sacrifice and dedication to achieve a new life for all Chileans within the framework of the nation's free institutions."[110] Allende's commitment to democracy was integral to his commitment to socialism; he regarded Marxism as a theory that could guide Chile in laying the economic foundations for the social equality that he and his party advocated so passionately.

The Popular Unity government's fusion of democracy and socialism and its proclamation of "La Vía Chilena," a distinctly Chilean path toward social justice, resonated deeply with artists and intellectuals in and beyond Chile. Female and male protest singers, artists, poets, and playwrights, reaching toward democracy, wrote music and staged plays, creating art in support of Allende and his vision of a transformed Chile. At the same time, powerful interest groups in the United States were creating and circulating an opposing view of Chile's political development. President Richard Nixon and Secretary of State Henry Kissinger declared a socialist Chile to be part of the worldwide communist conspiracy against which they were defending America and the entire "free world." This position was advocated and backed by U.S. copper mining companies, which had controlled Chile's chief economic asset, and the

International Telephone and Telegraph Company, which controlled telecommunications in Chile. Nixon and Kissinger believed that Allende wanted to ally himself with Fidel Castro to bring socialism to the Americas.

The Chilean right wing had close ties to the American political, economic, and military establishment. Using the language of "democracy," which the United States, confusing economic and political systems, had increasingly juxtaposed to "communism," Allende's opponents attempted to establish themselves as democratic and cast him as an authoritarian who would destroy Chileans' freedom. They played the anticommunist card, portraying the Chilean socialists as tools of international communism. This tarred the Popular Unity government with two brushes, condemning them as internationalists who were disloyal to Chile and as communists who were, by definition, dictatorial. According to this conscious and cynical propaganda strategy, Allende and his Popular Unity government could then be portrayed as un-Chilean, as breaking with Chile's fundamental national identity as a democracy.

Unfortunately, hiding behind their identities as mothers while acting as vigilantes helped El Poder Femenino to win popular support. If, according to maternalist thought, country and family are homologous, defense of one is automatically defense of the other. By conflating motherhood and the nation, and claiming extralegal rights to protect the country according to its own vision of reality, El Poder Femenino had a ready-made language with which to present itself as the national savior. Even the military, which was preparing the coup to be carried out on 11 September, could claim to be merely acting on the popular will, as the right-wing mothers defined it. The military claimed to be protecting the family and the nation, which the women conflated. This logic, which grows out of the division of labor by sex, can be manipulated to create a sense of chaos in order to undermine a democratic government, as it was in Chile. But the same logic can also be turned against authoritarian governments, helping to create a public space in which to promote the tenets of democracy.

Democracy in the Country and in the Streets

Confident and vivacious as an actress accustomed to moving on a public stage, Teresa Valdés invites solidarity, automatically assuming shared
views about democracy and justice. As part of Mujeres por la Vida
(Women for Life), a group of seventeen women who coordinated some
of the major women's groups opposing the dictatorship of Augusto
Pinochet in the 1980s, Teresa Valdés showed a flair for the dramatic and
a willingness to appear ridiculous. Although drawn from the center and
leftist political parties, which constituted the opposition to the dictatorship, Women for Life was committed to social change broadly con-
ceived. Claiming equity before the law, in the economy, in the political
arena, in medical treatment, and in the home, Mujeres, like so many
other groups of women before them, made a plea for equality on the
basis of difference.[1] But they also showed an audacity and a willingness
to act outlandishly that points to the way street demonstrations can
alter public perceptions and develop strategies to undermine even the
most repressive dictatorships.

She breezed into my office in New York in 1986, carrying *arpilleras,*
burlap tapestries that mothers, sisters, and wives of those who had disappeared in Chile made to bear witness to what Chileans were suffering.[2] Appliquéd testimonials, the *arpilleras* showed people being kidnapped and tortured, women mixing huge vats of soup in communal
kitchens, the police teargassing crowds, and gravesites with "N.N.," for
no name, on the tombstones.[3] Like so many liberal Chileans traveling

abroad, Teresa had smuggled out these tapestries made under the auspices of the Vicaría de la Solidaridad (Vicariate of Solidarity) of the Catholic Church to raise money for public relief.[4] These seditious cloth narratives told stories about what Chileans were enduring under the Pinochet regime. Valdés and her friends worked with women of the *poblaciones,* the working-class and squatter communities that were suffering the most from the loss of relatives kidnapped by the military dictatorship and from the double-digit inflation that made it increasingly difficult for all but the most privileged to survive economically. Since the 1980s, Valdés, a sociologist by profession, has continued to participate in movements of working-class women and to chronicle their lives.[5]

Although Teresa Valdés had been in jail in Chile following the coup of 11 September 1973, she was one of the lucky ones. Brought up on charges, she actually came to trial, was defended by human rights advocate José Zalaquett, and regained her freedom. Others, such as Nieves Ayress, were not so fortunate. Union members, students, foreigners, men with beards, long-haired women in pants, someone the concierge found suspicious or did not like—all disappeared, carted off by the truckload.

Juanita Alvarado, a working-class woman leader with whom Valdés has shared many campaigns, recalls that the connections between middle-class feminists and working-class activists in Chile were relatively untroubled in the period from 1970 to 1973, while the Popular Unity government reigned. During that flowering of democracy, women like Alvarado had been able to attend the university (she was the first in her family to do so). She had even pursued a master's degree in social work and therefore was not intimidated by—or deferential to—the college-educated women with whom she allied to defeat Pinochet. During the Pinochet regime, she worked in community-based organizations; after the transition to democracy in 1990, she directed the Equipo de Pobladoras (Working-Class Women's Community Group).[6]

Paradoxically, the coup on 11 September 1973 had contributed to popular solidarity by democratizing terror. Many union members, student activists, and artists—anyone involved with leftist political parties during Allende's Popular Unity government—were detained. Most of those murdered (94.5 percent) were young men, nearly 61 percent under thirty years old, and 73 percent under 35.[7] Women from all walks of life found themselves in the dark about what was happening to loved ones. Like Virginia Moreno Ayress, women who had lost relatives wrote letters and stalked police stations, courts, and army depots, trying to discover whether their husbands, children, sisters, or parents were dead or alive. When all possibilities for public life seemed to have disappeared, such women inadvertently created new ones. They held impromptu vigils for their lost family members. They graduated to hunger strikes in the headquarters of the United Nations in downtown Santiago. They took the stage, making themselves and the spaces they occupied periscopes from the closed world of the dictatorship to the open air of a potentially democratic public.

Since these women kept meeting as they tried to ferret out their relatives, they began to form friendships, which coalesced into loose organizations with strong bonds. To help women seeking out their relatives, a coalition of religious Catholic, Lutheran, Jewish, and other denominations formed the Comité Pro-Paz (Committee for Peace). Until Pinochet dissolved it in late 1975, it served as a human rights bureau, but it also provided legal and material aid, and gave birth in 1975 to the Agrupación de Familiares de Detenidos Desaparecidos (Association of Families of the Detained and Disappeared), which became one of Chile's foremost human rights organizations. The government, hoping to crush opposition, dissolved the Comité Pro-Paz. Following its dissolution, the cardinal archbishop of Santiago, Raúl Silva Henríquez, launched the Vicaría de Solidaridad (Vicariate of Solidarity), which was solely in the hands of the Catholic Church, and therefore answerable only to the pope. Organized in January 1976, the Vicaría gave support to the survivors of the military coup by providing legal advice, clinics, and jobs. Under the protection of the bishop of Santiago and the Vicaría de Paz, which set up workshops for women to make the tapestries, some women earned a living and found ways to express their grief by working in sewing cooperatives. Their workshops became safe havens to grieve and to publicize what was happening in Chile. The Vicaría also helped women organize around social issues in their neighborhoods. They developed networks in working-class Santiago to provide medical care, food, and childcare for women forced onto the labor market after the men who supported them lost their jobs or disappeared into Pinochet's jails, networks that provided connective tissue for incipient forms of egalitarian democracy. Following the imposition of a military junta led by Augusto Pinochet, the government was quick to declare that the "real" woman was a mother and housewife.[8] Within three weeks of the coup, Pinochet appointed his wife, Lucía Hiriart de Pinochet, director of the newly created Secretaría Nacional de la Mujer (National Secretariat of Women) and the Mothers Centers. According to Teresa Valdés and Alicia Frohman, some of these centers later served as vehicles for expressing opposition to the dictatorship, much as they had helped organize women's opposition to Allende. In most areas, however, the Chilean people, women among them, were silenced between 1973 and 1978. In 1978, attempts to resist the power of the dictatorship through street demonstrations and public gatherings focused on holidays, the most important of which was March 8, International Women's Day. A full resistance movement re-emerged in 1983 and did not end until after a referendum in 1988, in which the majority of the population voted against Pinochet's continued rule.[9]

THE REBIRTH OF STREET DEMONSTRATIONS

Resistance to the dictatorship first emerged in the unions and among women from the shantytowns. Their demonstrations quickly attracted feminist activists, who wanted to contribute their skills.[10] Double-digit inflation after 1974 had made it increasingly difficult for all but the most privileged of families in the shantytowns to survive economically. Some of the women who had joined raids on bakeries during the last days of the Popular Unity government suffered even more from the coup that overthrew it. As husbands and sons—who had been the principal wage earners—disappeared, poor women frequently became the sole support of their families. In the first hours of the coup, the army invaded former Popular Unity strongholds such as La Legua and La Victoria. Many of the men and some of the women, such as Nieves Ayress and Margarita Durán, were captured and held in clandestine prisons; others disappeared and were never seen again. Many women were left alone to sustain their families. Men who survived faced excruciating exploitation, execrable working conditions, and possible death if they tried to stand up for their rights.

Out of desperation and to save their children from starvation, women began to pool their resources in soup kitchens and community gardens. Those who hosted food kitchens in the back yards of their shanties risked being viewed as resistance leaders and having their houses marked as centers of political agitation. At a time when merely acting in conjunction with other people could attract the wrath of government, the *pobladoras* from around Santiago began forming what sociologists Naomi Rosenthal and Michael Schwartz have called "primary movement groups" and then "local movement associations."[11] By primary movement groups, they meant groups of neighbors simply meeting over a fence or going to a meeting and standing together. A local movement association included the branch of a union or a clandestine political group that was organizing in that neighborhood. Even women who did not join the organization might participate in some of its activities.

Avoiding what they considered political activity—that is, joining clandestine political parties and trade unions—*pobladoras* such as Alicia Cáceras talked about organizing "to feel human" again.[12] Cáceras distinguished organizing for human dignity, necessities, and human rights from what was previously called "political" goals. She claimed that, to the extent that the women were aware of politics, they were opposed to using force. She recalled, "We did not dedicate ourselves to a military way out. But we fought for a solution that was based on the rediscovery of the feeling [of being] human. A human [who] will make decisions and bring them to reality. For example, [we pursued] the idea of civil disobedience."[13]

Despite the vulnerability of women from the *poblaciones,* they found their way into demonstrations outside the shantytowns in the first organized resistance to Pinochet. As early as 1975, women from the shantytowns began to protest against police violence. Irene Rojas Morales recalled, "The first time [1975] was a total surprise for the *carabineros* [the hated national police]. At that time, nobody in Chile protested. And then suddenly a group appears that insists on ending [detentions]: screaming things. The *carabineros* were strongly involved in the torturing. The first reaction was one of surprise. They arrived with all of their equipment, such as water canons. They arrested some of us; they threw tear gas; it was such a strong repression."[14]

The economic situation under Pinochet worsened, with real wages plummeting in 1976 to 62 percent of their 1970 value. Health care expenditures fell to 70 percent of what had been spent during the Popular Unity government in the early 1970s, and the education allocation fell by half.[15] Economic hardship fell most heavily on the people who lived in working-class neighborhoods. Communists, Socialists, left Christian Democrats, and members of the revolutionary MIR (the Movimiento de Izquierda Revolucionaria, Movement of the Revolutionary Left) worked underground to draw together separate local, regional, and national networks. But women formed and maintained the soup kitchens, the childcare centers, the clinics, and the schools. They rewove the broken threads of people's lives and formed the new social fabric. Having viewed politics from the sidelines, women from the shantytowns became instrumental in re-creating public life in Chile.

On 8 March 1978, International Women's Day, two years after Nieves Ayress was released from prison, shantytown women joined with families of the detained and disappeared, teachers and union members, students and journalists, under the auspices of a group calling themselves the Sindicato de Empleadas de Casas Particulares (Union of Domestic Workers). At their meeting at the Caupolicán, a theater in downtown Santiago, women from all walks of life gathered to assess the situation in which they were living and to demand an end to state violence. By 5 P.M. the doors had to be closed because the space was full. Women from the Agrupación de Familiares de Detenidos Desaparecidos wore photographs of their missing relatives. Others held signs calling for reductions in the cost of living. Under banners displaying red flowers and doves, crowds of women carried on a festival of life to commemorate those who had died at the hands of the regime. A popular mass was followed by a performance of the *cueca sola,* which became the emblematic dance of the Folkloric Group of the Agrupación de Familiares de Detenidos Desaparecidos.[16] A romantic Chilean folk dance, the *cueca* usually consists of two people, waving handkerchiefs in playful and seductive ways. But dancing it alone pointed to the partners who were missing. Not viewing women as a threat, the security forces stood by and let the women meet in peace.

Conditions changed radically in April 1978, when Pinochet decreed a self-amnesty. The automatic amnesty exonerated everyone in the armed forces for crimes committed between 11 September 1973 and 11 March 1978. The government released many of the remaining political prisoners, but Pinochet's attempt to avoid any future historical reckoning infuriated many workers. The Confederación de Trabajadores del Cobre (Copper Miners Union, CTC) called an impromptu protest demonstration, which was brutally repressed. The Agrupación de Familiares de Detenidos Desaparecidos occupied three churches and the UNICEF headquarters in Santiago, where they organized a hunger strike that lasted seventeen days.[17] Having already organized a ten-day hunger strike the year before at the offices of the U.N. Economic Commission for Latin America, the Familiares continued their strategy of invading safe places to register their opposition to the government and to carve out alternative spaces in which to uphold democratic ideals. In the biggest demonstration since the coup, May Day 1978 provided an opportunity for Chileans, including large numbers of women, to show their opposition to Pinochet's government by congregating in a downtown square to demand civil and political rights.[18]

On 6 March 1979, women from the Agrupación de Familiares de Detenidos Desaparecidos attempted to celebrate International Women's Day in the Santa Laura soccer stadium. They were met by police who sealed off the stadium and tried to drive out the women demonstrators. On 5 March 1980, even greater repression of Women's Day activities occurred, as the police suppressed a demonstration in Santiago at Cariola Theater and arrested fifty women. During the early 1980s, repression on International Women's Day worsened, with fourteen women arrested in 1981 and similar numbers beaten and imprisoned in 1982. Taking over the major parks became part of the celebration, as women liberated areas of the city to serve their goals. Over the next few years, commemorations grew larger as more working-class women from the *poblaciones* joined the protests.[19]

TAKING TO THE STREETS

Had the women of the shantytowns not already been mobilizing, the recession of 1982 to 1983 might have left them and others despondent, as one-third of the population fell below the poverty line. They might not have followed the resurgent copper workers when the CTC called for a national strike in April 1983. Though the cost of a bus ticket into town (at the price of two pounds of bread) might deter women from the shantytowns from participating, they overcame their fear. At first in small numbers, they took part in demonstrations far from the safety of their own shantytowns, in areas where their poor dress made them highly conspicuous.

Resistance led to another state of siege. The government enacted the Constitution of 1980, which embedded the amnesty and created a "protected democracy." In answer to the Orwellian question about who, in fact, needed protecting, the Constitution answered by making the military the guardian of the state and by creating a senate of thirty-eight members, of whom nine were appointed for life. Presidents who had completed six-year terms gained permanent membership, which meant that Pinochet would become a senator for life. Combined with the votes of the nine appointed senators and those of the right, his appointment made amending the constitution extremely difficult.[20] Yet, even with all its faults, the Constitution of 1980 was viewed as a step toward returning the country to civilian rule, and large numbers of Chileans voted for it.

As unemployment rose to 30 percent, adding to the misery of people in the poor neighborhoods, politics exploded into a mass outburst of discontent in 1983. The Comité de Defensa de los Derechos de la Mujer (Committee for Defense of the Rights of Women, CODEM), made up of women from the shantytowns, had been launched in 1981 by leftist women to protect the interests of the poor. Along with the copper miners of the CTC, they organized the first Day of National Protest for 11 May 1983.[21] Taking care to provide a variety of ways people could demonstrate, they suggested keeping children home from school, avoiding food markets, calling in sick to offices, and turning off all lights from 9:30 to 9:35 in the evening. Most provocative of all, the organizers of the protest counseled beating pots and pans at 8 P.M., thus reclaiming and cleansing the public space that the right-wing women of El Poder Femenino had appropriated[22] Although there was little the authorities could do to the general population, they took out their wrath on the people in the *poblaciones*. On 13 and 14 May 1983, the national police and other units invaded working-class neighborhoods on the south side of Santiago. Among the worst hit was San Miguel, where Nieves Ayress's family had lived and worked. Surrounding the settlements, the police invaded at 5 A.M. and called out all the men over fourteen years old. They searched the houses for leftist literature, carried the men over to the playing fields (really empty lots at the edge of the neighborhood), and beat many of their captives.[23]

On 11–12 August, eighty-two people were killed by eighteen thousand marauding soldiers let loose in Santiago to repress demonstrators participating in the Fourth Day of National Protest, the largest demonstration in a decade.[24] In conjunction with the protests and in opposition to the violence, a group of sixty women calling themselves the Movimiento Feminista (Feminist Movement), led by sociologist Julieta Kirkwood, stood on the steps of the National Library in downtown Santiago, holding a poster that read "Democracia ahora. Movimiento Feminista Chile" (Democracy now. The Chilean Feminist Movement). Whereas in 1978 the *pobladoras* had launched movements for social change, now the largely middle-class, college-educated women joined them and sought to give issues of female equality and citizenship the same weight as other demands for democracy. The feminists came up with the slogan, "Democracia en el país y en la casa" (Democracy in the country and in the home), which became the shibboleth for the women's movement of Chile in its struggles against Pinochet, bringing together public and the private concerns of women for the first time.[25] By incorporating women's rights among other rights that they hoped to establish, the Movimiento Feminista of Chile (known by the name of the building they occupied, La Morada) joined with the *pobladoras* and women from the political parties in making sure that the struggle for democracy and human rights in Chile included women's rights.

The mobilizations did not come soon enough for those who suffered the worst repression. That fall, Sebastián Acevedo, a man who had lost two children to the junta, immolated himself in his front yard in the city of Concepción. His death served as a last straw. Women from the Christian Democratic Party, led by Graciela Bórquez, called together about seventy women activists from a variety of political parties for a press conference. Noting that violence and injustice were sweeping the country, they claimed that as women they could overcome the sectarianism that prevented the development of a strong and united opposition to Pinochet. Arguing that "Freedom has a woman's name" (referring to the fact that *Libertad* is a feminine noun), they outlined a vague program of commitment to life entitled "Today, not tomorrow, for life."[26] Then they went on to see whether they had a constituency for their movement.

Among the group that had organized the press conference, seventeen journalists, teachers, workers, artists, and professionals, calling themselves Mujeres por la Vida (Women for Life, since they opposed the politics of death that had overtaken Chile for a decade), planned another women's meeting at the Caupolicán Theater on 29 December 1983, not knowing who would attend. Over ten thousand women came from thirty organizations to rally against the dictatorship. At the meeting, they talked about the conditions they had endured during the previous decade; they sang songs; they cried.[27]

Following the success of the Caupolicán Theater meeting, the sixteen organizers began to act together as a political coordinating committee for thirty women's organizations. Though the coordinators were not *pobladoras,* Movimiento de Mujeres Pobladoras (Movement of Women from the Shantytowns, known as MOMUPO) was. Though the facilitators were not primarily feminists, Movimiento Feminista and MEMCH-83 (Movimiento Pro-Emancipacion de la Mujer Chilena, 1983, Movement for the Emancipation of Chilean Women, 1983 version) were leaders of the feminist movement in Chile. Since MEMCH-83 was itself a coordinating body for twenty-four gender-centered organizations, it is clear that concern about domestic violence, women's leadership, and sexual repression had become a part of the movement to liberate Chile from dictatorship.[28]

Mujeres por la Vida used street demonstrations in an effort to create a more egalitarian notion of popular democracy. The protests they organized amounted to civic rituals in which they reclaimed the city of Santiago and then the entire country from Pinochet and the military. By publicly confronting the violence of the military, they overcame the secrecy that enhanced the power of the authorities. They pitted their own female bodies against those of military men, raising questions about social relations structured in gender. Without homogenizing class and political differences, Mujeres por la Vida was able to focus on common goals.

María Asunción Bustos, known as Mirentxu, was one of Mujeres por la Vida's coordinators. The daughter of Basque refugees who had fled to Chile to escape the triumph of Francisco Franco in the Spanish Civil War, Bustos well remembers the loneliness and sense of desolation her family experienced as exiles. When the coup occurred in Chile, she was determined that whatever happened, she would stay and fight. Along with her family's commitment to social justice, she absorbed from her left-wing father a willingness to risk her dignity for a good cause.[29] A person with powerful capacity for joy, she remembers with a special smile the organizers' elation at the Caupolicán meeting. Having suffered alone, each woman there realized that she was part of a mass movement much greater than herself.

Participants in the mass movement differed in what they hoped to achieve. Many wanted to institute popular controls over legislation and the economy, but were not interested in altering the relationship between the sexes. They hoped to level the playing field so that the working class and the leaders of the political parties would regain power. Some groups of women were primarily concerned with improving their family's quality of life. Feminists wanted to redress the balance of power between men and women. The groups Mujeres por la Vida organized held divergent views about what they wanted in place of the dictatorship, but they all agreed on the need to end the violence.

Other groups hoped to end government repression by overthrowing it. Before the Caupolicán meeting, a new, underground revolutionary group, the Frente Patriótico Manuel Rodríguez (Manuel Rodríguez Patriotic Front), launched its activities in mid-December 1983. Along with the resurgent MIR, their goal was to push the mass movement to take up more militant tactics in the street, and even to take up arms if necessary to defeat Pinochet.[30] Mujeres por la Vida and the rest of the women's movement offered an alternative, hoping to create a new, democratic civil society in the process of defeating Pinochet. Not limiting themselves to the kinds of conscious intellectuals Jürgen Habermas thought were responsible for creating a public sphere in the eighteenth century, Mujeres por la Vida presumed that playing the part of citizens living in a democratic society might help develop people's capacity for living a democratic life.[31] Civil disobedience became Mujeres por la Vida's way of creating democracy, and 8 March 1984, International Women's Day, became the first test of their strength.

INTERNATIONAL WOMEN'S DAY AND DEMOCRACY

Chileans started commemorating International Women's Day in 1915—two years after the Russians—when a group of women in the southernmost city of Chile, Punta Arenas, organized the first march. But with the rise in the 1930s of the leftist branch of the women's suffrage movement, known as MEMCH, the celebration became intrinsic to the fight for women's rights.[32] When MEMCH, whose members were close to the Communist Party, suffered from postwar red-baiting and was driven out of the women's coalitions, the holiday lived on in the labor unions. The demise of MEMCH just when the Radical Party organized the Asociación de Dueñas de Casa (Homemakers Association), followed by the Christian Democrats' organization of the Mothers Centers, robbed Chilean women of the possibility of an organized leftist feminist movement. But International Women's Day continued as a holiday tied to the fight for the rights of women factory workers.[33]

No one I have talked to from Mujeres por la Vida remembers when she first celebrated International Women's Day or when the group decided to resurrect it in resistance to the dictatorship. In an effort to create a collective memory going back to before the Pinochet dictatorship, the organizers were searching for a past steeped in joy as well as in struggle. Some may have heard of the 1955 march, which began at the Plaza Vicuña Mackenna, at the heart of the traditional working-class area. The women chanted, "Down with milk (prices). Down with bread (prices). Down with the cost of books for studying."[34] Other potential celebrants may have joined the labor unions, which carried on the tradition of honoring International Women's Day throughout the 1950s and 1960s. From 1970 to 1973, during the days of the Popular Unity government, International Women's Day won the government's strong support. In 1972, in one district of Santiago alone, there were sixty-two events organized in connection with the holiday.[35] After the imposition of the dictatorship, the case was, of course, entirely different. But as early as 1976, only two and one-half years after Pinochet seized power, women, under the auspices of the Union of Domestic Workers, organized a celebration on 8 March at Don Bosco auditorium in downtown Santiago, where commentators recalled the origins of International Women's Day and spoke about political prisoners and those who had disappeared. From then on, not a single year lacked its women's holiday.[36]

On 8 March 1984, the first International Women's Day after Mujeres por la Vida was formed, two hundred women demonstrated by joining hands and singing the national anthem in the Plaza de la Constitución in front of La Moneda, the presidential palace that Pinochet had bombed in 1973. The police attacked the demonstrators, arresting about twenty women and beating up those they did not take to jail. Within a half hour, one hundred women gathered for a rally in front of San Francisco Church, just off the Alameda and up the street from the famous torture center at Londrés 38. The women demanded "Democracy now" as police swooped down and arrested ten more women, including psychologist Mirentxu Bustos, sociologist Julieta Kirkwood, teacher María Antonieta Saa, union leader Claudia García, and media consultant Carolina Fernández, all from Mujeres por la Vida. Those women remaining outside of the prison called a meeting at Cariola Theater in solidarity with their arrested sisters and in support of the return to democracy in Chile.[37]

At first Mujeres called for a single demonstration on 22 March 1984, in O'Higgins Park, to show women's solidarity and demonstrate their outrage at the repression of the march on International Women's Day. Mujeres flooded the foreign embassies with letters outlining human rights abuses in the country and publicizing women's decision to fight for the reestablishment of democracy. Mujeres also returned to the rhetoric of "womanhood." In explaining who they were, they said:

> We are Chilean women from a variety of fields: workers, professionals, students, peasants, artists, and housewives, women of all ages who have survived more than a decade of a system of death, whose most visible signs are: assassinations, exiles, detentions and disappearances, secret prisons, torture, imprisonment, repression against dissidents and every kind of abuse of power and arbitrary action against the most oppressed people. We accuse the military regime of throwing our nation into the greatest crisis of its history, a crisis that is not only political, economic, and social. It is a crisis of the future, a crisis of life. We live in a general climate of violence in which those who promote misery, unemployment, the drugging of hundreds of thousands of young people who lack hope.... Despite [our] pressing fear for ourselves as a people, we are also hopeful for a new dawn where life can once again have possibilities.[38]

Because the Eighth Day of National Protest was scheduled for 27 March, Mujeres effectively committed themselves to a state of permanent mobilization, naming March as "Women's Month." Denouncing the human rights abuses and claiming that "silence and indifference support the regime," the women declared in a letter to the foreign ambassadors, "We who wish to put an end to this regime of death are the majority. We have the force of reason and of morality [on our side], in opposition to the force of arms and avaricious interests." The women vowed to "struggle to regain freedom and create a clean and dignified homeland for our children and our children's children."[39] The women strategically invoked the language of motherhood, not citizenship, as if only appeal to a universal would have any power to persuade. For attempting to organize such a series of protracted demonstrations, thirty-three women were arrested and nine union leaders were taken into custody. Another eleven people, including a three-month-old and a four-year-old, died during the campaign.[40]

Later that year, on 22 December 1984, following the beginning of a state of siege in November, a group from Mujeres por la Vida, with Teresa Valdés among them, decided to commemorate the anniversary of their first mass meeting with a dramatic act. They overcame their terror by returning to National Stadium, where so many, including Nieves Ayress, had been tortured. Hiding banners under their clothes in the heat of December, the demonstrators attended the final games of the championship soccer match. Coordinating their action, with hearts palpitating, they unfurled a banner bearing their most recent slogan, "No +" (No more), meaning no more violence, no more dictatorship.[41] The crowd protected them, and they got away without being arrested. Symbolic politics had its place in the resistance movement and even those thought to be interested only in soccer were willing to protect opponents of the regime.

International Women's Day demonstrations continued in 1985, setting the stage for other escalations, as women confronted the Pinochet government with the devastation it was causing. MEMCH-83, now made up of women such as Paulina Weber, who had just returned from exile, declared March 1985 to be Women's Month.[42] Showing the commitment of certain women to drive Pinochet from power, the increasingly intense mobilizations ridiculed military power by forcing it to confront the bodies of women. On International Women's Day, 8 March 1985, women demonstrators gathered in Plaza Italia and Bustamante Park, in the heart of the city of Santiago, and proclaimed their solidarity with victims of the earthquake of 3 March. Police closed in with tear gas, shooting polluted water from mobile water cannons.[43] Not limiting their activities to the downtown area, Teresa Valdés recalled with a giggle how she and Mirentxu Bustos rode the subway with drenched hair and clothing, forcing people to notice that women were actively resisting the dictatorship.[44]

With psychologist Mirentxu Bustos and psychiatrist Fanny Pollarolo among them, Mujeres was especially sensitive to helping women overcome their fear of facing the police and confronting the issue of violence against women. Mujeres joined with other women's groups in July 1985 to hold a public meeting about the brutalization of women under the regime, showing that the systematic use of rape and disfigurement practiced on women from 1973 on was designed to shame them and cause them to retreat from struggle.[45] The demonstrations were designed to liberate women from thinking of themselves as victims or as having brought their suffering upon themselves. By transforming women's self-respect, Mujeres attempted to prepare them for full participation in a democratic polity.

With the state of siege lifted a few months earlier, the Fourteenth Day of National Protest was called on 4 September 1985 to celebrate the fifteenth anniversary of Salvador Allende's election. Ten people died that day, including Marisol de las Mercedes Vera Linares, a twenty-two-year-old student who was sitting around a fire with friends in a Santiago street. A truck carrying soldiers pulled up and simply fired into the crowd, killing her.[46]

Even with this level of violence, on 30 October 1985, Mujeres por la Vida organized another demonstration in their continuing effort to overthrow Pinochet. In the largest mass action in twelve years, Chilean women tried to reclaim Chile for democracy. Mujeres por la Vida organized three columns of well-dressed women of all classes to gather in Las Condes, a rich neighborhood of Santiago. Fancy dress was an important part of the defense strategy, since police are generally rougher on working-class women than on middle-class women, who may have powerful male relatives. Carrying signs designed by Lotte Rosenfeld, an artist who belonged to Mujeres por la Vida, they proclaimed, "Somos +" (We count more [because we are the majority]). The women held up their hands in a gesture indicating that at least their hands were not covered in blood. As the police attacked one column of women, nearly a thousand others reached the central meeting place, where the first column later joined them. All the women were soaked again when the police turned their water hoses on full force. Collective action seemed to be reaching a crescendo, promising radical change in 1986.

THE YEAR OF DEMOCRACY: 1986

Although the plebiscite ending the rule of Augusto Pinochet and the army junta was not held until 1988 and the new government of Patricio Aylwin did not take power until 1990, 1986 was the turning point, the year in which public proclamations about democracy and what constituted it became widespread. Among the advocates of democracy, Mujeres por la Vida believed that they could shape a new society from the old one.

In April 1986, while participating along with eighteen other organizations in creating the Asamblea de la Civilidad (Civic Assembly), the embryonic institution of democratic government in Chile, Mujeres por la Vida continued to focus most of its energies on popular mobilizations of women. Whether celebrating International Women's Day, carrying on a boycott of products that sponsored the government's television news programs, or trying to educate the pope about what was transpiring in Chile, Mujeres por la Vida voted with its feet, as well as insisting on representation in political bodies established by the opposition.

The annual International Women's Day celebration scheduled for 7 March 1986 set the stage for Mujeres' other efforts in the campaign for democracy in Chile. Mujeres por la Vida invited women from throughout the world to demonstrate with them and coordinated the activities of a variety of political and social groups. In a letter sent to all ambassadors to Chile inviting them to march on the most important day of international women's solidarity, Mujeres explained their commitment to democracy: "We believe in real and deep democracy as the best way to guarantee respect for human rights for everyone and to make Chile a free, just, and united country."[47] Barred from demonstrating in the Plaza de la Constitución in front of La Moneda, Mujeres had moved the demonstration to Forestal Park, which was public space, as they explained in their letter to the ambassadors. Their intention was to mobilize as women, "in a short and peaceful act."[48] There is no question that Mujeres, although made up of women who had been battered by sexism in the political parties, were highly sophisticated political actors and strategically played the women's card. Despite the use of the term *women,* they maintained their diverse interests and identities.

Although the seventeen women from Mujeres por la Vida who called the demonstrations were largely middle-class women, they were only the conveners. Many of those who participated in the demonstrations were from shantytowns, which, as always, bore the brunt of the repression. But to have the maximum effect, the demonstrations were usually called for central Santiago. Overcoming women's fear of being vulnerable in the center of the city was a first step in liberating the popular masses, especially women, and allowing them to assume their place in the city and in the nation. Mujeres por la Vida took on the responsibility of teaching women who had never been activists how to protect themselves while confronting the police. A measure of the organization's eagerness to build a cross-class alliance, to create a truly democratic movement by enabling everyone to survive police confrontations, is the handout written by Mirentxu Bustos and Fanny Pollarolo about how to prepare for the demonstration. Knowing that the police were likely to use tear gas, Mujeres urged women not to eat for at least two hours before the march. Taking nothing for granted, they counseled loose clothing and comfortable shoes. Most of all, they were conscious that makeup, especially mascara, could harm women once the tear-gas started flowing, so the flyer told women to use little or no eye makeup. They told them to put cream on their faces and lips to avoid irritation and to bring smelling salts—salt and ammonia in a bottle with a narrow neck—to help with faintness. Guiding the women as if for battle, Mujeres urged all participants to control their breathing when the gas filled the air and then take deep breaths after it passed.[49]

With detailed maps of downtown, the organizers of the 7 March 1986 demonstration made sure women of all classes could maneuver in the city. This was to be a silent march organized in three columns, each led by three women carrying signs. Coming from three points of a triangle, the columns of women were to meet in Forestal Park. All marchers would wear stickers saying "No +." Each organization would announce its calling. For example, the *pobladoras* who organized the food kitchen at La Victoria bore signs saying "No to hunger because we are the majority, the food kitchen of La Victoria." Each column had monitors charged with first aid, legal counseling, and security. In case the women were driven off, they were instructed to reconvene at the central meeting place. The leaflet instructed the marchers that "in case of repression, remember that our principal power is in organization and solidarity."[50]

Their slogan was "We Say No + [More]." Each line of the chant was followed by a chorus of "No more!" It went as follows:

On International Women's Day, our day, we the Chilean women say,
  "No more!" No more deaths, assassinations, and acts of torture!
No more exiles or arrests
No more!

No more political prisoners

No more!

No more hunger, misery, or unemployment

No more!

No more empty plates on people's tables

No more!

No more economic corruption

No more!

No more drugs or prostitution of our youth

No more!

No more spying, CNI [the secret police force that replaced DINA in 1977], and security agencies

No more!

No more patriarchal authority

No more!

No more dictatorship

No more!

We tell you this forcefully because...

We are the majority!

We are they who love democracy

We are the majority!

We are the majority who desire a new Chile, one filled with hope

We are the majority!

We are those who are for a free and unified Chile

We are the majority!

This is the truth: We are the majority. We shall fight, with clean hands, until we overthrow [the dictatorship]. Captain General, listen to this, we are the majority! And because we are the majority, we will win.

Women's word [word of honor].[51]

A variety of women's groups led by Mujeres por la Vida confronted police and soldiers in riot gear on the route of the march. Armed with tear gas and water cannons spewing from armored vehicles, the military let loose upon the women, who were chanting, "Justice and liberty," "For life," "We are the majority," and "1986 is ours, women's word." Eluding the police attacks, the women escaped to the downtown area, where they spent hours singing and dancing for democracy.

Undaunted by the repression on International Women's Day, Mujeres and fourteen other women's organizations organized a demonstration for 20 March 1986: a "Day of Democratic Rights," preempting the National Day for Democracy which the opposition had scheduled for 20 May.[52] Crowds of women exhorted people to "Vote for democracy." They filled all the major avenues and plazas with mock ballot boxes. They carried them to supermarkets and stores, set them up outside churches where mass was being said, and put them up outside soup kitchens in the *poblaciones*. Claiming that in the absence of democratic institutions, women planned to turn the streets into voting centers, they marched to the Central Railroad Station on the Alameda and to the National Library. They joined with the Association of Families of the Detained and Disappeared on processions to the gravesites of women who had died violently at the government's hands. Proclaiming their discontent, women used empty pots, kazoos, and tambourines to make noise.[53] In these, as in a variety of other demonstrations held in Chile until 1988, when Pinochet was forced out by a plebiscite, Chilean women tried symbolically to create a democratic public space in Chile.

Mujeres por la Vida devoted June 1986 to escalating protests, picketing some of the largest supermarkets and targeting pharmaceutical, detergent, coffee, and soft drink companies that sponsored the government's television news broadcasts. Arguing that these products helped promote the government's lies, Mujeres por la Vida carried out demonstrations on four Saturdays in June. These mobilizations highlighted the linkage between women's role as consumers of the products necessary to maintain ordinary life and women's role as active citizens. In a shop-in, the women filled their carts with the boycotted products and put stickers on them saying, "Don't finance lies, don't buy ———." Mujeres reasoned that even those who were afraid to march or participate could refuse to buy certain products without facing reprisals. The women advised readers of the stickers that by avoiding the tainted products, they too could contribute to the work of the Civic Assembly, which since April 1986 had been meeting to formulate goals for a new, democratic Chile.[54]

Because of Mujeres por la Vida's visibility and their ability to carry out frequent mobilizations, they represented all women's organizations in the Civic Assembly. María Antonieta Saa, a socialist teacher and one of the founding members of Mujeres, was their delegate and drafted the *Pliego de las Mujeres* (Women's Demand). Although many of the women felt that the liberal and leftist men who made up the majority of the Civic Assembly generally ignored or actively disparaged women's issues, Saa participated on behalf of the women's organizations because they wanted their program to be integrated into Chile's new democratic institutions. Saa, a lifelong feminist who as a child had signed a letter to her mother "Your daughter, the president of Chile," was the ideal person to represent women's interests among a group of men concerned with more traditional notions of political democracy.[55]

The Civic Assembly was made up of the Christian Democrats and all the leftist parties except the Communist Party. The Assembly attempted to formulate a shadow government to negotiate a transition to civilian government in Chile. In spite of ideological conflicts and different historical memories about what had brought the downfall of the Popular Unity government, the members of the Assembly tried to hammer out a future program for a democratic Chile.

Although Mujeres por la Vida's members pledged to devote themselves to social change while remaining apolitical, participating in the Assembly challenged their own commitments. To them, being apolitical meant not promoting the interests of their own political parties over those they thought represented the particular interests of women. Those who found it hardest to leave their personal party commitments behind, like Saa, persuaded Mujeres por la Vida that failure to participate in the Assembly would doom women's interests to extinction in any transitional government.

Since their list of demands represents the most detailed description of what the organized women of Chile wanted from democracy, it is worth dwelling on this. Because of their belief that patriarchal society relegated them to a secondary place, they thought it especially important for them to organize as women rather than simply as citizens: "Because a truly democratic society cannot exist without the active and equal participation of women, it is impossible to conceive of a truly democratic society that does not democratize the place of women."[56] Here the prodemocratic women were deliberately playing on the collective memories of what El Poder Femenino had achieved. Whereas the right-wing women had claimed to speak for women regardless of political affiliation or class, while pursuing an antidemocratic program designed to bring down the legally elected government of Chile, Mujeres por la Vida and the other women's groups hoped to promote the transformation of everyday life. As Teresa Valdés said, "We have brought women massively into the political process [not just to promote general social change but] in defense of our concerns and priorities as women."[57]

Not content merely to change the regime, the affiliates of Mujeres por la Vida argued with their bodies and their words for direct democracy and the reform of social relations. They were concerned with human rights broadly construed, including an end to domestic and state violence.[58] They called for the release of political prisoners and the return of those forced into exile. They deplored the increase in female heads of households, then at 40 percent, and the growth of prostitution. The document highlighted the need to reestablish maternity laws, along with price controls on basic necessities. Having faced the diminution of social services, the *Pliego de las Mujeres* vowed to fight for the reestablishment of universal health coverage, guaranteeing protection for pregnant women and nursing mothers and complete prenatal care.[59]

Adding a social dimension to what previously constituted civil rights, the demands included increased construction of houses, free education for women as well as men, forgiving water and electric bills for people in poor communities, eliminating unemployment, increasing wages, and ending the International Monetary Fund's control of the Chilean economy. In keeping with women's recognition of the work entailed in rearing children, they demanded increased salaries for women who performed public services, such as caring for children and teaching kindergarten.

Their vision of democracy called for gender equality before the law. They asked that rapists and batterers face quick and effective judgment. Mujeres demanded that women's participation in all political and social organizations be guaranteed. They underscored the need for legislation prohibiting sexual discrimination in every arena. They demanded sex education and equal wages for equal work. And they wanted to remove the distinction between "legitimate" and "illegitimate" children that the Pinochet government had instituted. Looking toward democracy, they urged that the rules governing the family be democratized. They wanted the government to educate the population about how to create and maintain egalitarian relations. And they exhorted Chile to ratify the United Nations Convention against All Forms of Discrimination against Women, the international Equal Rights Amendment (which the United States has still not ratified, though Chile has).[60]

Members of the Civic Assembly, including Saa, were arrested and held for forty days after calling a National Strike on 2–3 July 1986. Eight people died, mostly in Santiago, as a result of the army's practice of shooting into crowds of demonstrators. Fighting back, Mujeres organized an international solidarity campaign to win the release of the Assembly delegates and led street demonstrations when Saa and the others appeared in court. Finally, on 18 August, Saa was freed, along with the rest of the Assembly members.[61]

July 1986 saw increased mobilization and attempts by Mujeres and their allies among the women's groups to persuade the Civic Assembly to recognize the continued need for mobilizing. In a well-worked-out document, the women urged the Assembly to join Mujeres' protest meeting scheduled for 24 July. Attempting to ratchet up the pressure on Pinochet and the military, Mujeres called for solidarity from women throughout the world. They also implored the pope, the Chilean bishops, and all the parish organizations to speak out against the regime. July was to be the time for coordination.

Mujeres clearly believed that the Civic Assembly was being weakened by the men's competition for power. The document chided the men for letting personality conflicts divide them, for dragging their feet, and for not educating the population enough about what was going on in Chile and what the opposition was trying to do about it.[62] The women exhorted the political parties allied in the Assembly to come up with a unified proposal, to show their solidarity with the Association of Families of the Detained and Disappeared, and to support the relatives of those executed and wounded. Almost impatiently, Mujeres urged the Assembly to follow the women's lead and call a Second Day of Democracy, a mass activity modeled on their 20 March 1986 demonstration.[63]

In a document issued around 11 July 1986, Mujeres pointed to the government's strategy of promoting fear and apathy to prevent resistance. They urged the Assembly to consider how to overcome quiescence through collective action. Mujeres and its allies worried that three months after the Civic Assembly was first launched, people were not sufficiently aware of its existence. The women excoriated the Assembly for failing to call enough on the masses and for the reformers' unwillingness to carry out mobilizations.[64] But the battle was joined, and the view of Mujeres por la Vida and most of the women's organizations was that mobilizations and direct democracy ought to be an important part of the transition.

When news came in July 1986 that Pope John Paul II was planning a visit to Chile, Mujeres por la Vida drafted a letter and attempted to deliver it to the papal nuncio on the evening of 24 July 1986 in a march through the fancy shopping area of avenida 11 de septiembre. They asked women to assemble at seven in the evening and to "wear a shopping face" but hide candles and matches in their pocketbooks. The march was to be a slow and silent procession, led by women related to victims of repression, to the residence of the papal nuncio. The women were armed with a letter exhorting the pope to notice what was really going on in Chile during his visit the following April. The women used stickers to change the name of avenida 11 de septiembre, which commemorated Pinochet's coup, to avenida 4 de septiembre, the date of the election of Salvador Allende. Mujeres limited their stickers to those saying "Somos +" (We are the majority) and "No +" (No more).[65] Holding candles, the women chanted, "No more dictatorship," as the police swooped down, arresting more than sixty women as they arrived at the nuncio's dwelling.[66] Mujeres followed up the march on 30 July with an open letter to the Supreme Court. In it they claimed that "women in keeping with their *natural role as guardian of the moral values of the family,* for which the indispensable supreme value is justice, feel an obligation to show our profound disquiet" (my italics) in the wake of the escalation of government violence.[67] Again Mujeres used the rhetoric of "women," strategically trying to turn gender to their own advantage.

On 28 August 1986, as the repression intensified, Mujeres por la Vida emphasized their place as women who had seen the social situation deteriorate. Arguing that "everyday we encounter anxiety about feeding our families, about clothing, educating, [and] healing our children," they went on to exonerate themselves: "Women, as mothers, workers, squatters, professionals, peasants, students, as Chileans, urge the political and social leaders to assume their historic responsibility of leading the Chilean people to liberation." They joined with a variety of organizations in calling for a forty-eight-hour national strike beginning on the sacred date of 4 September. The goal was to end the dictatorship and establish democracy.[68]

In one of their most creative efforts to educate large numbers of people through mass demonstrations, Mujeres por la Vida hit upon a unique juxtaposition of demands, associating a clean environment with democracy. The document was addressed to "Public Opinion," and argued for the "decontamination of the political environment." They asked people to keep their cars off the streets on 4 September. They called for all factories to shut down for twenty-four hours. They urged people to save their lungs and avoid all the downtown areas and commercial centers. They promoted the idea that "clean air equals a clean nation," and claimed that they wanted the air to be "free of gasses used by the armed forces, [so that they could] establish a clean environment in which to study, work, act, and play." They argued that this campaign of "national decontamination would return Chile to a situation in which Chileans [could] breathe good air" in their country.[69] Having traveled to Nairobi for the second U.N. World Conference of Women in 1985, Teresa Valdés may have been conscious of environmental campaigns such as the Green Belt Movement Wangari Matthai was helping to lead in Kenya. Situating Chile's struggle for justice and democracy in the context of similar campaigns waged by women throughout the world against authoritarian governments and against the degradation of every aspect of life, Mujeres por la Vida promoted the metaphor of environmental safety as a correlate of political transformation in Chile.

The mobilizations of 4 and 5 September 1986 and the Manuel Rodríguez National Front's attempt to assassinate Pinochet on 7 September led to increased repression and a new state of siege, robbing people of the rudimentary civil rights they had recently regained. Among those targeted were Mujeres members Fanny Pollarolo and María Antonieta Saa. Pollarolo, known simply as Fanny, was arrested and remained in solitary confinement for fifty-five days, charged with promoting violence and social disorder.[70] At the end of September, Mujeres joined others in protesting against the state of siege. And in the first street action following the imposition of martial law, women from a variety of organizations papered the streets of Santiago with flyers calling for the establishment of democracy.[71]

THE STRUGGLE FOR DEMOCRACY CONTINUES

Through the following year, 1987, periodic mass mobilizations under the leadership of Mujeres por la Vida continued, but dissent grew among the thirty organizations that belonged to the opposition. Mujeres persevered, coordinating demonstrations all over Chile for International Women's Day. Drawing together widows of executed leaders, mothers of the disappeared, youth, victims of domestic violence, poor housewives, and those who suffered stereotyping as women, MEMCH "83" and Mujeres por la Vida organized a wide variety of women, four hundred of whom signed a call to demonstrate.[72]

During the first week in March, over two hundred events took place in *poblaciones,* schools, workplaces, and professional societies to mark International Women's Day. The sense of promise was marred by the death of a male supporter on 6 March in a drive-by killing as he was joining a demonstration.[73] But, with foreign visitors in attendance, Mujeres celebrated March 8 under the banner "United we fight for democracy and life." Mujeres por la Vida organized a meeting on 9 March to discuss the Chilean women's movement and its connections to women

abroad. On 10 March there was a peaceful demonstration in front of
Congress and then dancing and singing in the streets, as women from a
variety of organizations blocked traffic until police rolled in with jeeps
shooting tear gas. The police dispersed the women and the male students and workers who had joined them, beating and arresting demonstrators. Repression led to additional gatherings, such as the one on 11
March to express outrage against the brutality.[74] When the pope arrived
on 1 April 1987, having refused to meet in Rome with Graciela Bórquez
and other members of the delegation of Chilean women who had tried
to inform him about the poverty and injustices prevailing in Chile, Mujeres por la Vida protested in front of the public jail, asking aid for 396
political prisoners on a hunger strike and calling on the pope to intercede with General Pinochet to win release of all political prisoners.[75]
John Paul II did nothing.

Returning to the National Stadium on 25 August 1987, Mujeres por
la Vida demonstrated once again. This time the theme was "regaining
hope," and they called for a general strike to overthrow the dictatorship. They sang Schiller and Beethoven's "Ode to Joy," the theme song
of the opposition. They claimed that the demonstration would assert
solidarity through joy, song, and laughter.[76] On 11 September 1987, the
fourteenth anniversary of the coup, Mujeres por la Vida organized a
tableau in front of the Church of the Divine Providence. Dressed in
black, the women silently bore witness to their opposition to the
regime. Although they intended to stay from 1 P.M. to 1:30, the police
routed them within fifteen minutes. A similar activity that morning in
front of the National Library had led to the arrest of three women.[77]

The popular mobilizations accelerated along with the political process.
The time had come for the plebiscite Pinochet had provided for in the
1980 constitution. Although people could only vote "yes" or "no" to
Pinochet's remaining in office another eight years, the plebiscite would
provide a chance for people to show what they thought. Scheduled for
5 October 1988, opposition groups had to decide what their strategy
would be. The dangers as well as the possibilities of transforming the government after seventeen years of authoritarian rule were not lost upon the
women. Not only was the plebiscite not an election, but the men in the
opposition still didn't understand what Mujeres and other women's
groups expected from democracy. Capitalizing on a voter registration
drive for the plebiscite to raise consciousness about what democracy
might mean for women, Mujeres por la Vida went into action, along with
grassroots organizations that provided social services in the *poblaciones*.[78]

Mujeres por la Vida launched their campaign on 11 July 1988 with a meeting uniting many sectors of the opposition. Linking demands for human rights and democracy, Mujeres attempted to rouse the masses using a 1930s ballad, "Don't Forget Me," and forget-me-nots to remind the population of those who had disappeared into prisons, torture chambers, exile, and unmarked graves. With signs asking, "Where will the exiles, political prisoners, disappeared, and victims of assassination vote?" Mujeres, the Agrupación de Familiares de Detenidos Desaparecidos, and other women's groups mounted a campaign to recall what was at stake in the plebiscite. The first segment of the operation culminated on 29 August 1988, the day the government planned to announce its candidate— Augusto Pinochet. On that day, at precisely 2:00 P.M., one thousand silent women, dressed in black, organized into forty brigades of twenty-five members, spread out in downtown Santiago, opening packages of silhouettes inscribed with thumbnail biographies of the disappeared. Hoping for the maximum impact at an hour when Chileans were out walking and police presence was minimal, Mujeres organized their action precisely. After ten minutes, they left the silhouettes and the signs that they plastered all over the walls as a reminder to people about human rights abuses by the government. One of the most visual of the actions of Mujeres por la Vida, the campaign entailed having the police seen attacking representations of those who had disappeared, thus performing publicly what they had been doing in secret for fifteen years. By these means, Mujeres linked human rights and women's struggles in the popular imagination and succeeded in having the media record the confrontation.[79] Continued efforts to defeat Pinochet were fruitful, and Pinochet lost the referendum. But the struggle for democracy was just beginning.

The success of demonstrations like the ones on 11 July and 29 August made them seem simple, but nothing could be further from the truth. Personal, class, and political antagonism divided participating groups, who agreed only on the need to get rid of Pinochet. Men and women from the Agrupación de Familiares de Detenidos Desaparecidos and Catholic groups that worked closely with the Vicaría de la Solidaridad entered into shaky alliances with Mujeres por Socialismo, feminists from La Morada, and the women's groups in MEMCH-83. Political antagonists such as Christian Democrats, Socialists, and Communists had to accept their differences and work together. Pobladoras coordinated in Mujeres de Chile, and journalists, teachers, and labor leaders from other groups had to agree on symbols and chants that would not offend anyone, coordinate activities with women and men from the four corners of Santiago, and make provisions for meeting all possible responses from authorities. Women and male allies met daily and weekly for a month before the big demonstrations. They met in small groups in their neighborhoods and in citywide gatherings where they argued passionately and sometimes bitterly about what should appear in the pamphlets and flyers. Small groups discussed the themes they wanted to promote. Patricia Verdugo and Jimena Duque of Mujeres por la Vida often proposed images, and Lotte Rosenfeld usually designed them, but everyone had to agree about what they wanted the demonstrations to achieve. Commitment to overcoming the military dictatorship—and the determination to learn new democratic practices that could be put in place once Pinochet was overthrown—was all that held such diverse groups together.[80]

Fighting a double battle to bring down the dictatorship and prevent men in the democratic opposition from ignoring women's need to end sexual discrimination, violence against women, and sexism, a coalition of women planned another demonstration for International Women's Day. Still rejoicing from the October plebiscite, Mujeres proclaimed that because of that victory and the hopes for the new democracy, "[we] will be fundamental actor[s] as we have been up to now, and united we will achieve our demands and our goals."[81] The call included a catalog of their dreams: "We wish to sing, dance, cry and shout with pain and pleasure, hatred and love, frustration and hope. These sentiments brought us to victory in the plebiscite [and] enabled us to fight for fifteen years.... This is how we developed a democratic consciousness."[82] In a novel twist, the flyer announcing the gathering called on men to take care of the children so that the expected crowd of twenty-five thousand women could attend the meeting at 7 P.M., a time when women would usually be preparing dinner.

On 7 March 1989 in Santa Laura Stadium, more than twenty thousand women linked their celebration of International Women's Day to their aspirations for democracy. Following up on this massive demonstration, various women's groups put together a paper called "Women's Demands for Democracy," focusing on civil rights for women, reproductive and parental rights, and workplace reforms. As part of their proposals, the women again called for ratification of the United Nations Convention against All Forms of Discrimination against Women and passage of an equal rights amendment to the new constitution; the creation of a cabinet-level organization to formulate legislation about women; and an end to discrimination in education.[83]

One of the most significant of the organizations helping to shape the new constitution and elect representatives was the Concertación Nacional de Mujeres por la Democracia (Women's National Coalition for

Democracy), formed early in 1989 by women's groups and individuals who hoped to influence the Concertación de Partidos por la Democracia (Alliance of Parties for Democracy), which consisted of most of the opposition parties. The Concertación Nacional de Mujeres, preparing for the presidential and congressional elections in December 1989, made proposals regarding every area of social, political, and cultural life. The women offered their agenda, and even the right-wing parties could not ignore it.[84]

Although few women candidates ran for office, the gender issues appeared for the first time as a significant element in social and political policy rather than as a separate category—of so-called women's issues. The election to the presidency of Patricio Aylwin, a Catholic, conservative Christian Democrat who nevertheless supported many of the claims of the women's movement, helped raise issues that had appeared in the *Pliego* as the new constitutional government came to power in 1990.

The need for mobilizing did not diminish, since Pinochet remained head of the armed forces and continued to exercise power in the "protected democracy." When Pinochet packed the Supreme Court in early 1990, his appointees fired one of the few magistrates viewed as an independent jurist. Mujeres por la Vida added odors to its usual sight jokes. The women gathered on the second floor balcony of the Hall of Justice, from which they silently dropped rotten fish heads and decomposing shellfish. Above them a banner read, "La suprema está podrida" (The Supreme Court is a rotten fish).[85]

PERMANENT MOBILIZATION

Mujeres por la Vida continued to mobilize as a means of overcoming the fear of participants and establishing a space in which to express their views of democracy. Most of the women in Mujeres por la Vida, who came from parties or movements committed to socialist principles or Christian values, wanted Chile to carry out social transformation along with political change. Mujeres por la Vida and the disparate groups whose public demonstrations they organized believed that being in the streets meant they would get a hearing with the parties as well as in a newly formed democratic government.[86]

Once the opposition parties were again in a position to mediate between civil society and the state, however, they attempted to stifle the popular movement. Mujeres por la Vida, for their part, wanted to continue their "dual militancy." Determined to overcome the sectarianism of the political parties and unions to which they belonged, Mujeres por la Vida committed itself to promoting the interest of women and the family as goals of the parties. The members of Mujeres had not abandoned participation in political parties when they joined the social movement. But they also hoped to maintain the autonomy of the social movement of which they were such an important part.

For seventeen years, women who had been hurt economically as well as personally by the loss of a spouse or child participated in workshops, where they made *arpilleras* or organized communal kitchens in order to feed themselves and their neighbors. By turning what had been their private activities into public services for themselves and others, *pobladoras,* many of whom had never thought of themselves as citizens before the coup, began to connect violence in the home and political repression outside. Mujeres por la Vida helped provide them with an explanation for why, despite hardships, public participation in protests seemed like a liberating activity and why many of the women did not want to give up public life to return to their homes full-time to serve husbands and children. Teresa Valdés has said, "Apart from fear, [what stifled women] was conforming to the wishes of husbands and families that the women remain repressed."[87]

In fact, according Fanny Pollarolo, the demonstrations helped women conquer their terror of the government as well as of battering spouses. "This is a vicious cycle because the only way to overcome fear is to confront the situations that cause it."[88] Celebrations such as International Women's Day played a significant role in transforming ordinary Chilean women from fearful housewives to militant combatants against violence in the country and in the home.

The Chilean opposition was far-flung, and Mujeres por la Vida was only one of many women's organizations that helped to undermine the dictatorship of Augusto Pinochet. But Mujeres' significance lies not in the charisma of individual members—some of the most talented and convincing women on earth—but in their ability to respect the differences among the groups whose demonstrations they organized. Mujeres also understood the power of constant mobilization to enhance the courage and carry out the democratic education of masses of women with diverse views and class positions.

Most of the leaders of Mujeres por la Vida were young, accomplished professionals from the middle classes. Whether they had grown up in patriarchal military families, like Teresa Valdés and Fanny Pollarolo, or in refugee families from the Spanish Civil War, like Mirentxu Bustos, they were politically sophisticated. The genius of women like Graciela Bórquez, a lifelong Christian Democrat, was to use their political experience in the pursuit of views of social justice inconceivable without feminism.

For many, feminism was the new movement in their lives. When asked about the slogan, "Democracy in the country and in the home," former Mujeres por la Vida members frequently attribute the saying to "the feminists," as if to a separate group. Many of the leaders of Mujeres had long been associated with leftist parties and labor unions, and their strongest commitment—the issues about which they felt most clear—involved issues of economic and social equality. But, unlike traditional political leaders, who attempt to mute differences and win over large groups of people to party doctrine, Mujeres por la Vida respected the differences among *pobladoras,* shantytown women, mothers of the disappeared, makers of *arpilleras,* and single mothers with whom they engaged in daily contact.

As women of all races engaged in Civil Rights struggles in the 1960s United States learned, fighting for the rights of others often sensitizes activists to their own oppression. Despite their public militancy, women professionals and *pobladoras* might appear at planning meetings with black eyes and other evidence of battering. Buttressed by one another's support, Mujeres por la Vida and the other women's groups in the Chilean resistance committed the ultimate treachery against the male-dominated parties and unions when they refused to remain silent about domestic violence and thereby added another set of demands for democracy.

If Mujeres por la Vida failed to change Chile in 1986 as planned, or even in the plebiscite of 1988 and the election of 1989, Mujeres and the other Chilean women's groups succeeded in raising people's consciousness about how authoritarianism works in personal relations as well as in government. Although Chilean women ceased their mobilizations, they continued to participate in the state-run women's bureau, Servicio Nacional de la Mujer (National Service for Women, SERNAM), and in international conferences such as the fourth United Nations World Conference on Women, held in Beijing in 1995. As a result of Chilean women's extended ideas about democracy and human rights, they succeeded in getting the Chilean government to discuss many of the programs for women's rights as human rights promulgated in Beijing. Although Mujeres por la Vida does not exist as a formal organization in a democratic Chile, former members populate social organizations, research groups, and Congress, taking demands for the emancipation of women of all classes into every level of public life. As Fanny Pollarolo has said, "Having lived a collective life as a member of Mujeres por la Vida, creating such community on a larger scale seems anything but utopian."[89]

CHAPTER 4

Searching and Remembering

On a beautiful spring day in 1991, I went with Mabel Bellucci to march with the Madres de Plaza de Mayo in Buenos Aires, Argentina. Arm in arm, a crowd of about a hundred, mostly women and young people, walked in a large circle behind a line of women wearing white kerchiefs and carrying a banner calling for justice. Many of the leaders had been marching at 3:30 every Thursday afternoon since late April 1977 in an attempt to bring to justice those who had attempted to crush a social movement by destroying nearly an entire generation of young people.[1] After the chants and the repeated circles around the obelisk, people said good-bye and strolled away. Our group, with Madre Nora Morales de Cortiñas in the lead, went to have coffee in a nearby café. Nora de Cortiñas is an energetic, slightly built woman with a sense of purpose in her step. She moves quickly but always seems to have an ear open for an odd turn of phrase or a joke. Her wry sense of humor alone seems like a triumph, since one of her sons was captured and carried off in April 1977, about a year after the Argentine military took power.

One of the few Madres to call herself a feminist, de Cortiñas seems to have egalitarian relations with people of all ages. Not one to demand deference for what she helped accomplish—creating one of the world's most important movements for social justice and human rights—she doesn't give deference either. In spite of all her suffering, she has an optimistic nature. As we spoke in 1991, she offhandedly remarked that her husband had suffered even more than she had. Taken aback, I asked what she meant. "I only lost a son; he also lost a wife."[2] Any woman activist knows immediately what she means. Her husband, now dead, had grown up in a household where his mother made special efforts to protect him. De Cortiñas prided herself on being a housewife and mother until the government intervened in her everyday life and forced her to confront the state. In the company of women she did not know, she spent her days going from one government or religious office to another, seeking her missing adult child. Together these women had found a way to confront the government in the pursuit of justice. Risking the same abduction, torture, and death as their children, the women drew together.

To a certain extent, the women were reborn, as if giving birth was not enough. Having loved but not necessarily understood their children, the women gradually began to fathom, through their own confrontations with brutal and callous representatives of the regime, why their children had tried to address some of the worst characteristics of their society and why some had turned to militant action to defeat a government they thought defended only the interests of the wealthy and well connected. Some young people became involved with liberation theology and made a commitment to the poor, as Madre Hebe de Bonafini's son Jorge seems to have done before he was abducted.[3] Even those who had taken up arms to promote social justice deserved trials, as Nieves Ayress's mother remarked in Chile. Authorities in Argentina who could abduct tens of thousands and create 340 concentration camps equipped with torture chambers could easily have secured lawyers to indict alleged terrorists and bring them to justice. As human rights activist Antonio Elio Brailovsky later explained, "Those who said the junta was trying to defend [Argentina] from terrorism could not and did not want to assemble the evidence to prove that those who were arrested had committed the crimes they attribute[d] to them."[4] Instead, the junta in Argentina chose to punish those with whose ideas they disagreed, whether or not they had engaged in illegal activities.

For more than twenty-five years, the Madres de Plaza de Mayo in Argentina have been assembling evidence against the juntas and their apologists, trying to overcome collective amnesia to account for the thirty thousand people who disappeared. They have done that through constant mobilizations, particularly those centered on the Plaza de Mayo. In the course of struggle, they have grown from despairing parents into social activists. Their chief tactic has been the use of street mobilizations.

Although the Madres were not the only ones to fight the junta, nor
the first, they were, according to one of their founding members and
first leaders, Renée Epelbaum, "the first to have done it publicly."[5] They
became publicity hounds, staging performances before the cameras. Instead of campaigning secretly, the Madres were the most public citizens
in Argentina. "From the beginning, the Mothers went to the streets and
the others worked from their offices," says Madre Carmen de Guede.[6]
Fighting for answers to what happened when anywhere between ten
thousand and thirty thousand people, mostly in their twenties and thirties, had disappeared, these ordinary housewives turned themselves into
the crack troops of a movement that couches justice in terms of ethics
and historical memory. While providing their loved ones with a history,
the Madres de Plaza de Mayo, first unconsciously and now consciously,
wage a battle for human rights that includes economic and social rights
of the kind that no international body has yet affirmed. As Hebe de
Bonafini explained, "When a woman gives birth to a child she gives life
and at the same time, when they cut the cord, she gives freedom. We
were fighting for life and freedom."[7] She herself lost two sons and a
daughter-in-law in what the military called the Dirty War, which overtook Argentina between 1976 and 1983.

Élida Busi de Galletti lost her child, 31-year-old Liliana Galletti, on
13 June 1977. On a hunch, de Galletti went to the military base in the
fashionable Palermo section of Buenos Aires on her daughter's birthday,
5 September 1977. De Galletti baked her daughter a cake and took it to
the base where she thought Liliana might be a prisoner. "I went and tore
the cake into crumbs and [threw] them at the foot of a tree because I
thought that my daughter might be there....I thought that maybe from
some window Liliana might be looking at the trees....It seemed to me
that it was an act of madness, something without reason....Later I
learned that all of us did similarly unreasonable things. All of us."[8]

De Galletti kept going to different human rights offices without making any progress. Then someone told her about a group of mothers who
gathered in the Plaza de Mayo every Thursday at 3:30 P.M. She found
twenty women marching in a line, but she was afraid to join them. Since
no one invited her to enter the group, she left and went home. The next
time she came, she sat down on a bench crying. A mother seated near
her asked if de Galletti too had had a family member carried away. She
recalls that at that time they did not yet use the word *disappeared*. De
Galletti said yes, and added that she was afraid to join those who were
circling the pyramid at the center of the plaza because they seemed so

brave and self-assured. The other woman admitted that she too was intimidated about joining them. De Galletti finally entered the ring of
marching women. However, feeling like an outsider to their "clan," she
quickly left. The next week she returned, overcame her fear, and joined
the Madres on their march. When someone from the group asked who
of hers had disappeared, she finally understood that she wasn't alone.[9]

During the 1970s and 1980s, Latin America became synonymous with
military dictatorships, under which approximately ninety thousand people were secretly kidnapped and never seen again. In Argentina, approximately ten thousand were murdered and from ten thousand to thirty
thousand disappeared. The vast majority of those tortured in Argentina
died in the clandestine centers in which they had been imprisoned. Others were "transported" and killed along the roads, allegedly in armed uprisings; still others were stripped, drugged, and dropped alive from planes
flying from military airports. Because many of those abducted, held without charges, tortured, and frequently assassinated were under thirty, and
their mothers set out to find them in increasingly public ways, the Argentine case became emblematic of the problem of "the disappeared."

With state terror desecrating life in the mid-1970s, the women whom
officials called "Las Locas" (the crazy women) gave their children material reality in the only way possible: denying their deaths, the mothers
carried out processions, replacing the bodies of those who had disappeared in detention with their own marching bodies, seen every Thursday at 3:30 P.M. in the Plaza de Mayo. Despite the danger to themselves,
the women demonstrated to break the silence and to reestablish the
sense of a community united in the pursuit of justice. Their campaign of
direct action served as an irritant and a challenge to a government that
thought it could act with impunity, as well as to those who act lawlessly
in the twenty-first century.

Few people outside human rights circles spoke with the Madres when
they began their weekly mobilizations in 1977, and even fewer wanted to
acknowledge what was going on in Argentina. From 1971, when the
country was ruled by a moderate military government, through the period from 1973 to 1976, under Juan Perón and then his widow, María Estela Martínez de Perón (known as Isabelita), over a thousand people were
ambushed and "disappeared."[10] Right-wing paramilitary groups, among
them the Alianza Anti-Comunista Argentina (Argentine Anti-Communist
Alliance, also known as the Triple-A), assassinated leftists, civil rights advocates, and those who worked with the poor and seemed interested in
reform. The Triple-A, consisting of certain high-ranking right-wing mili-

tary officers such as Mohamed Alí Seneildín,[11] off-duty police, taxi drivers, and ordinary right-wing citizens, justified its extralegal activities by claiming that it was in a war to the death with revolutionaries.

Among the first of two hundred deaths for which the Triple-A was responsible were a radical priest and a senator who was a civil rights activist.[12] The right wing targeted left-wing activists, most notably the Montoneros (left Peronists) and the Ejército Revolucionario del Pueblo (People's Revolutionary Army, ERP), the group that Nieves Ayress's attacker claimed abducted his brother. By November 1974, the government decreed a state of siege against the leftist threat, declaring martial law and empowering the police and army to do as they pleased.[13] Those who never returned were described as having been carried off (using the passive voice), and then as having been disappeared (making *disappear* into a transitive verb). Four months before the military coup on 24 March 1976, General Jorge Rafael Videla explained that he and other Argentines were prepared for as many deaths as necessary to achieve the country's security.[14] When he, Admiral Emilio Eduardo Massera, and Brigadier Orlando Ramón Agosti of the air force took power as leaders of the first military junta, they began their task with gusto.[15]

Campaigns for social justice in the 1960s and 1970s aroused a generation of young people throughout the world. Unequal distribution of resources during the Cold War intensified struggles for civil rights and political change, ranging from the Civil Rights movement in the American South to wars of national liberation in former European and American colonies. The Cuban Revolution of 1959 aroused hopes among those seeking to redress injustices and fears among those who wanted to protect their own wealth and power. Generational antagonism emerged everywhere, but nowhere with more violence than in Latin America. Latin American military leaders, including those who had been trained in counterinsurgency techniques at the School of the Americas in Panama, considered all serious efforts at social reform to be part of a communist conspiracy that had to be crushed. Young people who hoped for a better world and would-be revolutionaries became targets of state terrorism, carried out through largely secret death squads. Nieves Ayress faced such military policies in Chile. The children of Renée Epelbaum, Nora de Cortiñas, Laura Bonaparte, Hebe de Bonafini, and María del Rosario Cerruti confronted state terror in Argentina.

The Argentine military, carrying out what they called the Proceso de Reorganización Nacional (Process of National Reorganization), declared war on those they considered subversives: workers, union activists and their lawyers, leftists, socially conscious doctors, journalists, Jews, students, and young people, particularly from the working class.[16] The secret kidnapping, detention without trial, torture, and murder of up to thirty thousand, of whom 3 percent were pregnant when they were arrested, continued from 1976 until the regime was replaced by a democratic government at the end of 1983.[17] Claiming to defend Argentina from leftist subversion, the junta carried out a national cleansing campaign. Speaking a year after the coup, General Ibérico Saint-Jean, the governor of Buenos Aires Province, outlined the goals of the dictatorship when he proclaimed, "First we will kill all the subversives; then we will kill their sympathizers; then all who remain indifferent, and finally we will kill the undecided."[18] Remaining silent, acting circumspectly, and averting one's gaze became means of surviving in Argentina, a comportment the Madres reversed through their insistence on working in public, where they established new civic rituals. By taking back the streets they attempted to reclaim civil society.

The Madres developed public performances to counteract the secret rituals practiced by the junta.[19] The Triple-A and later the Work Groups of the security forces frequently invaded people's homes during the night or at dawn, in groups of six to twelve masked men in civilian dress. To avoid being mistaken for common criminals, the Work Groups informed police about their activities and advised them to stay away, just as they did in Chile.[20] In carefully orchestrated ceremonies of terror, the abductors put a hood over the victim's head, beating and humiliating the subject of their search and other members of the family. They raped women and sometimes even tortured children to get parents to talk. Ransacking homes and taking booty were part of the job. Once detained, the subject lacked any right to contact family or lawyers. When the prisoners reached the site where they were to be held, they were stripped and tortured to break their will and destroy their solidarity with others. In some camps, prisoners were kept naked and chained to the walls or otherwise bound. Sometimes they were forced to sit in the middle of a room on the floor and remain silent. If they spoke or moved, they were beaten. They were left to rot in their own excrement or taken to lavatories in convoys of prisoners. And they were usually hooded or blindfolded.

One prisoner recalled:

> With the hood on, I became aware of my complete lack of contact with the outside world. There was nothing to protect you, you were completely alone. That feeling of vulnerability, isolation and fear is very difficult to

describe. The mere inability to see gradually undermines your morale,
diminishing your resistance.... The "hood" became unbearable, so much so
that one transfer [a euphemism for execution] day, I shouted for them to
have me transferred: "Me...me..." The hood had achieved its aim, I was
no longer Lisandro Raúl Cubas, I was a number.[21]

The excruciating pain and terror between torture sessions were interrupted by the sounds of others being tortured. Frequently the jailers
feigned executions; some of them were real. Waiting—for the torturers
to fetch you again or for the appearance of new prisoners who were
friends or family—created a state of almost constant terror. Some people were released and brought news about what was transpiring to a
populace cowed by fear and unwilling to listen.

When civilian government was restored in 1983, the government
commission established to investigate the disappearances produced
concrete evidence regarding 8,960 people, which the commission estimated to be perhaps half of those who disappeared.[22] According to the
Madres, who refused as a group to participate in the hearings, nine
thousand was less than one-third of those who were abducted. As people disappeared from the camps, new ones were abducted. Since only
witnesses, family, and friends could firmly attest to someone's having
lived, and whole groups and families were captured and killed, the final
number will never be established conclusively.

Some captives were released after years in secret detention centers.
Some had served as photographers or engineers or as "staff" in ESMA (the
clandestine center in the officer's club of the Escuela Superior Mecánica de
la Armada, or Naval Mechanics School), where Admiral Massera attempted to use Montonero leaders to help him develop a populist political
party modeled on Peronism.[23] But most of those kidnapped died under
torture or were murdered. Sometimes the jailers even told prisoners that
they would be set free. They then took them to the outskirts of cities and
staged guerrilla attacks, killing prisoners whom they claimed had been
underground in terrorist gangs. Some of the prisoners were taken—frequently in Ford Falcons—to the outskirts of the city and shot above their
own graves. In the cemeteries, mass graves mysteriously appeared with
"N.N.," for "not named," on wooden crosses or other crude markers.[24]

Élida de Galletti, who had torn up her daughter Liliana's birthday
cake in September 1977, learned after the junta was overthrown that a
woman who had been held in Banfield concentration camp had news
about her daughter. The woman, Liliana Sambrano, had been taken to

Banfield on 7 September 1977, where someone in a nearby cell called out that she was Liliana Galletti and had studied humanities. Galletti thought they would all be turned over to the Poder Ejecutivo Nacional (National Executive Power)—that is, they would be formally charged, get lawyers, see their families, and stand trial in open court. The witness then heard the guards tell people in Galletti's cell to eat little because they would soon be traveling. A few hours later, Liliana Sambrano was sent to clean the cell where the other Liliana had been. The clothes were folded up, and she presumed that the other Liliana had died that day. Élida de Galletti dated the decline of her family from her daughter's disappearance, which contributed to her husband's death and drove her son into exile. She herself died in September 1990.[25]

Those outside people who acknowledged the disappearances in the 1970s supported the dictatorship by arguing that the victims must have done something to be treated so badly. Others simply pretended not to know that their fellow citizens were being abducted at home and in the streets and were being tortured and murdered, sometimes in detention centers a stone's throw from their house or estate. After representative democracy was restored in Argentina, when an investigative committee talked to neighbors of the former clandestine torture centers, such as Orletti Mecánico in Buenos Aires, people admitted that they had known from the screaming that the garage was a torture center.[26] Others had simply moved away.

No human rights group has ever been able to ascertain how the junta thought it could simply kidnap thousands of young people without having to answer to their families. Believing that terror would cow the entire population, the junta pursued its policy of exterminating all those it considered to be leftist sympathizers. Parents went to the courts, the Ministry of the Interior, police stations, and army barracks, looking for their children, as Élida de Galletti did. When fathers had to return to work, the mothers continued their rounds, trying to ferret out their children. By robbing citizens of the ritualized processes of indictment and trial and by withholding the bodies of victims, most of whom were in their twenties and thirties, the junta effectively obliterated an entire generation and attempted to silence those who remained by denying their history. The Madres retaliated by publicly documenting what was going on and refusing to remain silent. They became keepers of the historical record and campaigners against future impunity. Against all odds, they tried to turn public opinion against the junta.

GOING PUBLIC

What happened next has already taken on mythical proportions. Out of terror and repression, a group of relatively inexperienced housewives and mothers became a social movement. Early accounts claim that, without prior planning, fourteen mothers descended on the Ministry of the Interior, the office that controlled the federal police and the courts. Shooed out by the staff, the fourteen mothers supposedly found themselves, by chance, in the Plaza de Mayo. Recognizing each other from the various waiting rooms where they went searching for their children, the women sat down on benches and began to trade stories. Since all assembly was prohibited, the police disrupted their impromptu meeting and told them to move on. Getting up from the benches, small groups of the women began to stroll arm-in-arm on the circular walk around the column in the plaza. As if vowing to make a pilgrimage, they decided to return the following Thursday at 3:30 P.M. Each week, more and more women joined their ranks, and by June 1977, some hundred mothers completed the *ronda,* or walk around the monument.[27] For nearly thirty years, the Madres have pursued their children's struggle for social change and refined their techniques of direct action.

One of the first Madres, María Adela Gard de Antokoletz, whose thirty-nine-year-old son, a prominent civil rights lawyer, was carried off in November 1976, recalled the evolution of the *ronda* in heroic terms after Azucena Villaflor de Vicente and two other Madres were abducted at the end of 1977: "And so, driven by the words of Azucena at our head, fourteen of us filled with fear gathered in the plaza. What were we fourteen going to do in the plaza? Absolutely nothing.... But we went with resolution and we continued going Thursday after Thursday. We didn't ask anyone about their ideas or what their kids did, or what was the ideology of the family. Just the fact of having a disappeared person [in your family], only this was enough to establish a brotherhood [*sic*] among us women."[28]

Gard de Antokoletz, like other mothers, had combed official offices looking for her son. Some women recognized each other as they went from agency to agency. The women gradually became comfortable with others who shared the same sorrow. One origin story says that several of the women gathered at Villaflor's house, and she became their informal leader. Nora de Cortiñas remembers Villaflor as "a person worthy of respect, one to whom one might go for protection, who always had ideas about what should be done, who always encouraged others to share in the work, who always was ready to do more."[29] Another early Madre remembered that in addition to visiting each other's homes, the women also met in churches. They were at the church of Stella Maris when Villaflor suggested that they should make an appearance in the Plaza de Mayo, where they might be able to present a petition to someone at the Casa Rosada, Argentina's West Wing.

The more heroic version places the origin of the Madres in the office of the vicar of the navy, Monsignor Eugenio Gracelli. Of all the officials visited by the family members of the disappeared, Gracelli was the only one who seemed to share their concerns. Instead of ridiculing the mothers, Gracelli welcomed them. He and his private secretary asked them detailed questions about their children's lives. He urged the parents to come back to see him in a few weeks; when they did, he looked into a substantial file box and reported that a son had been shot or that nothing was known about a missing daughter. When no other official would acknowledge that anything untoward was taking place, Gracelli seemed to validate the mothers' concerns. They later learned that he was reporting their information to the captors of their children.

Of all the women who became acquainted at Gracelli's office, Azucena Villaflor was the most politically conscious. From a working-class family of Peronists, she had had a job as a switchboard operator in a factory and probably had been involved in labor struggles when she was young.[30] She married a fellow Peronist who shared her devotion to the memory of Juan Perón and his first wife, the charismatic Evita Perón.[31] Since Azucena's husband made a good living selling kerosene, she left the paid labor force and became a housewife and at-home mother to their three sons and their daughter.

Her second son, Néstor de Vicenti, had quit the architecture department at the university to become a leather maker so that he would have time to devote to the poor. When he was kidnapped on 30 November 1976, along with his girlfriend, Raquel Mangin, Azucena Villaflor followed the path of so many other parents before her. She went to the Ministry of Interior, to the offices of the bishop, and to the vicar of the navy. One day in mid-April 1977, at the vicar's office, Villaflor, by plan or by design, called out to everyone in the waiting room that it was no use looking for their children individually; authorities were ridiculing their sorrow, and it was time to unite in their search for their children. Juana de Pargament heard Azucena Villaflor make the same suggestion at the Ministry of Interior. The two women left together, bought some prepared food to eat as they walked, and headed for the bishop's office.

When they arrived, he refused to see them.[32] According to a third account, Azucena said that they were wasting time talking to priests and going individually to police stations to make inquiries about each of their children; she suggested it was time to go to a public place.[33] Another woman recalls that at that point someone pulled out her agenda and they decided to meet at the Plaza de Mayo on 30 April 1977.[34]

Located in the financial district of Buenos Aires, at the center of the downtown shopping district, the Plaza de Mayo is the symbolic capital of Argentina, its sacred secular space. Around this square are grouped the Ministries of the Army and Navy, the presidential palace, and the Ministry of the Interior. The cathedral and the *cabildo,* or colonial city hall, also border the plaza. The square is filled with palm trees, benches, and walkways, encompassing a space large enough to hold a hundred thousand demonstrators during the days of the Peronist rallies. A bit off-center in the plaza is the pyramidal monument commemorating the 1810 May Revolution against Spanish domination.[35] Paradoxically, it was in the Plaza de Mayo (then called the Plaza de Victoria) that the Argentine Assembly burned all the instruments of torture in May 1813, making their use illegal. One hundred years later, the Madres occupied the square to protest the torture of their children.[36]

Beginning 30 April 1977, the Madres marched on Thursdays at 3:30 P.M., as the abductions continued, multiplying the numbers of disappeared and adding new Madres to the processions. Some mothers, such as Hebe de Bonafini, lived outside of Buenos Aires. From La Plata, about sixty kilometers southeast of the capital city, de Bonafini came to Buenos Aires when she could and helped organize similar Wednesday afternoon demonstrations in La Plata. When she joined in May or June 1977, she had lost one of her two sons; shortly after, her remaining son and her pregnant daughter-in-law also disappeared. For her as for the others, the ritualized meetings once a week at the plaza provided emotional ballast as they all continued to search for their children.[37] With the weekly assemblies as a fulcrum, the Madres added other activities, keeping themselves in the public eye in order to counteract the terror of the silence about the disappearances.

Having little political knowledge at the beginning, the Madres learned a great deal. Over the course of their development, the Madres' identity changed. As Élida de Galletti explained:

> With the passage of time, the group had been growing, not only in number but in maturity. Their work, confrontation, and their school, the street. The dialogue, the interchange of ideas, the avid reading of every possible source

of information or commentary, aided their analytical abilities. And many issues they had known intuitively began to become conscious. There was no room for sectarian positions or differences in fundamental beliefs. Having a child disappear is what made us sisters: the same pain, the same struggle.[38]

Like most people who protested against human rights violations during the dictatorship, "they did so only after their own kin, not those of their neighbors, disappeared. The Mothers protested as victims, not as citizens," according to one observer.[39] Their public problem was how to make Argentina realize that what was happening to the Madres was also happening to the country as a whole. The Madres saw themselves initially as individual mothers searching for their own children. "Our task began with each one's search for her own child. Then we realized that it was necessary to look for all the children, and this was the most difficult transformation, one toward which not everyone was disposed," according to Hebe de Bonafini.[40] María del Rosario Cerruti recalled her own early behavior: "When you go out to the street like that you don't have a clear motive, you have the anxiety of the loss of a child, the desperation, and when you begin to fight you realize the struggle isn't about a child, it's about a system that destroys everyone who thinks, everyone who disagrees. So one child is converted into thousands of children and the struggle takes on a different meaning."[41]

In the first days of the Madres, when grief was paramount, it was customary, according to de Bonafini, to say "that my child did not do anything; they took him away because he was a professor, artist, or lawyer."[42] Viewing themselves and their children only as victims was a very powerful position, one that gave them moral capital. But then the Madres diverged from other parents whose children were taken from them during the Dirty War, acting collectively and searching for all the children.

Simply by becoming Madres, women became conscious of what their role in society had been. As Hebe de Bonafini explained: "My life had been the life of a housewife—washing, ironing, cooking and bringing up my children, just like you're always taught to do, believing that everything else was nothing....Then I realized that that wasn't everything, that I had another world too. You realize you're in a world where you have to do a lot of things."[43]

At first shrewd rather than politically sophisticated, the Madres transformed their initial sense of victimization into a strategy. They played on the contradiction between their society's sentimentalized view of mothers and the interests of the junta. For example, they would have been bad mothers if they had failed to look for their children. Only by hunting for those carried away could they defend family values. Metaphors of birth and rebirth are popular among the Madres and those writing about them. Among the most poignant is one from Hebe de Bonafini: "Nuestros hijos nos parieron" (Our children gave birth to us).[44] Alejandro Diago, who closely studied the Madres, claims that "they negate the idea of maternity that had come down through the generations, the notion that it is exclusively an individual act."[45] De Bonafini argues that the Madres raised new possibilities for women, the most important of which is the possibility of the "socialization of motherhood."[46] In the parlance of the Madres, the socialization of motherhood became a metaphor for a political system in which social need would supplant wealth and power in the distribution of resources. The Madres increasingly followed in their children's footsteps. Giving the lie to Jorge Luis Borges's claim that "Argentina was not a nation but merely a territory where democracy was an abuse of statistics and where people occasionally had virtues as individuals but as social beings only defects," the Madres fought for and continue to fight for the kind of political system that would provide everyone with equal access to food, health care, schools, and political rights.[47]

If it seems strange that there were no fathers among the group, it was not entirely accidental. Certainly, the men had to return to work. But the absence of men meant more than that. "Men think before doing something. I think a mother doesn't think if her child is in danger," says Madre María del Rosario Cerruti. "Many of the men stayed home, believing they could do nothing. It seems that men have less resistance to all this. Women seem to be stronger."[48] Cerruti also claimed that the exclusion of men was sometimes a strategic choice: "If the police insulted the [men], they would have hit back and they would have been taken. When we insulted them, they thought, what can these old women do?"[49] Hebe de Bonafini said that they excluded men because they believed that women would not be beaten and they would be more convincing if they acted as mothers without men.[50] The cultural power of mothers to establish morality and shame the junta was the only power the Madres had, and they attempted to use it wherever they could.

They also learned how to weld together women of different classes and different priorities around an identity as mothers of the disappeared. An important part of democratic organizing is learning how to unite people. When U.S. labor leader César Chavez was asked about his organizing strategy, he responded that first he talked to one person, and then another, and then another. Although politically inexperienced, some of the mothers had paid attention to activist children. Since the primary problem the Madres had in meeting clandestinely was how to set up their meetings, they tried to remember what their children had done. Aware that police were everywhere, the Madres spoke in code on the telephone. According to Nora de Cortiñas, if they were to meet in the Violet Tea Shop, for example, they would refer to a meeting at the Cafe of the Flower. Instead of giving the real time and day, they would give a time and day before or after. At first, they lost track. In the middle of a coded message, a Madre might interrupt to ask whether that meant the day before or the day after.[51] Even when everything worked, Ford Falcons drew up to places where the women gathered, simply to harass them.

At first, the Madres hoped that there might be some government officials who would help them find their children, but experience taught them to take matters into their own hands. On 11 July 1977, three months after the women began marching, three of the mothers, Azucena Villaflor, Beatriz de Neuhaus, and María del Rosario Cerruti, visited the minister of the interior, General Albano Harguindeguy, while sixty other mothers marched outside in the plaza. Harguindeguy, a crude man, began by gossiping about the irresponsibility of the younger generation. He claimed that his own niece had been involved in politics and now had run off to Mexico, where she had become a prostitute. He suggested with a lascivious grin that perhaps their sons had simply gone on sexual escapades.[52] The women were outraged. María del Rosario Cerruti recalls lighting into him, telling him that Francisco Franco, who had died in 1975 after ruling Spain for thirty-six years, also "assassinated many people, but he always signed [the execution decrees himself]." She went on: "You all are cowards because you assassinate and sign nothing [in your own names]."[53] The outraged Madres returned to the plaza, and no major official of the dictatorship ever agreed to meet with them face to face again. In not so subtle ways, Harguindeguy had tried to shift the terrain. As mothers obeying the cultural norms of their society, the Madres occupied the moral high ground. By removing the disappeared children from the household and placing them in the brothel, Harguindeguy attempted to move the discussion into the streets, where he thought mothers had no power. María del Rosario Cerruti was able to match him. She disputed his claim to morality by comparing him unfavorably to Franco and challenging his manhood. In this and other attacks on the dictatorship's authority, the Madres learned to wield motherhood as a weapon.

The Madres' use of symbolism became their greatest weapon. Although Argentina is one of the most secular countries in the Americas, symbols, rituals, and practices of Catholicism nevertheless abound. In the Madres' search to awaken the conscience of the nation, they employed familiar religious symbols and ceremonies. Though many of the early Madres were Jewish, they were familiar with Catholic rites and drew upon Catholic symbols and ritual practices to form a community capable of revealing what was happening around them. They thought first of putting nails, such as those used to crucify Jesus, in their lapels, later considering olive branches for its symbolism of healing and restoration. Neither caught on. But, among people influenced by Catholicism, pilgrimages are a way of cohering those who have little else in common. In secular terms, a pilgrimage or act of moving together provides a visual image of solidarity, the embodiment of missing people, and hopes for their return. No ritual is more potent than a pilgrimage, and for the Madres, a defining moment came with a religious pilgrimage to Luján, about 65 kilometers northeast of Buenos Aires.

The pilgrimage to the sanctuary of the Virgin of Luján took place annually in the 1970s on 1 October and normally attracted about 150,000 people. Taking the opportunity of a large public assembly, which would otherwise be prohibited, various human rights organizations decided to join the faithful. Azucena Villaflor, an ardent atheist, refused to take part even in a political pilgrimage, but other Madres decided to go. Organizers were concerned that it might be difficult to recognize other Madres. The Madres had been gathering in Buenos Aires and La Plata and different women came to each event, so amid a crowd of hundreds of thousands, they were afraid they would not recognize one another. They decided to wear white kerchiefs, later to become a powerful symbol. According to one account, before the march to Luján, María del Rosario Cerruti suggested that they buy white fabric to make head scarves so that they would be identifiable. Since there was no time for the purchases, they eventually wore white diapers on their heads, thereby marking themselves as mothers. By Aída Suárez's account, Azucena Villaflor suggested the scarves to make the Madres noticeable: "Azucena's idea was to wear as a kerchief one of our children's nappies, because every mother keeps something like this, which belonged to [her] child as a baby."[54] More recent memories claim that Madre Eva Castillo Obarrio suggested that they wear diapers as scarves to mark them as members of a group, perhaps even persuading some people at the pilgrimage that they were members of a religious sect.[55]

After the disparate groups of Madres arrived in Luján wearing their white scarves, they lined up to receive communion together. Several generals and Cardinal Juan Carlos Aramburu were in attendance, and priests circulated through the crowd. As the Host was placed in their mouth, the mothers prayed that their children would reappear. The priests withdrew in horror, as if they had been contaminated by contact with the Madres. Juana de Pargament, María del Rosario Cerruti, and Hebe de Bonafini quickly gathered beneath a large sign made up of photographs of their children. They circulated among the throng carrying the sign until a young man offered to hold it. He took it and ran off.[56]

The Madres' faith in the young has been both their strength and their chief weakness. Keeping their lost children alive by bringing their assassins to justice has been the Madres' chief purpose in life through nearly thirty years of street demonstrations. Along with newspaper columns, public commentary, and later travel abroad, the Madres have sought out young people who remind them of their children and who seem to share their offspring's faith in fighting for social justice. Hebe de Bonafini recalled that in 17 October 1977, when Monsignor Plaza, the archbishop of La Plata, gathered Catholic schoolchildren to support the regime, the Madres came from Buenos Aires to demonstrate with their sisters in La Plata. They marched to the cathedral with a group of Marist priests. Once in the building, they explained to the young people how children their age and a bit older had been kidnapped and were being held—no one knew where. Instead of celebrating with guitar music and food, the young people held a conference about what was going on in their country. The next morning, they tried to get the archbishop to mention the people who had disappeared in the mass he was offering, but he refused.[57]

As the numbers of Madres demonstrating on behalf of their lost children grew, many realized that they needed a structure for their organization. They planned a public event, a fantasy retirement party for María Adela Gard de Antokoletz and Josefina Barros. The meeting was set for 18–19 October 1977 in Pereyra Park, about 40 kilometers southeast of Buenos Aires on the road to La Plata. Azucena Villaflor and María del Rosario de Cerruti seem to have formulated the strategy. They named Hebe de Bonafini, Nora de Cortiñas, Beatriz de Neuhaus, Gard de Antokoletz, Juana de Pargament, and three others as the Madres' underground leaders. Carrying food and flowers for the "retirement party," they met and created a cell organization.[58] This form, which some of the Madres undoubtedly understood, if only in retrospect, from

Montonero and ERP children, was designed to coordinate Madres from different places to disseminate information. Equally important was the Madres' decision to separate the cells so that each Madre knew the names and addresses of only a few others. If Madres were abducted and tortured, authorities would not be able to destroy the whole organization. Despite the reputation for spontaneity acquired by groups such as the Madres, the Madres were in fact highly organized.

Their organization was divided into five geographical districts, and again into neighborhoods. Each district had a delegate who was not one of the inner ten. Each delegate had five Madres reporting to her. These five in turn organized three or four other Madres; each of these also had three or four Madres who reported to them; and these three or four organized another two or three, so that almost all the Madres were linked without everyone knowing the others. Nora de Cortiñas became the coordinator, alerting people about foreign visitors and calling public demonstrations.[59]

The Madres' willingness to take to the streets for public performances gradually made them attractive to journalists. Just when the Madres consciously realized their need for the press remains a mystery, but on 5 October 1977, Mother's Day, they published an ad in *La Prensa*, the leading newspaper in Buenos Aires, listing the names and identification numbers of 237 mothers of the detained and disappeared. While everyone else in Argentina hid, hoping the military would not notice them, the Madres put themselves in the public spotlight. Although many of the Madres were from working-class or lower-middle-class families, some of the original Madres were from the upper middle class and a few were members of the elite. Their status seldom helped; even close relatives of generals disappeared. But one of the early Madres was kin of the owners of *La Prensa*, a possible reason the newspaper succumbed to entreaties to publish the material. Showing the corruption that went along with terror, the newspaper charged the Madres a higher rate because they were desperate. The paper refused to publish the names of the detained and disappeared, and it accompanied the ad with an editorial denouncing terrorism. Yet the Madres, by their sheer audacity in printing their names and identification numbers, showed the public that at least one group of women was not afraid.

In late October 1977, the Madres joined three hundred relatives of the disappeared and human rights activists in a march on Congress, where the junta had their offices. The demonstrators wanted to present a petition with 24,000 signatures, calling for an investigation of the 537 disappearances human rights groups could document. Many reporters went along. Not realizing that antagonizing the press is the cardinal sin of politics, the government arrested journalists from CBS, United Press International, Associated Press, and the BBC, along with some Madres. The Madres entered the building by a back door, but none of the commanders were in their offices. Sister Alice Domon entered the building with Azucena Villaflor, her son and daughter-in-law, and Hebe de Bonafini. Domon, a member of a foreign missionary order, worked in the slums of Quilmes, a working-class suburb of Buenos Aires. A staunch supporter of the Madres, she was outraged at the way young labor militants had been disappearing. Her closeness to the Madres made her an object of official scrutiny.

The police, wielding tear gas and batons, drove away demonstrators outside the building. Then, at 7 P.M. they arrested everyone inside. They commandeered public buses to carry the demonstrators to the fifth precinct police station. In a humorous footnote, one of those arrested called out to Nora de Cortiñas, who was outside, that they were being carried to "la quinta," the fifth precinct. De Cortiñas mistook the meaning of "la quinta," thinking they were being taken to the presidential palace of Olivos, also known as "La Quinta," and shouted "Great!"[60] Several foreign journalists were among the large group arrested. The government, perhaps fearing the foreign press, released the reporters, the Madres, the nun, and the other activists at around 3 A.M. However, by arresting members of the press, the government made some permanent enemies. Many of them provided the Madres with publicity, if only from abroad.[61]

Unfortunately, the periodic dramatic acts the Madres carried on in front of the press only punctuated the sad tedium of their real work—visiting the commissaries, searching for their children. At times, they were charged as loiterers, for which there was a thirty-*centavo* fine or fifteen days in jail. Many of the women chose jail. Referring to the thirty pieces of silver paid to betray Christ, they remarked that thirty *centavos* was too small a price to pay for their children.[62] The Madres' pictures were taken, their phones monitored, their lives threatened. Again they had recourse to religious practices. According to Hebe de Bonafini, they were usually forbidden to speak in jail, but not to pray. "So we start praying at the top of our lungs for others to know that the Mothers are there." When the interviewer asked her about whether she was religious, she slyly replied, "No. But we know how to pray, especially when we are arrested."[63]

THEY WOULD NOT QUIT

Repression grew. The Madres' activities were closely monitored, and the women were frequently arrested at their Thursday marches. The worst time for them was late 1977 and early 1978. Ten family members and friends of the disappeared, including two Madres, Esther Ballestrino de Careaga and María Eugenia Ponce de Bianco, and the French nun Sor Alice Domon, were kidnapped from the Church of Santa Cruz where they were meeting secretly on 8 December 1977. Along with the other Madres and family members of people who had disappeared, they had gathered to put together the names and money for an ad to run on 10 December, the anniversary of the passage of the Universal Declaration of Human Rights. As they left the church, Alfredo Astiz, a young naval officer who had infiltrated the Madres organization, embraced those he wanted detained. They too vanished. The Madres knew only that their companions in battle had disappeared, until after the junta was forced to step down and survivors of the camps began to testify.

Pieced together from the testimony of former captives, the story reveals the depravity of the military. Esther Careaga and María Eugenia Ponce were brutally gang-raped at ESMA. Two days after the raid on the church, another French nun, Léonie Duquet, secretary to Bishop Novak of Quilmes, was captured, although her only connection to the Madres was sharing a house with Sister Alice Domon. That same day, Azucena Villaflor was abducted in the street by one of the ubiquitous green Falcons.[64]

Villaflor was next seen by prisoners at ESMA who knew nothing about the Madres but were shocked to see a housewife in custody. Lila Pastoriza, a survivor of ESMA, remembers Azucena tenderly: "I was accustomed to seeing militants, but this woman reminded me of a housewife; it was like seeing an aunt inside [the torture center]. This seemed strange."[65] Azucena asked a prisoner, Ana María Martí, her name and whether she knew anything about Azucena's missing son.[66] She also inquired about Astiz, whom she knew as Gustavo Niño. A day or so after her capture, Azucena was hideously tortured. The two French nuns fared no better: they were tortured and gang-raped, and then they were forced to pose in front of a Montonero poster for a picture their torturers sent with a bogus ransom note. The threat to the junta's reputation abroad led the army to call Navy Work Group 3.3.2 to ask what they knew about the nuns. The navy denied any part in their abduction.[67] ESMA survivors later recounted that none of those associated with the

Madres survived for more than five days. According to one account, their bodies were deposited in a lagoon in the delta of the Paraná River.[68] Yet the Madres continued to march, as other mothers, frantic that they were unable to find their children, joined the original group and carried on their symbolic pilgrimage under the gaze of soldiers armed with rifles and bayonets.

Esther de Careaga, one of those detained and disappeared at Santa Cruz Church, was especially heroic in the face of state terror. One of the few Madres who had any prior political experience, de Careaga fled from political repression in Paraguay with her sixteen-year-old daughter. When her daughter was abducted, de Careaga went looking for her child. Arrested herself, she was beaten but then released. Her daughter, though raped and subjected to torture with electric cattle prods, was also freed after a few weeks. Quickly sending the teenager out of the country for her protection, Esther de Careaga, a member of the Communist Parties of both Paraguay and Argentina, remained with the Madres. The Communist Party of Argentina avoided criticizing the junta, hoping to prove they were not terrorists, and de Careaga confronted them. Determined to fight until all of the disappeared were freed and their tormentors punished, she was helping to gather names for the Human Rights Day ad on the fateful evening of 8 December 1977 when she was captured. The Madres were devastated, having lost de Careaga, Ponce, Azucena de Villaflor, and Alice Domon. From December 1977 to the World Cup games in June 1978, when foreign journalists flooded the city and helped the Madres gain more international publicity, the Madres had to turn to other methods to keep their message alive. They began to write their stories on paper currency, on the hundred-*peso* and later the five-hundred-*peso* bill. On bills worth about a dollar, across the face of a hero of the independence movement, they wrote their children's names, when they were abducted, and who they thought was holding them. They circulated the money at fairs and large markets, where it would be hard to remember just who had passed the bill. Since no one wanted to hold onto the money once they noticed its message, the currency circulated quickly. From the Madres' perspective, this was ideal, since they reached many people. One Madre recalls that in the absence of access to radio, television, or daily newspapers, they had to be ingenious about publicizing what had happened to their children.[69]

International press attention certainly aided the Madres. After nearly forty years of attempting to bring the World Cup to Argentina, the games had finally been scheduled to take place in Buenos Aires in June

1978. Not just a sport, soccer is intimately connected to Argentine nationalism, and by chance Argentina was one of the contenders in 1978. Although the Peronists had succeeded in securing the competition, the military junta made it into a ritual to enhance its own power. Not since the 1936 Olympics, according to French journalist Jean-Pierre Bousquet, had a sports event been so politicized.[70]

European human rights activists tried to organize a boycott of the World Cup, but it would have been such an indignity for Argentina had the games moved that Montonero poet Juan Gelman sent a letter from underground to *Le Monde* urging Europeans to make the trip. He claimed that the World Cup would be a "festival of the people, a gigantic press conference that would inform the world of the tragedy that our people is enduring."[71] During the week when the Europeans considered their boycott, the numbers of Madres on the *ronda* diminished from several hundred to fifty. Many Madres were afraid of antagonizing their countrypeople, who were more concerned with the games than with the disappearances. Certainly those fifty who demonstrated were considered traitors by jeering passers-by. Despite the adverse publicity abroad, the games went on as scheduled.

Argentina's opponent, the Dutch soccer team, brought bouquets of carnations to the Madres in the plaza. As the games opened at the Monumental Stadium of the River Plate on 1 June 1978 with almost eighty thousand spectators in attendance, at the Plaza de Mayo, "one hundred women who had been dispersed around on the benches gathered quickly around the pyramid, having covered their heads with white kerchiefs and begun their slow procession."[72] Before television cameras in the plaza, Madres began telling their stories. An official, followed by forty men in uniform, approached the Madres and told them they had to leave because the state of siege precluded demonstrations. But with the cameras and microphones of the international press running, the police dared not attack. The Madres continued their march for at least a half-hour before they dispersed. The black-and-white photographs and television footage showed women who appeared even more vulnerable because, unlike most demonstrators, they usually carried their pocketbooks. Their images appeared in newspapers—including sports pages—all over the world.

The generals denounced the women, claimed that the world press was in the hands of subversives, and denied that there were kidnappings, concentration camps, and disappearances. The Madres were accused of being traitors who gave the country a bad name by drawing the press. Although at least forty-six people were abducted during the World Cup, the Madres' visibility may have saved most of them.[73]

Following a demonstration of over 2,500 human rights activists in late 1978, the military junta, trying to isolate opponents, separated the Madres and other demonstrators from their sacred secular space.[74] Authorities closed off the Plaza de Mayo with metal fences and mounted police. Although the doors of the cathedral on the plaza were barred to them, the women found refuge every Thursday at other churches. Hebe de Bonafini remembers that the Madres, finding it impossible to stay away from the plaza, staged forays, sometimes on Thursday mornings, sometimes on Friday afternoons, just to walk in the square. The danger continued. They were accused as subversives, saw husbands and children lose their jobs, and faced opprobrium from their neighbors, who believed that they and their children were threats to the Western, Christian values the junta claimed to be upholding against a communist threat.

Madre Aída de Suárez reflected upon the importance of the plaza: "For the Mothers, the square signifies the best of our lives because the square is the place of our children.... [T]he square is the most important thing left to the Mothers.... From 30 April 1977, we've always been there because this square is ours."[75] Another Madre added, "After so many marches I came to think that [the plaza] was a small, liberated space separate from the rest of the country."[76] Serving two purposes, the plaza became the Madres' stage as well as their home, the space where they coalesced most fully.

On 22 August 1979, the Madres took a bold step by registering with the government as a legal association, thus carving themselves a space in civic life. Their statement of purpose committed them to Judeo-Christian values and claimed that they wanted to know where their children were, with what they had been charged, and when they would be brought to trial. In their statement of purpose, the Madres declared their opposition to "any kind of terrorism, whether from individuals or the state. We believe in peace, brotherhood, and justice. We desire the implementation of a democratic system in Argentina that respects the fundamental rights of people."[77] With the help of an association of women from the Netherlands, the Madres purchased an apartment where they could meet regularly while the Plaza de Mayo was closed to them.[78]

THE BEGINNING OF THE END

It would be nice to say that by attracting the press through their visual props and ritual processions, the Madres won the support of their countrypeople and forced the military to step down, but in fact defeat in the 1982 Malvinas or Falkland War did that by demonstrating the weakness of the armed forces and belying the junta's claims to have brought Argentina to the pinnacle of greatness as a world power. Worsening economic conditions and not the disappearances had begun to rouse Argentina from its lethargy. In April 1979, there was a general strike, the first major labor demonstration since the junta had taken power three years earlier. Then, on 7 November 1981 and 30 March 1982, two additional strikes attracted fifty thousand workers each. Their demand for "Peace, bread, and work" led to numerous arrests, including six Madres, who were detained following the second strike.[79] On 2 April 1982, seemingly in an effort to raise its prestige after the economy had devastated the middle as well as the working class, the junta invaded the Malvinas Islands, known in Great Britain as the Falklands. Using nationalism to unite the country, the junta went to war. Although a few prominent individuals, such as Raúl Alfonsín of the Radical Party, opposed the war, the Madres were the largest group that refused to march to the drum of nationalism. Madre Carmen de Guede explained that the Madres "were against it because the military were using it to try to raise their prestige, to try to glorify themselves. We felt they were killing people pointlessly. They wanted to keep their hands soaked in the blood of our young people."[80]

The Malvinas War lasted from April to June 1982 and effectively discredited the military commanders. The long-standing dispute about control of the islands could have been settled in August 1968, when the British tried to get Argentina to negotiate. But control of the Malvinas roused passion on both sides. The war was a financial disaster for Argentina. Even if Madre Renée Epelbaum exaggerated when she claimed that Argentina's two-and-one-half-month occupation of the Malvinas almost equaled U.S. per capita spending during the ten years of the Vietnam War, the disaster was far-reaching.[81]

Unlike other opposition groups and the unions, which supported Argentine claims to the Malvinas, the Madres protested against the military. Again taking advantage of the anniversary of the Universal Declaration of Human Rights on 10 December to draw attention to Argentina's violation of fundamental rights, the Madres claimed that the Malvinas War

was merely a continuation of the Dirty War. Because of Argentina's igno-
minious defeat, the junta announced that they would hold free elections
for a constitutional government. But they refused to set a date. By December 1982, six months after the war's end, nine million workers
throughout the country declared a general strike.[82]

The climate of opinion toward the Madres had changed over the
years. Even amid growing dissatisfaction and political strikes by the
working class, the Madres had faced hostile neighbors when they carried out their twenty-four-hour March of Resistance on 10 December
1981. The Madres began to demonstrate on the night of 9 December,
and they occupied the plaza in one way or another for twenty-four
hours. In the southern hemisphere's hot December sun, none of the
shopkeepers around the Plaza de Mayo would permit the Madres to buy
cold drinks or use the bathrooms. Nevertheless, about eighty Madres
made it through the day, the night, and the next day. When the vigil was
complete, the Madres moved to the cathedral at Quilmes, one of three
churches in Argentina that supported human rights activists. The
Madres sat down in the church and started a ten-day hunger strike, demanding the release of all the disappeared and a full account of what
had happened to them.[83]

It is doubtful that the Madres realized in 1981 that they would be
demonstrating even after the junta was replaced by a civilian government. It is even more unlikely that they realized, when they set out to
hold their vigil for human rights in 1981, that the anniversary of the
Universal Declaration of Human Rights would become their signature
event, commemorated every year thereafter. A year later, still under the
dictatorship, authorities barred the Plaza de Mayo before the Second
March of Resistance on 10 December 1982. Undaunted, the Madres,
joined by a sister group, the Abuelas de Plaza de Mayo (Grandmothers
of Plaza de Mayo), and the Families of the Detained and Disappeared,
marched up the Avenida de Mayo, chanting their demands: "Free all
political prisoners; bring the disappeared back alive *(Aparición con
vida)*; restore the disappeared children to their families."[84] This time
shopkeepers opened their stores, permitted the women to use bathrooms, and nurtured those they had so often scorned as traitors to their
country. The March for Life on 16 December 1982 attracted all the
human rights groups and the unions. More than 200,000 people
demonstrated before the police shot into the crowd, killing one and
wounding sixty. Yet the genie was out of the bottle. By February 1983,
the junta announced that elections would be held on 30 October 1983

and that ninety days later a new president would be installed.[85] On 8
December 1983, the Thursday before the junta stepped down on 10 December, thirty thousand people joined the Madres in the plaza.[86]

A week later, the Third March of Resistance took place to register
opposition to the self-amnesty the armed forces had decreed the preceding April. The Madres scattered silhouettes of the missing all over
the city. As Chilean-American poet and critic Marjorie Agosín recalls,
"Not only did thousands of human outlines, some of them pregnant,
appear on walls and doors throughout the city, but the Mothers
marched around the plaza carrying these silhouettes. One time, the
Mothers asked observers to lie on the pavement, and they assigned each
the name of a missing person. Using these symbols, the Mothers managed to personify the missing, to demonstrate that these were not just
names and dates, but living, breathing human beings" whose mothers
still sought them.[87] The crowds took up the Madres' chant to bring the
disappeared back alive, by which they meant that the government
would investigate the policy of exterminating opponents. Presuming
that justice entailed bringing every torturer and killer to trial and having them jailed for their crimes, the Madres assumed that the government would punish the guilty.[88]

THE POLITICS OF SPECTACLE

The politics of spectacle concentrated attention on what was happening
in Argentina from 1976 to 1983. Not that it was hard to know when
people were abducted from restaurants and kidnapped in the streets. As
the longtime editor of the English language *Buenos Aires Herald,*
Robert Cox, who was forced into exile in 1979, recalled: "It was not...
possible for anyone living in Argentina not to know. The blind were
blind because they did not want to see, not because there was nothing
to see, nor because they were eyeless."[89] To improve vision and arouse
people from their lethargy, the Madres acted crazy. And, as the Madres
readily admit, they were crazy for marching up and down in broad day-
light when people were disappearing.[90] By marching week after week,
wearing their white kerchiefs, carrying pictures of their abducted children, and drawing silhouettes on walls and sidewalks, they forced people to see what they did not want to see.

Though the Madres were neither the first human rights group nor the
most effective in finding out what had happened to those who had been
abducted during the Dirty War, they were the most visible—and thus

the most interesting to foreign cameras. Religious symbolism helped them attract an audience. "With serious faces, eyes questioning, scarves on their heads, they began to march as if in a religious procession. And the photos, true ritual icons, their hands perspiring. [They were] peaceful processions, supplicating assemblies. Later, with time, the forms became more politicized [with the introduction of] signs, insignias, chants, angry faces in protest."[91]

The Madres may have begun their searches as naive housewives, but by the period of the transition, the Madres represented an alternative political option. Sophisticated in vying for moral power, they used the rhetoric of motherhood. But most of the Madres no longer believed that motherhood alone justified their right to act as citizens. Unconcerned with collective guilt, the Madres expected their country to investigate the way individuals participated in state violence. They wanted their children vindicated, but most of all they wanted social justice, a commitment they inherited from their children. In their public displays, the Madres conjured up those who had disappeared into what the Nazis had called "night and fog." By emphasizing their children's physicality, if only in photographs and silhouettes drawn on streets and walls, the Madres had literally embodied civil society for seven years, when state terrorism crushed most forms of resistance and other human rights groups worked more circumspectly. Through the use of processions modeled on Catholic rites, the Madres enacted a civil society in which they and their missing children could make claims to citizenship. They had no intention of giving up their campaigns for social justice simply because a new government had been elected.

CHAPTER 5

Memory through Mobilization

In the week before the Madres' thousandth march around the Plaza de Mayo on 27 June 1996, the Madres' House, on Hipólito Irigoyen down the street from the Congress building, resembled a cross between a socially active convent and a youth center. Simply dressed women scurried about in search of lists they needed to continue their work. Phones rang, and women lowered their voices out of habit, protecting the anonymity of their callers. Journalists waited patiently for the audience promised to them. Teenagers, some with violet hair and black leather jackets, came looking for wires or paint for the huge folk figures and signs they were preparing for the demonstration. A low buzz provided background noise for the action, punctuated by louder questions and statements about Hebe de Bonafini. De Bonafini, who has been the leading spokeswoman for the Asociación de Madres since the 1980s, is a hero to some and an abrasive autocrat to others, including some former allies. Nevertheless, like her or not, she represents the Madres' insistence on telling about the atrocities of the Argentine dictatorship of 1976 to 1983 and continued acts of repression in the present.

At the Madres' House, Hebe de Bonafini was a subject of concern: she had lost weight, her voice was cracking, and her doctors said she must cut back. Outsiders visiting the Madres sat in the small dining room that serves as a waiting room. A journalist and a cameraman chatted as they waited for Hebe de Bonafini to come so that they could take pictures for an article that would help publicize the march. The other Madres offered tea and went about their business.

My Argentine friend Alejandra and I had made an appointment to meet Hebe de Bonafini, whom we knew from newspaper pictures dating back to the mid-1980s. I had also seen her from afar over the years, as she led marches and addressed demonstrations. When she arrived, she looked thinner but also bigger. She was filled with the sense of purpose that has driven her and the other Madres since they realized that by insisting on a full historical reckoning of what went on during what the military called the Dirty War, they had an important part to play in shaping their country's future and fulfilling their children's political and social goals. De Bonafini came in, took charge, and immediately began arranging her schedule: she wondered whether we would mind if she spoke to the journalists first. Reporters are the Madres' lifeline, helping them get their message out. They always want to publicize the names of criminals walking among them. The Madres, who join no political party, hold a distinguished position on the left. Having broadened their notion of injustice beyond the disappearances, the Madres associate state violence and the disastrous economic straits in which Argentina continues to find itself.

While we waited to see de Bonafini, we gathered pamphlets and clippings that the Madres have arrayed on shelves in the dining room and looked at photographs of the Madres, especially Hebe de Bonafini, sanctified by the famous white kerchief, meeting with political leaders from all over the world. To pass the time and cover our sense of being intruders when we wanted to belong, we began to read. The material scattered around for visitors like us includes flyers, pamphlets, and the monthly periodical, the *Madres de Plaza de Mayo,* that the Madres publish since 1984. The journal includes articles by a variety of men and women who share the Madres' sense of urgency about keeping the record straight in the saga of crime without punishment in Argentina.

With disappearances as the Argentine government's preferred form of terror, making people and ideas visible has been the central dynamic of the Madres' effort to keep their version of history alive through street demonstrations. As my friends and I emerged on 27 June 1996 from the subway into the freezing late afternoon light of the Plaza de Mayo, we discovered a festival. Vast banners and huge puppets hovered just above the heads of the tens of thousands gathered to march with the Madres. Milling about, looking at the groups with signs and collecting the flyers everyone was giving out, it was hard to remember how dangerous it had been for the Madres to mobilize during the dictatorship and how few had supported them. In fact, the crowd was not as united as it had first

appeared. Once the movement began, it was hard to say who was leading and who following. But it was clear that there were distinct groups
and different banners.

The members of the Asociación de Madres de Plaza de Mayo, with
Hebe de Bonafini in the middle of a large phalanx of elderly women, had
probably started marching. But they might have begun at the same time
as their former colleagues, the group known as Las Madres de Plaza de
Mayo–Línea Fundadora (Founding-Line Madres of the Plaza de Mayo).
They withdrew from the Madres in January 1986, but they share the
Plaza de Mayo every Thursday afternoon at 3:30 P.M. And they continue
to demonstrate and speak out about abuses of human rights and about
the worsening economic crisis. Close to the Founding-Line Madres, but
marching with their own banners, the Abuelas de Plaza de Mayo
(Grandmothers of the Plaza de Mayo) add another dimension to the
ronda. The Abuelas, founded under the name Abuelas Argentinas con
Nietitos Desaparecidos (Argentine Grandmothers with Missing Little
Grandchildren) in October 1977, five months after the Madres first assembled as a group in the Plaza de Mayo, devote themselves to finding
grandchildren, of whom there may be as many as four hundred, captured as infants or born to pregnant women who were abducted and tortured while they were pregnant and usually murdered after giving birth.

MAKING SPECTACLES OF THEMSELVES

The Madres and Abuelas transformed the Plaza de Mayo into a democratic space that afternoon, as they had on so many other afternoons
and evenings when they came together in pursuit of their version of justice. In contrast to the Madres' commitment to making its views known
in public, the junta did its work in silence and secrecy. In an attempt to
control public perception of what was transpiring in Argentina, the military tried to remove the Madres from the public eye after the World
Cup of June 1978. Unable to openly repress the women while the eyes
of the media were upon them, the junta waited until their guests had
gone home. Then the junta secured the Plaza de Mayo, erected metal
barriers, and permanently posted a police cavalry to keep out the
Madres. The Madres, hoping to maintain their collective identity although they could no longer march in the plaza, incorporated as an association on 22 August 1979.[1]

The military not only terrorized the population by imposing silence
about the disappearances; they also began both to deny their crimes and

to pardon themselves. On Army Day, 29 May 1979, the junta tried to legislate its view of recent Argentine history when General Roberto Viola, then head of the junta, referred to "those who have disappeared forever," and attempted to gloss over the question of responsibility. He claimed that although "the army regretted" what had happened, "there would be no explanations." And the always quotable military governor of Buenos Aires province, General Ibérico Saint Jean, added that "all Argentines would benefit from throwing a...blanket of silence over the disappeared."[2] The Madres countered the image of a blanket of silence with the idea of a spectacle by speaking for those who were absent to anyone who would listen and by appearing everywhere they could find an audience.

Because the Madres insisted on acting in public, the junta was increasingly forced to come out of the shadows to defend itself. To counter adverse international publicity, they hired Burson-Marsteller, a leading New York ad agency, to initiate a defensive campaign before September 1979, when the Inter-American Commission on Human Rights of the Organization of American States was scheduled to hold hearings about human rights abuses in Argentina.[3] The ad campaign attempted to promote the idea of Argentine rectitude by distributing cards people could mail to Amnesty International proclaiming that "somos derechos y humanos" (we are right and human), a play on the expression *derechos humanos,* or human rights.[4] The government got tens of thousands of people to plaster their cars with decals carrying this self-righteous slogan, and billboards and signs echoed the statement in an attempt to discount the stories of disappearances. Thrilled by the Argentine victory at the Youth World Cup in Japan, a popular radio sports announcer exhorted his audience to march on the Plaza de Mayo, where the Madres had snuck in, to demonstrate that real Argentines, not human rights advocates, were "derechos y humanos."[5] Before the Inter-American Human Rights Commission arrived, the government dismantled the torture center at ESMA (Escuela Mecánica de la Armada, the officers club of the Naval Mechanics School), apparently killing some of the prisoners and sending others to more clandestine camps.[6] At the same time, the junta decreed Law 21.068, called "The Presumption of Death Law," which said that anyone who had been missing for more than three months between 6 November 1974 and 6 September 1979 could be considered dead. The government offered reparations.[7]

After the junta turned to Madison Avenue, the Madres intensified their identity as *locas.* Appearing crazy and uncompromising became a way to get the attention of their fellow citizens. If fear governed so-called reasonable behavior, then behaving unreasonably challenged the apparent rationality of government terror. But the Madres themselves underwent a change. Until the Madres were driven from the plaza in 1978, most of them probably believed that their children were still alive. The Madres' forced removal from the plaza seemed to put to rest their expectations of ever seeing those loved ones again and converted many of them to their children's political ideals. They moved toward what observers have called "the socialization of motherhood." Paradoxically, the Madres' renewed sense of loss intensified their commitment to young people and to fighting. They staged guerrilla forays into the plaza in 1978, 1979, and 1980, proclaiming the presence of their loved ones. One mother explained:

> I think that I'll never see my husband and my son again. But I think that they are present in all the young people who are with us and in our remaining children. I never say that I've lost them, lost them forever. We have them with us, not physically, but they are here with us. My two other children live at home with me, and every time we touch something that belongs to my son or my husband, we say, take care because that is Hector's, [or] yes, take it, but take care because that is Papa's. I never say "was" about them.[8]

The Madres' refusal to call the disappeared "dead" even caused friction with some of their allies. When Adolfo Pérez Esquivel, the founding director of the Servicio de Paz y Justicia (Service for Peace and Justice) of the Ecumenical Movement for Human Rights, received the Nobel Peace Prize in 1980 for his work in Argentina, he offered 10 percent of the prize money to the Madres, with whom he had worked. His commitment to them nevertheless failed to assuage the women when some of those accompanying him on his European tour denounced the thousands of deaths in Argentina. The Madres were outraged. In a document issued on 5 December 1980, the Madres claimed that they wanted and expected to see their children back alive and standing up for the same principles for which they had been abducted. And the Madres stormed back into the plaza in early 1980, never again to be separated from the polis in which they and those who marched with them created a democratic space.

From that space, the Madres defend their view of Argentine history against the military's self-amnesties and self-justifications. For example, on 28 April 1983, a year after the Malvinas War and six months before elections were to be held for a constitutional government to replace the dictatorship, the junta issued their Final Document. They admitted that "they had sometimes committed errors, as in any wartime situation, when [belligerents] sometimes exceed the limits [of justifiable activities] and violate fundamental human rights."[9] While officially acknowledging that kidnapping and disappearing people (always in the passive voice with no attention to who had carried out the abductions and murders) "was the [issue brought against them] that had the greatest legitimate impact on human sentiments," the junta still tried to justify its actions.[10] The government claimed that all those who had disappeared had been "terrorists" and could be presumed dead. The Madres continue to deny both statements.

THE MADRES DIVIDED

The disappearances had united the Madres; constitutional government tore them apart. Differences of class, religion, and politics were bound to divide the women. In the first years of the junta, when grief was paramount in the lives of the Madres, there was no need to discuss differences. It was customary then to claim that their children hadn't done anything. Early on, Juana de Pargament remarked, "Our children wanted every family to have a decent home, enough food and clothing, and they wanted every child to have the opportunity to go to school.... Our children worked in the *villas* as doctors, building homes, teaching. When people understand why they were taken, what they wanted, they are going to understand us and we'll have something better."[11] But after the return to constitutional government, Madre Graciela de Jeger explained that the Madres "don't want the names of the victims. We know who they are. We want the names of the murderers. We want them to tell us what happened. They have to explain what they don't want to explain. This is the meaning of *aparición con vida* (bring them back alive)."[12]

Initially, the arbitrary abductions of largely young people were enough to unite their mothers. At first, viewing themselves and their children as victims was a very powerful position, one that placed moral capital in their hands. But the Madres' removal from the plaza in late 1978 brought them into closer proximity with one another. While some went out to work and continued to be preoccupied with caring for their remaining relatives, a core of women began to spend more and more time in the center. Being in nearly daily contact with one another required more structure and engendered more conflict. The Madres had to work out routines and intensify their division of labor. Meeting two or three times a week forged the Madres into a more coherent group, but they gained their solidarity at the price of hierarchy. Increasingly, Hebe de Bonafini and those who admired her leadership skills moved to the top. Whereas in the first two years staying alive and finding answers had provided direction for the group, formulating strategy became more important after they were banished from the Plaza de Mayo.

The Madres had taken on a collective identity by the time Azucena Villaflor, Esther Careaga, and María Eugenia Ponce disappeared in December 1977. But Azucena had led by enhancing the self-confidence of those around her. Had she lived, she might have been able to help the other Madres intensify their skills at confronting the government. But she too might have had to establish more formal positions in order to maintain the organization.

The resumption of constitutional government on 10 December 1983 presented the Madres with all kinds of strategic problems. Because such a long period elapsed between the time the armed forces were discredited following the end of the Malvinas War in June 1982 and the actual transition to civilian rule, the Madres were desperate to save anyone left alive in the prison camps. The Madres looked for someone in the constitutional government who shared their determination to bring the military to trial. As far as the Madres were concerned, the first president, Raúl Alfonsín, should have used his position as commander in chief to take over the 340 clandestine torture centers in police stations and military compounds. Some centers, such as ESMA, La Perla, and El Vesubio, had been subjects of testimony by survivors. At ESMA, prisoners such as Sara Solarz de Osatinsky and Norma Susana Burgos remained alive in part because they had skills needed by Admiral Emilio Eduardo Massera of the first junta. He hoped to become the new Perón, the leader of a vast populist movement, and he regarded the left-wing Peronist Montoneros as possible foot soldiers in that effort. The two women formed part of a group known as "the staff" who worked on the files. These consisted of photographs and standardized forms with places for the names, aliases, dates of arrest, family data, membership information, and material about prisoners' familiarity with firearms and explosives, as well as their prison identity numbers.[13] The Madres wanted the new government to find the records, which would provide additional evidence to reconstruct the junta's actions. By publicly documenting the history, the Madres hoped to prosecute individual soldiers, sailors, and police and punish them for their crimes against humanity.

To do that, they would need to establish a historical record of what had transpired during the "Process of National Reorganization."

When lawyer Raúl Alfonsín ran for president on the Radical Union ticket in September and October 1983, the Madres met with him and pled fruitlessly with him to pledge to release all political prisoners within forty-eight hours of taking office. Subsequent evidence proved the validity of their claims that some prisoners were still alive when the military stepped down. Cecilia Marina Viñas was seven months pregnant when she was abducted along with her husband in July 1977. At ESMA she delivered a son. Though her mother continued to search for her grandchild, the family gave up hope that Viñas herself was alive. But shortly after Alfonsín took office in December 1983, she called home seven times, saying that the guard where she and others were being held occasionally let her use the phone. Her parents taped one conversation, in which she plaintively asked about her young son, whom she thought was safely with his grandparents. Despite the family's efforts to get the new government to find her, authorities did nothing. Her last call came in April 1984, leaving supporters to wonder whether she and others might have been found had the authorities investigated their cases.[14]

While the Madres were interested in saving lives, Alfonsín was concerned with restoring the rule of law. To do that, he reversed the military's self-amnesty and revised the military codes.[15] But he didn't move fast enough or forcefully enough for the Madres, who equated time with life. They were outraged by Alfonsín's failure to arrest the leaders of the security forces and put their fate in the hands of newly appointed civilian judges, or to provide subpoena powers to "a bicameral investigatory commission to condemn those responsible for the flagrant violations of human rights perpetuated in [the] country."[16] Instead of having Congress, which had full powers to subpoena the military, investigate the disappearances, Alfonsín appointed a board of distinguished citizens, which the Madres considered to be a weak body of inquiry, to form the Comité Nacional de Desaparición de Personas (National Committee on Disappeared People, CONADEP). Under the directorship of Eduardo Rabossi, Under-Secretary for Human Rights, and the chairmanship of novelist Ernesto Sábato, the committee drew only on voluntary testimony and had to complete its work by 20 September 1984. Rabossi, a committed liberal and an optimist, was surprised that the perpetrators were not in any hurry to unburden their consciences.[17]

Focusing on descriptions of abductions, torture, and executions and conditions in the clandestine centers where prisoners had been held, the committee lacked authorization to investigate the plans by which state terrorism took form, bring charges against individuals, or determine the line of command. The committee had no power to investigate who, if anyone, supervised the various branches of the police and the armed forces. Why, for example, were certain people killed and others kept alive? Who decided policy about torturing and murdering captives? Most importantly, how many prisoners remained alive when the junta stepped down? The Madres were not willing to proceed without a full explanation of why the junta targeted particular people and what happened to them in detention. Did the leader of the last junta, General Reynaldo Benito Bignone, give orders to have prisoners executed at the same time as he ordered their photographs and the records of their captivity destroyed? The Madres wanted the blanks filled in, and obviously their demand was anything but academic. As one Madre explained, "The systematic use of repression and state terrorism as a method of government is what [we] want to reveal and combat."[18]

Afraid of a cover-up, the Asociación de Madres officially boycotted CONADEP and refused to testify or share their substantial archives. Many Madres feared that airing horrific stories without prosecuting individuals would merely routinize the torture, making it seem as if it was destined to take place. As an organization, the Madres wanted the government to assess responsibility and assign blame to particular people. Asking for trial and punishment for the guilty was a call for full public disclosure about the history of the dictatorship.[19]

On 20 September 1984, ten months after deliberations began, CONADEP presented the president with a fifty-thousand-page document and a secret addenda—never released to the public—listing 1,500 officials implicated in the assassinations. Tens of thousands of people, but not the Madres as a group, mobilized to commemorate that historic moment. For the Asociación de Madres, the publication of the report was a first step to undoing history. They blamed the committee for turning in a list of corpses instead of providing indictments of those guilty of what they considered to be "crimes against humanity."[20] "If Congress passed a law that declared the abduction and disappearance of people as a 'crime against humanity,'" torturers would know, according to Renée Epelbaum, one of the original Madres and later president of the Founding-Line Madres, that someday they would be held accountable for what they had done.[21] Unwilling to accept a mere chronicle of atrocities that assigned no blame, investigated no union or party's complicity, and provided no meaningful explanation, the official organization of the Madres rejected the proceedings. They did not want a document like a medieval chronicle, in which calamities seemed to be acts of God. They rejected accounts that presented "a world in which things *happen* to people rather than one in which people *do* things."[22] The Madres' opinion was only confirmed when the book *Nunca Más*, made up of excerpts of the hearings, became an instant bestseller and required beach reading during the summer of December 1984–January 1985.

With the list of horrors circulating so freely but no indictments for the guilty, the Madres intensified their efforts to shape public opinion. According to their own history, they "wanted to have [their] own thought in the street."[23] There were two ways of getting their ideas out: through print and through constant mobilization. At the end of December 1984, the Madres launched a monthly newspaper, *Madres de Plaza de Mayo*, to succeed the bulletin they began in 1980 with the help of sympathetic journalists. The Madres' newspaper provided another public outlet in addition to the space they occupied in the Plaza de Mayo. But the street demonstration—a mixture of spectacle and shaming ritual—remained their preferred method of publicizing the historical evidence they had gathered about what had really happened during the dictatorship and how it was being covered up.

The Madres' continued criticism of Alfonsín and his democratically elected government provoked him to cruel retorts. Frustrated by lack of support from the Madres, he accused them—but not the former torturers—of promoting "subversive terrorism" that detracted from the national interest.[24] Since the justification for all the Latin American military dictatorships of the 1960s through the 1980s was that they were defending national security, in the name of which they tortured and murdered opponents they called "subversives" and "terrorists," the Madres were understandably outraged. As early as 13 December 1983, Alfonsín addressed the nation about his human rights program. He announced his decision to prosecute the leaders of the dictatorship as well as the left-wing organizations.[25] In what became known as the theory of the "Dos Demonios" (Two Devils), Alfonsín, and later *Nunca Más*, promoted the idea that Argentine society had endured a civil war between leftist guerrillas and the military, who were both equally responsible for the violence.

Outraged, the Madres responded to Alfonsín's most recent slurs in an editorial in January 1985, probably written by the editor, María del Rosario Cerruti, outlining their hopes for a nation committed to democracy and social justice:

To the president, who claims to be democratic, it is necessary to explain, once again, in case he's forgotten, what the meaning of "national" is to us. What is authentically national is a population who develop the wealth of this country for their own benefit; it is to receive an adequate wage, to have enough food, to have a home; it is to be able to educate our children, to have health protection, to improve our intellectual and technical capacity, to have our own culture and to have freedom of expression; it is to have armed forces to drive [trucks], planes and boats that transport troops and materials to places of natural disaster, who work with the people in an efficient and rapid way; it is to have a police force that protects freedom and respects all citizens; it is to have impartial judges who guarantee justice; it is to have duties and rights that can be exercised freely; it is simply to have the right to life, but with dignity.[26]

Moving at what the Madres considered a glacial pace, Alfonsín's administration nevertheless accomplished what few other governments going through a transition to democracy have been able to do: it indicted, prosecuted, and convicted leaders of three of the four juntas and the commanders of the military regions into which Argentina had been divided. By reforming the military code, which had jurisdiction over criminal acts carried out on military grounds, the new government succeeded in moving trials to civilian courts if the military did not indict or try offenders within a reasonable amount of time, and gave prosecutors rights of appeal to civil court.[27] When the Supreme Council of the Armed Forces failed to reach a verdict about the commanders of the junta after nine months of deliberation, the civil court took over the prosecution in April 1985. However, between April and December 1985, while the civil trial was underway, the government also indicted seven prominent leaders of left-wing groups.

As the trials began, the Madres used the streets to tell their side of the story of Argentine state terror. On 25 April 1985, they held the March of the Masks to Court. Constantly trying to get the attention of their countrypeople, as they had with the silhouettes in 1983, the Madres organized a pageant in which everyone except the Madres wore masks. The white masks, with high foreheads and hollow eyes, evoked those who had disappeared.[28] A particularly poignant moment occurred when one of the masked figures stopped to nurse her baby.

In contrast to the Madres' peaceful demonstrations, the military attempted a coup, leading the government to declare a state of siege beginning in October 1985 and lasting two months. At the end of December, the judges of the Federal Court found guilty and sentenced to life terms General Jorge Rafael Videla and Admiral Emilio Eduardo Massera of the first junta. The remaining junta members got from four and one-half to eighteen years, except for four who were exonerated.[29] In 1986, the trials of the twelve regional military governors and seven hundred mid-level officers wended their way from the military to the civilian court. On 2 December, the courts sentenced some of the most nefarious police officers, prison doctors, and military officers to between four and twenty-five years in prison, as the military grew restive.[30] Three days later, when the courts claimed that the statute of limitations had run out in the trial of naval officer Alfredo Astiz for the 1977 murder of teenager Dagmar Hagelin, Alfonsín issued the Full Stop Law, "Punto Final," which mandated that all potential defendants had to be tried by April 1987.

That law provided one of the few areas where the military and the Madres were united. In Alfonsín's defense, his friend and aid Carlos Santiago Nino claimed that the decree sped up the pace of the indictments. By March 1987, four hundred officers were on trial.[31] In reaction to the trials, mid-level military men attempted a coup during Easter week of 1987. On 13 May 1987—far too quickly, according to the Madres—Alfonsín sent Congress a draft of the Due Obedience (Obediencia Debida) Law, justifying the exoneration of mid- and lower-level officers whose trials were already underway. The law was passed on 6 June 1987.[32] Ignoring Nuremberg precedents, the government of Argentina claimed that there was no individual responsibility for crimes committed under orders. They did not include rape, kidnapping of children, or theft of real property among the protected activities because of the line of command, but the military was not satisfied with the reprieve. They organized four additional military uprisings in 1988 and 1989. In October 1989, President Carlos Saúl Menem (who succeeded Alfonsín in July 1989) pardoned the 280 high-ranking officers who, unaffected by the Due Obedience Law, were still on trial. Then, on 30 December 1990, Menem freed all the commanders who were still serving prison sentences.[33] Proving that in Argentina at least might did make right, the government provided evidence for the Madres' claim that the democratic government was still largely subject to military threats.

RIDICULE AND MEMORY

Dependent on presenting their views in the court of public opinion, the Madres renewed their use of shaming techniques to make their presence felt. They attended the initial trials of the commanders, wearing their scarves and sitting in silent protest. But each time Hebe de Bonafini tried to put on her scarf, the prosecutor had her remove it. In what would have been comic had it not been so deadly serious, de Bonafini simply replaced a scarf embroidered with names of the disappeared with a plain white scarf. The prosecutor asked her to remove that one as well, saying that she was wearing a political insignia. Outraged, she complained that the former commanders wore their uniforms and the police wore their caps; why couldn't she wear a plain white scarf? When the chief prosecutor judged her scarf out of order, de Bonafini complained that while they were absolving all the assassins, the court was condemning her simple white kerchief.[34] In democratic Argentina, fighting about scarves and thus appearing obnoxious helped to clarify political positions. With that in mind, the Madres around Hebe de Bonafini continued to act "unreasonably," mocking the government at every opportunity.

The Madres keep themselves in the public eye through periodic street demonstrations on holidays they created. The Madres of course have held weekly marches every Thursday since 30 April 1977. They also punctuate the year with annual commemorations: 24 March is the anniversary of the military coup in 1976; on 10 December, the March of Resistance celebrates Human Rights Day.[35] The Madres celebrate other dates in addition to these two anniversaries, in which the Madres consecrate themselves to achieving social justice and a government concerned with promoting human rights. For example, they mark turning points in their own history. These include the anniversaries of the abductions of 8–10 December 1977, decade anniversaries of the Madres' first march in 1977, the Madres' 450th march around the square in April 1985, the thousandth march around the square on 27 June 1996, and the twenty-fifth anniversary of the coup on 24 March 2001. Some years, the Madres join other groups, for whom significant holidays include 8 March, International Women's Day; May Day, in solidarity with the international working class; and 5 October, Mothers' Day in Argentina. The Founding-Line Madres, whose commitment to internal democracy led them to withdraw from the larger group of Madres in January 1986, marched at the end of May 1986 along with the Abuelas de Plaza de Mayo, the Latin American Federation of the Associations of Families of the Detained and Disappeared (FEDFAM), and the Families of the Detained-Disappeared for Political Reasons, to honor those who died in the junta's power.[36]

As unwilling participants in a managed transition to what some view as a "frozen democracy," the aging group of Madres has linked the past and the present.[37] Even at the cost of appearing ridiculous, the Madres convey their analyses of how the past lives on in current policies that subordinate social good to the obligation of paying an exorbitant national debt racked up by the military and its successors.[38] For those who feel that the Madres try to cover too many issues, saying, "You cannot fight against every human rights abuse in a democracy with the same dedication with which you fought against military abuses during the 1970s," the Asociación de Madres answers that it must. When critics say that neoliberal efforts to impose tuition for higher education and university entrance exams have nothing to do with human rights, Hebe de Bonafini and the Asociación de Madres insist that they do.[39] How far they are willing to go and how confrontational they are willing to appear—especially in defense of young people—has become an important measure of the continued urgency they feel about achieving a more just society by linking contemporary repression to its historical antecedents under the dictatorship.

KEEPING COUNT

In Chile, Guatemala, El Salvador, Bosnia, and South Africa, finding the bodies of those murdered by death squads and the military has become part of the process of seeking justice by documenting the past. Some of the most horrifying moments in the South African Truth and Reconciliation hearings of 1994 were the testimonies of security forces describing how they roasted prisoners alive on spits or beat activist Steve Biko and let him slowly bleed to death. In Chile, the controversial proposal of the "Mesón de Diálogo" (Dialogue Roundtable) in June 2000 turned on whether, without admitting guilt, the armed forces would disclose where the lost bodies were hidden.

Even that goal has become a source of conflict between the Asociación de Madres and the government. Right after taking power, Alfonsín ordered the exhumation of graves on the outskirts of cemeteries. With the help of physical anthropologists, the government undertook the process of identifying skeletons and decomposing bodies. During the dictatorship, bodies had been turning up on the banks and estuaries of Río de la Plata and the South Atlantic beaches. Rumors, later substantiated by the 1995 confessions of Naval Captain Adolfo Scilingo and others, supported anecdotal evidence from people living near naval bases, who heard planes take off late at night and return in the early hours of the morning. Decomposed bodies washed up on the shores of beaches in Argentina and neighboring Uruguay. Scilingo revealed that all high-ranking officials at ESMA and many at Bahia Blanca participated in "el Vuelo" (the Flight) in which drugged, naked, but still living prisoners were dropped into rivers or the ocean.[40] These remains supplemented those with gunshot wounds or signs of torture, which were sometimes dumped by soldiers in empty lots or burned with tires in camps such as El Vesubio, known for its perpetual black smoke.

President Raúl Alfonsín's effort to carry out massive exhumations after taking office in late 1983, though at one level a way of documenting history, met with the wrath of the official Asociación de Madres. "We respect those Mothers who want the exhumations, of course, but we don't, as an organization, agree with it," stated Hebe de Bonafini.[41] She went further, calling the display of the skeletons outside the medical departments and the photographs of the cadavers "a truly macabre circus." "Can you imagine the terror? Thousands of dead people thrown on tables and for what, to frighten people."[42] Her objection was not to the bodies; the bodies, the Madres acknowledged, were the bodies of their children. But by focusing on the dead, in her opinion, the government was simply trying to close the book of history without providing a full accounting. For the Madres, agreeing that their children—that all the disappeared, all of whom they claimed as children—were gone would turn the mothers of the disappeared into the mothers of the dead. Speaking again for the Asociación de Madres's official position, Hebe de Bonafini explained at the time that they were not interested in visiting the places that served as concentration camps and torture chambers and they did not want to see the exhumed bodies. They thought the killers should be brought to justice and serve their sentences.[43] They hoped the Under-Secretariat for Human Rights would not simply retrieve and identify bodies, but "identify the assassins." Some Madres claimed that they had no desire to examine cadavers while assassins remained free.

But frequently parents, such as Nieves Ayress's mother in Chile or Founding-Line Madre Dr. Laura Bonaparte in Argentina, received anonymous phone calls telling them that their children were being held at a specific place, or that their child's body could be found in a mass grave, or, as in the case of Marcelo Gelman, the son of sculptor and Abuela Berta Schubaroff and poet Juan Gelman, that the body had been reburied after it was discovered in a decomposed state.[44] Hebe de

Bonafini opposed public exhumations without the express consent of all of the families, arguing that the evidence about forced abduction, torture, and genocide was ample— there was enough historical documentation. According to de Bonafini, what the country lacked was the will to bring the guilty to justice.[45] As far as rituals were concerned, the Madres preferred street demonstrations or trials, with their procedures for establishing the truth.

For some relatives of the disappeared, and especially for the Abuelas de Plaza de Mayo, however, the bodies provided welcome clues. Some mothers and mothers-in-law of the disappeared, whose daughters or daughters-in-law had been among the women who were pregnant when they were kidnapped, embarked on efforts to find missing grandchildren. The Abuelas de Plaza de Mayo decided in 1977 to find the lost children. They focused on those abducted as infants and toddlers and sought out babies who might have been born to imprisoned women.[46] Not knowing whether or not a child had been born, many of the Abuelas were especially eager to find the bodies of the mothers. By examining the skeletal remains for fissures in the pelvic bones, forensic anthropologists could tell whether or not a woman had given birth. As early as 1980, the Abuelas gained support from geneticists. Latin American emigrant doctors and their U.S.-born colleagues developed ways of matching antigens in blood cells and later of examining the DNA of close relatives to see if there was a genetic match.

For example, according to Rita Arditti, Estela de Carlotto, one of the founders of the Abuelas de Plaza de Mayo and its longtime president, learned through exiled survivors of La Cacha concentration camp that her daughter Laura, whose body had been returned to her filled with bullet holes, had given birth in 1977 to a boy she had named Guido after her father. Grabbing Laura's child from her at birth, her attackers claimed to have taken him to his grandmother. To taunt Laura, the officers told her that her mother had rejected the child and did not want to have anything to do with either her daughter or her grandson. Unconvinced, the young mother told another prisoner that her mother would never abandon her or her child and would fight the military with all her strength.[47]

Another grandmother, Haydee Lemos, discovered her fourteen-month-old granddaughter on her doorstep in 1977, five days after her pregnant daughter Mónica and her husband were kidnapped. A decade later, according to Rita Arditti, a casual meeting between Estela de Carlotto and an old friend of Mónica's revealed that both had been at the

Pozo de Banfield (Banfield Pit) outside La Plata, where Mónica had given birth to another girl. By further chance, Lemos discovered that a child had been adopted by a policewoman and her husband. Through a complicated procedure of genetic testing, the Abuelas were able to prove that the child belonged to the Lemos family, who gained custody.[48] For the Abuelas, the chance to examine individual bodies offered the possibility of rescuing the life and personal history of another human being.

BREAKING APART

The basic disagreements between the two groups of Madres relate to three issues of principle: government reparations for those who disappeared, monuments and plaques, and exhumation of the bodies. The decision of the Asociación de Madres de Plaza de Mayo to boycott the hearings of CONADEP had not been unanimous. Many individual Madres shared the view of other human rights organizations that the committee might turn up new evidence about what had happened to those who had been detained and disappeared. Like other Argentines, they needed a "story" to help explain the sequence of events that had overtaken their families and their country. Some of the Madres did go to the camps to examine the bodies, seeking after so many years some connection to the physical embodiment of their children. Those mothers continued piecing together narratives about what had happened to their children after they were abducted.

The transition to constitutional government divided the Madres into two groups. The largest group remained with Hebe de Bonafini and kept the name of the Asociación, the apartment they had purchased, and the monthly newspaper. Those who left in January 1986, calling themselves the Línea Fundadora, the Founding-Line Madres, included many of the women who had first assembled with Azucena de Villaflor to march in the Plaza de Mayo in late April and May 1977. Even Hebe de Bonafini agreed that those who seceded had been instrumental in creating the Madres and had shared leadership during its early years.

The split, like most divorces, left less than the sum of its parts. Personality differences appear to be the main cause of the eruption. From the perspective of the Founding-Line Madres, the problem is with Hebe de Bonafini and the power she wields in her group. The Founding-Line Madres view de Bonafini as authoritarian, impatient with those who differ with her, corrupt, overly quick to take ultra-leftist positions, and prone to using coarse and insulting language as a means of provoking authorities and gaining attention for the Madres. In the year after the break-up, de Bonafini recognized that many of those who had seceded did not like the way she acted toward Alfonsín and the government, but she was convinced that she was right.

De Bonafini, in turn, considers the Founding-Line Madres to be elitists who looked down on her and many of the other working-class Madres. Many of those who left, like Renée Epelbaum, Nora de Cortiñas, and Laura Bonaparte, were either Jewish or married to Jewish men, although no one on either side admits that anti-Semitism might have contributed to the conflict. Marguerite Guzman Bouvard, who is close to Hebe de Bonafini and Juana de Pargament, tries to represent both sides of the conflict. To Bouvard, disagreements over whether to participate in the CONADEP hearings and whether to support the government's attempts to exhume bodies were the real divisions among the Madres.[49]

De Bonafini disparages the Founding-Line Mothers and their marches in the Plaza de Mayo: "Look how few of them [come] on Thursdays. Five, six, or eight [come] to the plaza with a megaphone to list the [names of the] disappeared. This is something totally...useless because at that level they have no resonance. It would be something else if they named those who did the repressing, but they would consider that too intransigent, something hard, and they only like acting like 'pacifists.'"[50]

Despite the bad blood, the product of a difference in style and the domination of Hebe de Bonafini as the leading spokeswoman for the Asociación de Madres, there are important strategic differences between the two groups. These sometimes mimic the political differences that might have caused their own highly sectarian children to have been antagonists. Critics such as Bouvard make the Founding-Line Madres appear more naive than they are when they underestimate the importance of the Founding-Line Madres' demands that they should choose individually whether they wanted to go to the hearings or attend the exhumations and that they should maintain their alliances with other human rights groups, including the Abuelas and the Families of the Detained and Disappeared. Familial values tie the Founding-Line Madres to the Families of the Detained and Disappeared, who also lost relatives, and to the Abuelas, whom the Founding-Line Madres have known for a long time.

The differences between the two groups may also be structural. Many associations committed to egalitarian relationships think that decentralization is intrinsic to democratic practices. This was a widespread belief of the New Left and the feminist movement of the 1960s in Europe and the United States. The contrary view is that division of labor necessarily leads to fixed hierarchies and more authoritarian structures. Clearly this was a charge that the Asociación de Madres and Hebe de Bonafini took to heart: once the Founding-Line Madres withdrew, the larger association formalized its procedures, and began to hold weekly meetings of the governing board and annual meetings of affiliated Madres groups from outside Buenos Aires. Nevertheless, Hebe de Bonafini is increasingly the group's principal spokeswoman. The Asociación de Madres is consistent and systematic, and it is willing to stand alone to make a political point. De Bonafini is right that her practice and that of her group would be classified as "hard," fixed as it is on principles and a determination to be an irritant that may well account for the continued impact the Madres have on Argentine society.

The Founding-Line Madres, by contrast, practice a more decentralized politics, based on what the New Left in the United States called "participatory democracy," or what Renée Epelbaum called "consensus." Less practiced in formal political programs, their structure is also more fluid: "Since we began in 1977, we have worked in the same way. There were no posts, no positions."[51] Following a system I have called "artisanal," all the members of the Founding-Line Mothers work at a variety of tasks, making commitments to the projects undertaken.[52] Seeming to regard the Founding-Line's way as consistent with the way the Madres began, Epelbaum also recalled that although she and Élida de Galletti initially wrote all the flyers and bulletins the Madres published and others took them to the printers, "We did what we knew best, each of us, and it had nothing to do with posts or positions. The Línea Fundadora is and has to be—as the Madres always were—a collective movement."[53] The Founding-Line Madres are certainly more open to a variety of strategies, working both in public and private to bring the past to light. Constantly opening their hearts to individuals, the Founding-Line Madres work in personal ways.

Those in the Asociación de Madres de Plaza de Mayo claim that the Founding-Line Madres are also more reformist, and thus less conscious of the ways capitalism and imperialism have affected movements of liberation all over the world. To Argentine journalist Alejandro Diago, de Bonafini gloated that several of the Madres who left with the Founding-Line had already returned to the Asociación in 1988. Moreover, she boasted that her group "continues to march, produce ideas, travel abroad to tell people their new [strategies] to keep renewing their work, while the others don't accomplish much."[54] Bouvard, possibly reflecting de Bonafini's opinion, argues that the Founding-Line Madres "intended to work within the political system as an interest group rather than as a radical opposition group that continued demonstrating and marching against the government."[55] This is the perennial charge of centralized groups against those that are decentralized, and is seldom accurate.

The charges Hebe de Bonafini frequently has made against the Madres of the Founding- Line—that they don't know how to organize demonstrations, spread the word inside Argentina and abroad, or develop new strategies—highlights something both groups know: the Madres, like other grassroots organizations, stand or fall on public attention. When critics charge that the numbers attending the Madres' demonstrations have diminished, the Madres of the Asociación answer that they are not running football matches. On the other hand, when their numbers soar, they proclaim them, as they did after the commemoration of the twentieth anniversary of the coup in 1996 and the twenty-fifth in 2001.

Although the Founding-Line Madres continue to march in the plaza every Thursday and on important holidays, they have diversified their public activities. They generate cultural events such as the street "occupation" at the Plaza Las Heras in December 1995 and the Bridge of Memory in October 1996, and they try to reach young people through school programs. Determined to make contemporary youth recognize themselves in those who were detained and disappeared, the Founding-Line Madres filled trees with large pictures of their children and put out some of their treasured items. Marguerite Feitlowitz quotes Renée Epelbaum as saying that they organized street festivals to celebrate their children's lives, not their deaths: "Their disappearance was someone else's crime, not our children's identity."[56] In 1997, the Founding-Line Madres helped students at the Colegio Nacional de Buenos Aires (National High School of Buenos Aires) honor ninety student predecessors who were abducted. The Founding-Line Madres developed a widely attended art exhibit about their children's lives. And in La Plata, Founding-Line Madres helped students to assemble biographies to place on plaques at the Colegio Nacional de La Plata.[57] Hoping to promote activism among the next generation of young people, the Founding-Line Madres link the lives of contemporary youth to past generations. Despite hurt feelings and anger on both sides of the Madres' divide, in fact both groups remain united in their desire for full disclosure, in their need to engage with fellow citizens in the public square, and in their commitment to mobilizing in order to express their political views. Both groups continue to march in the Plaza de Mayo.

As in postwar Germany, the issue of reparations has created antagonists, raising questions about whether reparations for survivors are entitlements or blood money. Nearly half of those abducted were working-class people, largely in their twenties and thirties, and many of them were parents of young children. Often the abducted provided the sole support for their families. Some family members lost their job while trying to save relatives. Grandmothers and other relatives who struggled to raise the surviving children needed the financial support provided by reparations. In 1994, under President Carlos Saúl Menem, the government legislated reparations to family members of the disappeared and other victims of "state terrorism," presumably including survivors. Since some richer families also had lost their wealth paying ransoms or turning over deeds to corporations (still in the hands of individual military officers), reparations were welcome to many. By 1997, when the government issued three billion dollars in bonds to cover the costs, about eight thousand people had claimed their funds under the 1994 law, and others had until the year 2000 to claim theirs.[58] At the same time, the government passed a law granting the children of the disappeared exemption from military service.

The Asociación de Madres under Hebe de Bonafini's leadership tried to make reparations synonymous with forgiving the military and "selling out." As de Bonafini sarcastically remarked:

> Money will never substitute for justice. Now they want to give $100,000 to every mother. What a sum! When there is no money for education, when there is nothing for seniors, when there is nothing for the mothers [of those who died in] the Malvinas [War]. When there is no money for health care. When there is no money for books. How interested this government is in buying our consciences.... We, the Madres de Plaza de Mayo, will never permit them to pay with money what they owe in justice. Our children's lives have no price; there wouldn't be enough money in the world to make up for [their loss].... This is the domestic [internal] debt; it is the debt they have to us, the debt of justice, the [price is] prison for the assassins."[59]

De Bonafini and the Asociación de Madres claim that being the offspring of someone who disappeared is no honor, and that no one should have to serve in the military. The Founding-Line Madres follow those victims of the Nazis who argue that nothing the perpetrators do can make up for their crimes, but they should at least take responsibility through reparations to the children of the disappeared, many of whom could not get an education or develop job skills without these benefits. A related issue concerns plaques, memorial parks, and the preservation of some of the torture centers. With Old Testament fervor, de Bonafini rails against icons that represent the death of the disappeared. When the families and friends of those who disappeared from the humanities faculty of the University of La Plata, where de Bonafini's daughter-in-law studied psychology, wanted to include a plaque for her, de Bonafini denounced them. Using the same arguments she leveled against the Founding-Line Madres, de Bonafini claimed that the only acceptable monument to the dead was continued commitment to the social struggles in which they engaged. De Bonafini excoriated students at the school of architecture at the University of La Plata for engraving the names of the disappeared on the steps of an amphitheater there. And she threatened to tear down plaques hanging in the courtyards of the school of anthropology and the school of psychology that include pictures and biographies of disappeared students. Some of those who hung plaques on police stations that served as clandestine prisons or collected photos and biographies of the students believe that de Bonafini should not dictate how others grieve.[60]

Taking her cue from those who say, "Don't cry, organize!" Hebe de Bonafini has little patience with what she regards as sentimentality, viewing such ideas as dangerous. On 23 March 1999, the day before the twenty-third anniversary of the military coup, de Bonafini and the Asociación de Madres were appalled by a ceremony at Costanera, on the outskirts of Buenos Aires. Mabel Gutiérrez of the Families of the Detained and Disappeared placed the first stone, dedicating a monument to the victims of state terrorism in what would be a thirty-acre Park of Memory.[61] Gutiérrez emphasized that such a monument would not "pretend to close wounds, nor would it end the quest for truth and justice." She assured the gathering that the monument did not indicate the sponsor's recognition of the death of the disappeared, nor an end to the struggle to punish those responsible, but that the park would simply be a place in which to remember.[62] With Carmen Lapacó of the Founding-Line Madres and Estela Carlotto, president of the Abuelas de Plaza de Mayo, in attendance, the ceremony to honor the dead proceeded.

Despite the care Gutiérrez took in explaining what they hoped to achieve with the park, a counterdemonstration took place. The Asociación de Madres de Plaza de Mayo, the Group Against Police and Institutional Repression, and the Ex-Detained and Disappeared for Polit-

ical Reasons opposed the monument and rejected the sponsorship of the
municipal government of Buenos Aires, a group they claimed was riddled with torturers.[63] Showing to some degree the simplification and
outright distortion of claiming that Alfonsín supporters were no different from the torturers, the group attacked Aníbal Ibarra, the cochair of
the City Council, who had been one of the two prosecutors of the military commanders and had helped the Abuelas locate lost children. Although the democratic government might be correctly viewed as too
moderate, Ibarra certainly was not one of those involved in genocide.

For de Bonafini and her group, monuments and exhumations are for
the dead, and she insists that the spirits of those who disappeared live
on. In one of the Madres' political flyers, written in the form of a letter
to a son, a Madre, calling herself simply "Mamá," writes that "all those
traitors who claim to be repentant are interested in assuring your death,
your total death, and they want to pay me for your death. I insult them.
When I look in their eyes, they lower their gaze. Do you know why? Because I look at them with your eyes and I speak to them in your voice."
The flyer, dated April 1995, is entitled, "To Give Birth to a Child Is to
Give Birth to Thousands of Children."[64]

MEMORIES AND COMMITMENT

The Madres continue to fight to shape the official history of the dictatorship, and they have been willing to risk everything to shock their
compatriots into remembering. The Argentine public is no more eager
to think about the past than it is to consider the financial debacle, some
of which was caused by the military dictatorship. The juntas carried out
atrocities in secret and effectively amputated an entire generation from
the body politic. Argentine governments, first by denying the disappearances and later by attempting to forget the disappeared, tried to
sever the past from the future. Matilde Mellibovsky, a Founding-Line
Madre, asserted that "they eliminated the generation that comes after
me, they isolated me from the future, they separated me totally from
any continuity." But she knew from the beginning that she wanted "to
recuperate [the past] through memory."[65]

Creating historical memories, even if the two groups of Madres differ about how best to prevent their country's amnesia, is intrinsic to
both groups and to their hopes for the future. The need to remember is
one reason why the Madres have granted so many interviews and written down so many of their stories. While many have argued that in the

face of structural adjustment and global economics, the forms of repression have become truly invisible, the Madres insist that in the past
they revealed the all-too-inhuman face of repression, and they know
how to do it again.

On the last day the junta ruled in December 1983, Hebe de Bonafini
outlined a theory of permanent resistance: "For us the struggle isn't
going to change; it's going to continue exactly the same. Instead of putting our demands to the military, we are going to put these demands to
the constitutional government."[66] Early on, the Madres expressed their
need to keep demonstrating, at first to prevent future army coups, but
then to "voice publicly, if necessary, our disagreement with policies or
decisions that we judge to be of dubious effectiveness or to be mistaken.
It is our obligation to do so, since this is the duty of all good citizens
within the framework of a pluralistic and free democracy in which dissent should be expressed in a civilized manner."[67] Though differing in
tactics and rhetoric, both groups of Madres extoll the need for direct
democracy. Only by open argument with those in power can they ensure that their version of history will get a fair hearing in Argentina. The
democratic project, which both groups of Madres pursue, of combating
the potential for state terrorism continues with the next generation of
activists.

CHAPTER 6

Youth Finds a Way

Avenging angels in T-shirts appeared in the late 1990s. They condemned those guilty of atrocities in Argentina and Chile. Demonstrators used baggies filled with red paint to toss at the buildings where the torturers lived and chains to link themselves to fences in raucous spectacles called *escraches* in Argentina and *funas* in Chile. Among those targeted for public shaming were junta leaders, secret police, soldiers, and their supporters; businessmen who administered the property seized when people were abducted; and physicians who supervised torture sessions or repaired the damage so that survivors could be sent back for more. Countering official denials with visual tableaux, children of the detained and disappeared returned to haunt those who murdered their parents. Young people put themselves on the line to help a larger public visualize what went on during the Dirty War and how authoritarianism continues to permeate Chilean and Argentinian society.

Although many people in Argentina and Chile want to forget, some young activists view themselves as survivors[1] and have taken to the streets to publicize what perpetrators hoped to hide. As time passed, some people discovered that they had been kidnapped at birth and "adopted" by friends of the torturers or by the torturers themselves; others lost their parents through disappearances or forced exile. Without becoming mired in a culture of death, these youthful demonstrators have found ways to acknowledge the social vision of their parents. By substituting ridicule and gallows humor for the choking fury the Argentines call *bronca,* they deliver a message to their fellow citizens about justice and direct democracy. By pointing a finger at those who killed and maimed with impunity, they hope to clear up the historical record and set a new standard for justice in their country. Using "megaphones, tambourines, songs, and music, with joy and openness," the young people show that they are committed and that "they have something to say and...want to contribute to the creation of a world in which they can live, a world of truth and justice, where they can overcome fear and reject [those who acted with] impunity and [carried out the worst forms of] censorship."[2]

Like the Madres de Plaza de Mayo, these young demonstrators are eager to reveal the systemic quality of the repression they believe still characterizes Argentine life. Some of them resemble the Abuelas de Plaza de Mayo. These young people are detectives who find their country strewn with clues about illicit social mobility at the cost of a sizeable number of people in their parents' generation. These young people, especially in Argentina and Chile, use stories that have been suppressed to reveal the true identity of those hiding their pasts.

The major change in the 1990s was the rebirth of popular demonstrations among human rights groups. Although the birth families of the disappeared continued to be active, they were aging. Many had died, including Renée Epelbaum and Élida de Galletti of the Founding-Line Madres de Plaza de Mayo and Serrano Solá of the Agrupación de Familiares de Detenidos Desaparecidos (Families of the Detained and Disappeared) in Chile. That is why the emergence of young activists all over Latin America, but particularly in Argentina and Chile, and the militant festivals of *escraches* in Argentina and *funas* in Chile became so important. The generation the dictators had hoped would cower in fear or simply forget had jumped onto the public stage and would not leave.

MEMORIES

In 1994, when friends of Carlos de la Riva decided to commemorate the twentieth anniversary of his abduction by the Triple-A (Alianza Anticommunista Argentina, or Argentine Anticommunist Alliance), they planned a memorial at the school of architecture of the National University of La Plata. They thought it would be a suitable occasion to honor the one hundred architecture students of that generation who had died or disappeared.[3] Hoping for a reunion, they made elaborate efforts to contact the families of their classmates. They organized a

commemorative meeting called "Memory, Remembering, and Compro-
mise," on 3 November 1994.[4] The University of La Plata, known as the
Sorbonne of Latin America, about an hour's drive from Buenos Aires, is
the closest any university in Latin America comes to having a campus.
On the outskirts of the quaint provincial city of La Plata, whose gaily
colored pastel houses and wrought-iron balustrades resemble the outskirts of many Mediterranean capitals in the 1960s, the university attracted students from all over Argentina. Like the Sorbonne, La Plata
has a reputation for being a center of intellectual and political ferment,
where ideas generated at home and abroad get a full airing. At the memorial ceremony in La Plata, many children, some the same age their
parents had been when they were detained and disappeared, felt for the
first time as if they had found kin.

> At the memorial at the school of architecture in La Plata we first got to
> know each other as the Children [los Hijos]. The organizers asked us if we
> wanted to say something, and at first none of us felt moved [to speak].
> After half an hour, when we got to know each other, we formed a group,
> hugging as if we were brothers and sisters and crying together. All of a
> sudden, someone grabbed the microphone and said he wanted to bring
> regards from a guy who hadn't been able to come. Someone else came alive
> and said something. Finally we all spoke, whether to give greetings or to
> say what we felt or to tell a story, and there was so much emotion when we
> finished and we left the stage that people came up to us saying: "I knew
> your father in such a place," "I knew him in some other [place]." Everyone
> greeted us in some way."[5]

The organizers of the La Plata meeting had worked hard to contact
family members from all over Argentina, and they worked even harder
to gather people for a meeting during Easter week of 1995 at the Julio
Cortázar workshop. Following this reunion, organizers set 13–16 October 1995 to gather in Córdoba. According to their press release—
which was sent over the internet on 19 October—the conference was attended by 350 family members of those murdered and disappeared
from fourteen regions of Argentina.[6] Again they reviewed their scattered memories: "Did you go to Devoto too? Were you there on that
Mother's Day when they allowed us to come for the whole day and have
contact [with our parents]?" "Yeah, I was there." "Hey, I was there
too." "Did you know that your mom was with my mom and your dad
with my dad?"[7]

   Coming together was cathartic because they could share their experiences with others who understood the loss and determination they

felt. They could express a variety of emotions and concerns without having to defend their feelings or explain that they wanted justice, not vengeance. "We don't want our cry for justice to be viewed as if we ourselves planned to exact justice with our own hands." Reversing the usual pattern by which youth try to win recognition for who they are, they tried to show who their parents were: "They denigrate our parents as subversives, guerrillas. Our parents had ideals, dreams, utopi[an ideas], goals for a different country. We want society to know who our parents were."[8] They publicized the claims of survivors. For example, Adriana Calvo, a survivor of Pozo de Banfield (Banfield Pit) and three other Argentine prison camps, remains bitter about the trials of the commanders in 1985. Although she was surrounded by microphones, she was not permitted to talk about her political commitments, but only about her abduction, torture, and imprisonment.[9] She says that a true system of justice would have allowed discussion about why people like her had joined political groups such as the Montoneros. She would have welcomed the opportunity to explain who the revolutionaries were and what they had hoped to achieve.

Even before the ceremony at the school of architecture of the National University of La Plata, a few children of the disappeared had joined the *rondas* with the Madres de Plaza de Mayo, and the teenagers stayed after to help the aging women. Then, at the conference in Córdoba, the young people decided to form their own organization, called Hijos por la Identidad y la Justicia contra el Olvido y el Silencio (Children for Identity and Justice against Oblivion and Silence, HIJOS), first in Argentina and later in Uruguay,[10] with outposts in Chile, Mexico, Venezuela, Spain, and Sweden, wherever exiles had gathered. I first heard about HIJOS from Alejandra Vassallo, who told me about their shaming rituals, or *escrache*. But I saw some HIJOS members at the march that the Asociación de Madres de Plaza de Mayo and the Founding-Line Madres de Plaza de Mayo (Línea Fundadora) held to commemorate their thousandth march around the Plaza de Mayo in June 1996. In Buenos Aires, the Asociación's offices were filled with signs and puppets. When I asked who had made them, one of the Madres replied, "the kids *[los hijos].*" Later on in the conversation, I learned that she was referring to a specific group of young people in their late teens and twenties, connected to the missing generation of the disappeared. A friend of Alejandra's knew a member of HIJOS, whom I tried to contact. The Hijo was well known to the Asociación de Madres, but like teenagers anywhere, this one seemed to move by night, leaving only fast food containers as evidence that she had been there. Finally the Hijo—or rather, the Hija—suggested that we meet at the demonstration, where I could identify her by her purple hair. Amidst a crowd of five thousand, among whom were hundreds of women with burgundy hennaed hair, this Hijo stood out, not only because her hair was really blue, but because she was dressed as a punk, with nose ring and black leather jacket in the cold air of a late June day in the southern hemisphere. She greeted me and then rushed off to help her friends unfurl their banner. By 1996, the HIJOS had been demonstrating for more than a year.

After the Córdoba meeting, HIJOS began a series of public activities designed to shame those to whom the government had granted pardons. According to the HIJOS's own account, their coming out had gained an audience because of revelations in March 1995 by former naval captain Adolfo Francisco Scilingo. His firsthand account of atrocities provided concrete evidence about what had happened to many of the disappeared.[11] During the military dictatorship, naked bodies in various states of decomposition had washed up on riverbanks and ocean beaches in Argentina, Uruguay, and Chile. Ariel Dorfman, an Argentinian who had escaped from Chile after the coup in 1973, wrote a novel called *Widows* nearly a decade later, about an unnamed place where bodies kept floating ashore.[12] After the coup in Chile, torturers used the phrase "going to Moneda" to mean being dumped over the Pacific, and "going to Puerto Montt" to mean being dumped over land.[13] But the largest number of bodies appeared along the Río de la Plata, which separates Argentina and Uruguay.

In 1995, Adolfo Scilingo approached the well-known Argentine left-wing journalist, Horacio Verbitsky, saying that he had a story Verbitsky would want to hear. Verbitsky was suspicious because members of the military were notorious for their wall of silence. Over a year, Verbitsky and Scilingo met as Verbitsky recorded Scilingo's testimony. The initial account, published serially in *Página 12,* was expanded and later published in Spanish as *El Vuelo* (The Flight). It told the story of the young naval captain, Adolfo Scilingo, who in 1977, while in his late twenties, had worked in the operations division of ESMA, the Argentine torture center through which thousands of people passed.[14] Scilingo became the toast of the talk show circuit. His grotesque account of almost falling from a plane as he tried to push a drugged but still living prisoner to his death provided graphic evidence about how two thousand or more prisoners had died. Captives were told that they were being transferred to other prisons and required vaccinations. To the sound of soft music, they received injections. Then, on Wednesday and Saturday nights, they were loaded onto planes, where they were stripped and thrown naked into the Río de la Plata by men like Scilingo.[15] Alone and together with HIJOS, Scilingo appeared on television and spoke on the radio. Not content with waiting to express themselves, and unaware of shaming rituals and their dynamics, the Hijos needed to break through the routinization of horror. They embarked on a practice designed to shock the public.

It was entirely fitting that young people should take the lead in commemorating their parents' generation: In the 1970s, nineteen- to thirty-five-years-olds were marked as seditious, hunted down, and attacked during the repression by the Triple-A and the juntas in Argentina, the Pinochet dictatorship in Chile, and the last days of the Franco dictatorship in Spain. This was the age group of Nieves Ayress and Margarita Durán in Chile; of the urban guerrillas of ERP and the Montoneros in Argentina, and of many of those trying to overthrow the dictatorship of Francisco Franco in Spain. In fact, young people traveling with their parents in the Basque Country in Spain in the 1970s and 1980s were treated as if they were all terrorists. Police routinely searched them and the cars in which they were traveling; authorities ransacked their apartments; they were arrested and frequently tortured, and denied access to lawyers. Those who openly participated in leftist movements devoted to social change were presumed guilty of violent acts whether or not evidence actually tied them to a crime.

In Argentina and Chile, former torturers inhabit the same streets and cafés as their victims, turning up so frequently that they seem to be stalking them. For some of these unindicted criminals, the leftists they imprisoned and tortured are probably still the most interesting people they know. From the point of view of former torturers, these are old relationships. Even after particularly grisly torture sessions, guards sometimes insisted that prisoners play cards with them or discuss their children's education.[16] Possibly ashamed of what they were doing, some guards and officers needed their victims to exonerate them; they needed to pretend that prisoners wanted and still want their attention.

In Chile there is a similar pattern. The Chilean MIR (Movimiento de Izquierda Revolutionaria, Revolutionary Leftist Movement), like the Montoneros in Argentina, was the object of particular brutality. The MIR, which followed the strategies of Ché Guevara, attempted even after his assassination to pursue a policy of popular democracy and popular revolution. Making alliances with the rural and urban poor and with the indigenous people known as the Mapuche, the MIR promoted urban and rural land seizures and popular mobilizations throughout the 1970s. The Villa Grimaldi, in the beautiful foothills of the Andes in Santiago, bears comparison with ESMA and other notorious concentration camps in Argentina. Now razed, with the land devoted to a memorial park, the Villa Grimaldi was the greatest achievement of state terrorism in Chile. Run by the intelligence service that reported directly to Augusto Pinochet, Villa Grimaldi became the center of attempts to expunge the MIR. According to Nieves Ayress, who had been a socialist and joined the MIR in exile after she was released from prison, the torturers honed their skills on people like her and then applied them to the MIR in Villa Grimaldi.

Following the Chilean plebiscite in 1988 where Mujeres por la Vida and other members of the opposition managed to convince the majority of the population to vote against keeping Pinochet in power for another decade, Pinochet stepped down. But the constitution dictated that he remain head of the armed forces for another eight years, and he became a senator for life. As what the 1980 Constitution had called a "protected democracy," Chilean political arrangements were even more rigid than those of many other states going through regime changes. In the election of late 1989, Patricio Aylwin was selected as president. As a conservative Christian Democratic senator, he had negotiated with the women who helped overthrow Allende, but later turned against Pinochet.

Upon taking office in 1990, Aylwin immediately ordered an inquiry into the violence that had occurred between 11 September 1973 and 11 March 1990. Nominally under the direction of Raúl Rettig, a widely respected jurist, aided by José Zalaquett, a noted legal scholar and democratic judge, the committee was empowered to investigate only those who died violently during the dictatorship. Nieves Ayress, Margarita Durán, Margarita Romano, and the other 150,000 who had undergone incarceration and torture in Chile could not tell their stories. There was no power to subpoena authorities. The blanket amnesty law (Law 2191) that Pinochet decreed in 1978 exonerated everyone in the armed forces and police for crimes committed between 11 September 1973 (the day of the coup) and 11 March 1978. As a result, no authorities could be brought up on charges.

The report of the Truth and Reconciliation Commission, known popularly as the Rettig Report,[17] which appeared in 1991, had much less resonance than *Nunca Más*. The Rettig Report reads like a chronicle. But, more importantly, with the military still firmly in Pinochet's hands and with the appointment of nine other conservative senators for life, the possibility of any kind of real change seemed slim. Nonetheless, Pinochet's arrest on 16 October 1998, at a London clinic where he had gone for back surgery, set the stage for change in Chile. He was held for possible extradition to Spain, where Baltasar Garzón, a national judge with prosecutorial power to initiate an investigation, had indicted Pinochet for human rights abuses. The long silence that Mujeres por la Vida had periodically interrupted with their street demonstrations was now broken. The promise of Mujeres in Chile and Madres in Argentina could now be taken up by a younger generation.

SHAMING THE PERPETRATORS

Silence often accompanies shame, and that is why the Madres, the Hijos, and Chilean practitioners of the *funa* make noise. Whereas the torturers try to pass unnoticed, the activists and their supporters make scenes. Opening up spaces in the public sphere, where even those in power must face their opponents, groups seeking a full accounting of the violence that overtook their countries have tried to expose evidence that others would prefer to keep hidden. Beginning in 1986, while the trials of the junta leaders were going on in civilian court, the Madres devoted the last page of their newspaper, *Madres de Plaza de Mayo,* to what they called "The Gallery of the Repressors," or the Rogues Gallery. With ample documentation, the Madres published material for a popular history of the dictatorship. Along with the official government publication that first appeared in 1985 and was reissued in 1995 in *El juicio que cambió al país* (The Trial That Changed the Country), the Madres' newspaper provided excerpts from the testimony of survivors of the concentration camps and families of the detained and disappeared.

Then Presidents Raúl Alfonsín and Carlos Saúl Menem began issuing amnesties. Some of the worst torturers went free because they were judged to have been "just following orders" *(obediencia debida),* and therefore deserved pardons. With no recourse to the courts, first the Madres and then the Hijos attempted to publicize the names of former officers, such as Jorge Acosta and Alfredo Astiz, who were responsible for some of the worst atrocities at ESMA.

While many outside the human rights community wanted to forget the past, some young people had a commitment to those other young and idealistic people—their parents—whose lives were cut short in the

1970s and early 1980s. Argentine journalist Gabriela Cerruti has written movingly about the effects of state terror on the everyday life of
young people during the dictatorship in her memoir, *Heredero al silencio* (Heir to Silence). Born in 1965, she grew up in Punta Alta, near the
naval base of Bahia Blanca, from which planes carried prisoners to their
death. Cerruti was close friends with the daughter of Naval Captain
Jorge Acosta. In the 1970s, Acosta was commander of Belgrano Naval
Base.[18] He later went on to officiate over ESMA's torture chambers,
where twelve people, including two French nuns, Azucena Villaflor, and
ten other family members of the detained and disappeared were tortured and condemned to death by Acosta. Also at ESMA, Acosta,
known as El Tigre, took one of the disappeared prisoners, known as La
Negrita, as a sex slave and then as a mistress.[19]

An alleged defender of Western Christian values, Acosta was a patriarchal tyrant. Cerruti recalls how he hated youth culture and how state
terror infiltrated his family life. For example, Acosta became enraged
when his daughter listened to popular records that Cerruti brought over
to the house. The lyrics speaking of "liberation" so infuriated him that
he called his daughter "trash" and threatened to beat her.

Cerruti is also conscious of the ways her mother, a schoolteacher,
tried to protect her six daughters. Cerruti's mother censored her daughters' references to "redness," "liberty," or anything having to do with
"society." Since any rebellious behavior against parents, let alone another authority figure, could result in accusations of subversion and
even disappearances, Cerruti's mother policed her daughters' behavior.
The mother became so terrified when her daughters were sneaking
around planning a Mother's Day surprise that even when she learned
what they had been plotting, she grounded them for a week for lying to
her.[20] As exaggerated as her fears may seem, they were no match for the
horrors of reality.

Cerruti, a teenager at the time of these incidents, interprets such ex-
cesses in relation to the terror the military tried to instill. As a prize-
winning investigative journalist, she tries to face down the perpetrators
and force them to acknowledge what they did. Failing that, she tries to
hold them up to public scrutiny. Likewise, the young people committed
to participatory democracy confront the ghosts of the past. They have
taken to the streets to force acknowledgment of what transpired in Argentina. Hoping to integrate what they know about history into the collective memory, they try to shame those who have escaped justice.

ESCRACHES AND FUNAS

On a beautiful Argentine summer day, 11 December 1995, the day after the forty-seventh anniversary of the signing of the United Nations Universal Declaration of Human Rights, young people came by bike, motorcycle, scooter, bus, truck, or car to rally in front of Congress in downtown Buenos Aires. Holding signs, young people stood beside their vehicles as they invited those on foot to join them and take advantage of the free transportation. They organized themselves to march. From a side street, a foam-rubber rat wearing a military cap rolled to the head of the caravan. With someone pedaling underneath the rubber skin, the "ratmobile" prepared to lead the parade. The bearded, long-haired, mixed-sex group of largely young people stood by on their bikes and affixed signs over their handlebars announcing an *escrache*.

Escrache, an obscure Argentinian slang word for revealing something hidden or uncovering a fact—roughly equivalent to unmasking someone or being "in their face"—was not a word on the tip of anyone's tongue, and it still raises questions.[21] Sergio Molina, an Hijo in Great Britain, defined *escrache* thus: "to place in evidence, publicly reveal, or show the face of someone who seeks anonymity." He went on to explain that "only a few of those responsible for 'genocide' are recognizable in Argentina. They are those the press has publicized, mostly former members of the military juntas, former Minister of the Economy [José] Martínez de Hoz, and famous infiltrators such as Captain [Alfredo] Astiz." He applauded the fact that "these people cannot appear in public except in the most reactionary or frivolous places. Outside of these, most people act outraged whenever they appear, and sometimes people even try to attack them. Wherever they are seen they generate repugnance, disgust and fury." But he laments, "Most of the criminals pass unnoticed and are perfectly comfortable because they are free to carry on with impunity." There's where the *escraches* come in:

> With the *escraches* we make these people visible, and we publicize the roles they played during the dictatorships. Neighbors learn alongside whom they live. The people at the bakery, the guys at the bar, and the people at the stores recognize them as torturers. So long as there is no justice, at least they cannot live peaceful lives: people in the streets recognize them for what they are, criminals. Their bosses in politics and the big companies (who generally know what they did) have to hide them or fire them to avoid the shame of those who know that they hire assassins, or the employers face losing the support of their clients.[22]

The first *escrache* took place on a hot Saturday afternoon at 3 P.M., when no one would be at work.[23] This particular demonstration had many targets, but the first was Vice President Carlos Ruckauf, who had signed one of the first decrees authorizing the "Annihilation of Subversion" and had given orders in 1975 to "let the bullets fly." These decrees, though issued under the militarized government of Isabelita Perón, established the pattern that legitimated the kidnapping and murder of the government's opponents.

The same *escrache* attempted to get under the skin of Aldo Rico. Rico, who had been a lieutenant colonel in the Malvinas War, led the Easter Uprising against Raúl Alfonsín in 1987. He attempted another coup seven months later. Saved from prosecution by Alfonsín's "Due Obedience" decree of 1987, Rico was at that time the *intendente* (mayor) of San Miguel in Buenos Aires province.[24] Though neither Ruckauf nor Rico was in his office that Saturday afternoon, the crowd condemned the impunity of those who had contributed to violence and lawlessness in Argentina. After shaming Ruckauf and Rico, the carnivalesque crowd moved on to the the Ministry of Education. The target of their ridicule there was Dr. José Luis Magnacco. An eminent gynecologist at Despido Clinic, he had supervised torture sessions to make sure that victims did not die until the torturers wanted them to. Even more important for a crowd that included some Hijos with siblings born in captivity, he had officiated at the births of children whose mothers were frequently manacled to cots while in labor and murdered after delivery. As a doctor who continues to treat patients, he drew the special wrath of the crowd, who began targeting him in mid-December, following up with weekly visits throughout January 1996 at Mitre Clinic, where he had his office. The clinic asked him to leave.[25]

The December 1995 *escrache* then moved to the house of the former director of the torture center nicknamed El Vesubio because the building emitted a steady stream of black smoke. The acrid smell and smoke resulted from burning rubber tires with cadavers of the murdered. From the former director's house, the political revelers went on to the home of another physician known to have supervised torture sessions. With this stop, they began a signature activity: throwing baggies of red paint at the walls to recall the blood spilled by those being *escrechado*. Although the demonstrators defaced property, their actions were mild compared to the violence that had overtaken their country for nearly a decade. The board that ran the building agreed and "decided to leave the stains to show that a torturer lived there."[26]

Heady with their nonviolent but raucous attacks on those untarnished by torture and murder, HIJOS finished up with two of the most hated officials of the dictatorship: Admiral Emilio Eduardo Massera and General Antonio Domingo Bussi. Admiral Massera, a member of the first military junta, was especially recognizable because of the great wealth he had accumulated by stealing property, including furniture and real estate titles, from those he persecuted. His audacity and total lack of shame about anything he had done, and his eagerness to speak about his unchanged views on television, made him an especially painful irritant. His position as the overseer of ESMA carried with it the memory of special horrors: pregnant women were brought from other torture centers to ESMA close to their delivery time. Scarcely one hundred of the almost five thousand people who passed through the doors of ESMA survived, but many of the survivors became dedicated witnesses. Though usually blindfolded, most prisoners learned to see beneath their masks. They also developed acute hearing. The official they saw or heard most often was Emilio Eduardo Massera, who seemed to enjoy interacting with the prisoners.

For this reason, Massera has been the target of many *escraches*. On 5 June 1999, for example, HIJOS led other human rights organizations in pointing out how Massera had violated the terms of his house arrest. Because of a conviction for trafficking in babies related to the kidnapping of infants, Massera and Jorge Rafael Videla, head of the original junta and the de facto president of Argentina until 1981, were put under house arrest by Judge Adolfo Luis Bagnasco. Bagnasco had sentenced Massera to remain in the rather luxurious accommodations of the Pacheco Barracks in Buenos Aires, but the Hijos learned that Massera preferred his luxurious apartment on fashionable avenida Libertador. After seeking Massera at the barracks, the crowd decided to carry out the *escrache* at his palatial home. It was clear that the police preferred to repress the *escraches,* and they bristled about the fact that under a moderate democracy, they had to identify themselves when imposing their version of the law. When a policeman started to arrest one of the demonstrators, the rest intervened, demanding that the officer show his badge. A scuffle ensued and the police, claiming that the crowd tried to seize his radio, arrested several demonstrators.

Massera fought back, bringing charges against the Hijos at the twenty-first precinct. He accused them of attempting to commit robbery, assault and battery, resisting arrest, and threatening his life. One of the Hijos said of the demonstration that "the minimum someone who commits genocide deserves is a little paint on his house." But at least Massera had to appear with his lawyer at court in order to present his charges. A human rights organization that spoke in defense of the Hijos argued that when criminals walk the streets, it is outrageous that those demanding justice are accused of disturbing the peace. He defended the *escrache* as a necessary means of carrying out the revelations that society requires.[27] The Hijos got off on a technicality.

Antonio Domingo Bussi was another target of the first *escrache* and of subsequent demonstrations by the Hijos.[28] A divisional general widely believed to have traveled to Vietnam under the auspices of the U.S. government to study torture techniques being used on the Viet Cong, Bussi seems to have been the technician who disseminated knowledge about different forms of torture to at least thirty-three clandestine centers. While Isabelita Perón was still president, Bussi had officiated over Operation Independence, supposedly directed against local guerrillas of ERP in the industrial city of Tucumán. Under the guise of rounding up "terrorists," he oversaw the decimation of dissidents, especially union activists in Tucumán.

Bussi became the military governor of Tucumán a month after the coup and continued until December 1977. Spared even the limited attention massacres and abductions attracted from foreign press in Buenos Aires, Bussi ruled Tucumán with an iron fist. An incident reported to the Argentine National Commission on the Disappeared in 1984 concerned Bussi's orchestration of executions by firing squad. Omar Eduardo Torres reported that "the first shot was fired by General Antonio Bussi. Next he made all the higher ranking officers take part. . . . Between fifteen and twenty people were murdered every fortnight."[29] Even more than Massera, Bussi seems to have benefited financially from pillaging union funds and the property of his victims. His constituency was composed of wealthy factory owners and landowners who benefited from his repression of the labor movement. Having built a political machine on the support of those he had enriched, and having destroyed most of the militant working-class leaders of two generations, Bussi was elected governor of Tucumán after democracy was restored.[30]

The Hijos were especially happy to end their first *escrache* at the mansion Bussi had acquired in a fashionable district of Buenos Aires. An Hijo writing for the organization's magazine five years later could scarcely contain his glee about playing kazoos, throwing paint, and dancing their mockery of Bussi as helicopters flew over the marchers.[31] Clearly the exuberance of the writer recalls what she and her fellow revelers felt in

1995: "We were so euphoric we couldn't go home....To carry on a bit more, to avoid ending such a glorious day, we all went to the Plaza de Once...where we finally exhausted our energy DANCING AND DANCING."[32]

Had the day- and night-long *escrache* taken place anywhere in North America or in Western Europe in the late 1960s or early 1970s, observers would have immediately likened them to Yippees, or Provos, or Situationists, or other young dissidents who ridiculed those in power while attacking them. Without knowing that Guy Debord and the Situationists had looked to the urban festival to parody consumerism and the objectification of workers, the Hijos developed a new form of urban festival to confront the old guard of torturers and those who preferred to forget. The implements of their shaming rituals were images, sounds, and symbols.[33] Nearly thirty years after the abductions began, a new generation honored their parents in their own way, by creating rituals of remembrance to pillory those who had eluded formal systems of justice. Much more than their parents, they were concerned with turning public spaces into popular forums where the merits and demerits of government could be discussed.

THE *ESCRACHE* AGAINST ASTIZ

Like all memory, that acted upon in *escraches* is partial. It could not be otherwise because, without a full accounting through trials or open public testimony designed to provide full disclosure, charges and counter-charges remain matters that are asserted and denied. The subject of the greatest infamy was former naval Captain Alfredo Ignacio Astiz, who infiltrated and betrayed the Madres de Plaza de Mayo and was well known to many survivors of ESMA. The blond, blue-eyed young man who reminded Azucena Villaflor of her son came to the Madres for solace and support one Thursday, giving his name as Gustavo Niño and claiming that his brother had been kidnapped. They never imagined that the young woman whom Niño frequently brought with him to demonstrations as his younger sister was a really a prisoner at ESMA named Silvia Labayrú.[34] He was the Judas who hugged the Madres to signal who should be abducted from Santa Cruz Church on 8 December 1977, and he shot a seventeen-year-old Swedish-Argentinian girl, Dagmar Hagelin, as she fled past a house where he had organized a stake-out. The dismissal of his case on 5 December 1986 because of the statute of limitations had galvanized Alfonsín to issue the Final Stop law that same day in order to speed the prosecution of other military personnel.

A young man of twenty-four at the time of the military coup in 1976, Astiz had risen through the ranks while infiltrating human rights groups and kidnapping people. By 1981, he was the naval attaché at the Argentine Embassy in Johannesburg. Then, as lieutenant (junior grade), he was forced to surrender to the British without firing a shot in 1982, after failing to take the island of Georgia in the Malvinas War. The campaign demonstrated the incompetence of the armed forces when their enemies were not chained to walls or reduced to jelly by torture. Even so, the end of the dictatorship left Astiz unscathed: in 1985 he was promoted to full lieutenant, and in 1988 not only became a captain in the Navy, but won a decoration for valor in his "fight against subversion."[35]

Astiz stood out in public, however, largely because of the efforts of the Madres de Plaza de Mayo and other human rights groups to publicize his crimes. Three women who had been prisoners at ESMA testified against him in a French court, which tried him in absentia and found him guilty of the murder of two French nuns, Léonie Duquet and Alice Domon, who were abducted and murdered along with three Madres and other family members of the disappeared in December 1977. Increasingly, ordinary people took notice of Astiz. At a Portuguese restaurant in Buenos Aires at the end of May 1997, a group of people in their twenties were celebrating when they noticed Astiz at a nearby table. One of the young men, a rugby player, Martín Alsogaray, the grandson of a general and the nephew of a Montonero who had disappeared, approached Astiz, who was eating with four young people. Alsogaray confronted Astiz, saying, "Son of a bitch, what are you, an assassin, doing here, freely walking the streets?" Astiz just smiled and remained seated. The young man and his friends made a scene and then exited the restaurant, saying that they were not going to eat beside an assassin.[36]

Astiz never offered any explanation or registered any remorse for what he did. A particularly visible symbol of state terror, Astiz eventually became a political liability. In January 1998, President Carlos Saúl Menem dismissed Astiz from the navy, and in March, Congress repealed the Full Stop and Due Obedience Laws. Although no one could be retried, new cases could now be brought to trial.[37]

In an attempt to improve his image, Astiz agreed to an interview with Gabriela Cerruti. The article appeared in June 1998 in the magazine *Tres Puntos,* where Astiz was quoted as having said that he remained "the man technologically most able to kill a politician or a journalist."[38] In an act of bravado, he seems to have admitted to Cerruti that "every day friends come to tell me that I ought to lead an uprising." Attempting, as torturers often did, to vindicate himself as a cultivated man who tortured and murdered in order to preserve his country, Astiz went on to say: "Do you know why a soldier kills? For love of country, for pride, for machismo, for duty."

Astiz was charged with "justifying criminal acts," a crime under Argentine law, and was ordered to appear in court at the end of February 2000.[39] Astiz maintained that Cerruti "distorted and changed the meaning of his sentences" and claimed that he had not granted an interview, but was just engaging in informal conversation. A witness on his behalf, "Zaza" Martínez, admitted that he had urged Astiz to meet with Cerruti as a means of improving his public image.

The real courtroom drama occurred even before his testimony. The hearing was set for 1 P.M., but Astiz had come into the courthouse early in the morning, when only a few police officers were around. Despite the fact that the courtroom could hold about a hundred people, at first only a few well-dressed young people were present. As Astiz was called to take his seat as the accused, the audience pulled off their shirts to reveal T-shirts that read, "Astiz is an assassin" and "Imprison those who commit genocide." Standing about six feet in front of him and the television cameras, the fifteen young people, children of those whom Astiz is believed to have murdered, shouted: "Try him for what he did, not for what he said," and "What happened to the Nazis will happen to you: wherever you go [to whatever town] we will [come after you and] track you down!" Apoplectic at the attack, Astiz rushed toward the door, which the Hijos had blocked. The police, at first taken by surprise like the rest of the audience, quickly escorted Astiz outside until they could clear the courtroom.[40] One of the demonstrators, Carlos (pseud.), whose parents were abducted when he was a month old, embraced the other children of the disappeared, who huddled together in the presence of the man who, for them, personified evil.

HIJOS's efforts at shaming former torturers have continued on the internet. True children of their generation, they use the web and e-mail connections to answer questions from all over the world about themselves and the former torturers. Starting from groups in La Plata, Córdoba, Mendoza, and Tucumán, HIJOS quickly spread to eighteen cities in Argentina and ten abroad. In 1996, the group in Venezuela established a website. Recognizing the need to use the Internet in order to get their message out beyond local and national borders, HIJOS is creating a virtual public forum that includes anyone with access to a computer. One of the principal sections of the site emanating from Spain (http://www.nodo50.org/hijos-madrid/h-portada.htm) is devoted to publicizing biographies of the torturers, providing descriptions of the torture centers based on the testimony of survivors, and offering personal accounts by members of HIJOS. Some of these appeared in Juan Gelman and Mara la Madrid's collection of reminiscences, *Ni el flaco perdón de Dios: Hijos de desaparecidos* (Not Even by the Grace of God: The Children of the Disappeared), which appeared in Argentina in 1997.

CHILEAN *FUNAS*

No group of Hijos has absorbed the spirit of the *escraches* more than the Chileans in their *funas*. The Chilean slang term *funa* means "revealing or displaying something." Beginning in September 1999, the Chileans began to demonstrate. Their predecessors, a small group of Hijos made up mostly of women, began meeting in Chile in 1996. Together with a group of activists known as Acción, Verdad, y Justicia (Action, Truth, and Justice), they organized their first demonstration downtown, near the Plaza de la Constitución, at the intersection of Huérfanos and Esperanza Streets—literally where Orphans meet Hope.[41] Almost a year after Pinochet was first detained in Great Britain, the group of young people called on survivors of the torture centers, the Agrupación de Familiares de Detenidos Desaparecidos, Families of Those Executed as Political Prisoners, feminists, and students to join together to shame the most notorious purveyors of violence.

Alejandra López is typical of the activists who engage in *funas*.[42] Raised by a politically active mother after her father, Nicolás López Suárez, a labor leader, disappeared in 1976 when she was five, she had become interested in working-class struggle and was writing a history of La Legua. La Legua, the working-class socialist center strongly committed to the Popular Unity government, had become a notorious drug center by 2000. But in 1973, La Legua, where Nieves Ayress worked before her detention, had been one of the few neighborhoods to offer armed resistance to the military coup. López, with a keen sense of history, wants to restore the memory of those times as a blueprint for the future. She knows that as many as 150,000 were tortured in Chile, out of a total population of nearly eleven million, and she feels an obligation to continue the work that previous generations began. She therefore devotes a lot of her time to participating in movements such as the *funas* in the hope of democratizing her country.

One of the first *funas* took place at the clinic of a cardiologist, Alejandro Forero Álvarez. He seems to have refined his skills in dealing with cardiac arrests while helping to resuscitate torture victims for whom DINA still had use and helping to murder those with whom the torturers had finished.[43] As activists hovered near death, he sometimes played good cop, winning their confidence and then betraying them. Other times he injected them with fatal illnesses or drugged them before they were thrown alive from helicopters. According to Pedro Alejandro Matta, a survivor of several Chilean concentration camps, including the Villa Grimaldi, many of Chile's leading cardiologists and gynecologists gained their skills by supervising torture sessions.[44]

Dr. Forero Álvarez seemed an obvious choice for a *funa*. A largely youthful crowd blowing horns went to his office at the INDISA clinic, where they had made appointments. Trying to humiliate him and publicize his past, the group made no effort to hold him at the clinic. They let him escape but made sure that his staff, neighbors, and patients knew what he had done.

Another *funa* took place in the countryside where a landowner had supervised the massacre of local workers. Knowing they could not expect participation in the rural area, where people still feared the landowner, the organizers of the *funa* rented buses and brought sixty activists to the site of the demonstration.[45] The next *funa* took place at the headquarters of the telephone company in downtown Santiago. Many leading torturers during the Pinochet dictatorship developed management skills and went on to civilian jobs in big business. Emilio Sanjuria Alvear, who had become an executive in the legal department of the privatized phone company, was the official in charge of administering the southern province of Temuco for DINA. Although he was widely believed to have been responsible for the massacre of indigenous Mapuche people under his command, those allegations had not deterred the phone company from advancing him to a high position. The activists chose the late afternoon, when crowds fill the avenue, for their demonstration. Many passers-by took the flyers and listened to the ditties the *funadores* made up to reveal the history of the man who was the subject of the shaming ritual. Another *funa* unmasked José Aravena Ruíz, "The Devil's Toy," who tortured to death four well-loved leaders of the MIR.

Operation Condor, a particular target of the Hijos, had been organized by Augusto Pinochet and the head of Chilean intelligence forces, Manuel Contreras Sepúlveda, who apparently reported directly to Pinochet, to coordinate state terrorist activities internationally. Although human rights activists and those trying to escape from repression knew by the late 1970s that people who had fled their country for safety were disappearing from their new countries, the structure of the international organization remained unclear. A hidden cache of two tons of documents, later called the Archive of Terror, was accidentally discovered in the police station of Lambare, a few miles from Asunción, Paraguay, in 1992, offering proof of what survivors had alleged: there had been an international conspiracy of the secret services of Chile, Argentina, Bolivia, Brazil, Uruguay, and Paraguay to kidnap, torture, and murder people that any of the signatories decided were their enemies. Chilean agents, for example, went to Buenos Aires to assassinate Sofía Cuthbert and her husband, General Carlos Prats González, Pinochet's predecessor as army chief-of-staff under Allende. Prats, a general committed to constitutional government who fought off the June 1973 coup attempt against Allende, could have been a credible leader of the opposition. During the last months of Spanish dictator Francisco Franco's life, he seems to have permitted Condor to carry out extraterritorial operations in Spain. Condor then established operatives in Brussels and Rome. Eugenio Berríos, a chemist who worked with Operation Condor, attempted to murder the Chilean Christian Democratic general Bernardo Leighton and his wife in Rome. And Operation Condor carried out the greatest act of terrorism on U.S. soil until the attack on the Federal Building in Oklahoma City and the World Trade Center: the 1975 assassination of Orlando Letelier and Ronni Moffitt in Washington, D.C.[46]

With Manuel Contreras finally in prison for the murder of Moffitt and Letelier, and Pinochet facing more than 150 (later, nearly 200) indictments for murder and torture, the only leader of Operation Condor who remained unscathed in the late 1990s was Captain Miguel Krassnoff Marchenko. Krassnoff had directed the José Domingo Cañas torture center, as well as the Brigada Halcón (Hawk Brigade of Chile's secret service) at Villa Grimaldi. Krassnoff had been responsible for capturing prisoners in one country and bringing them to another. He had ordered the kidnapping of Edgardo Enriquez in Argentina and Jorge Fuentes Alarcún in Paraguay and had them brought to Villa Grimaldi, which he helped run. As an experiment, he had Fuentes injected with rabies virus after he had been tortured for days in the notorious tower of the villa. Alleged to have supervised hanging a prisoner by his testicles while a fellow officer poured boiling oil on the prisoner's female comrades, who were close to death, Krassnoff prepared a list of 119 Chileans whom he had helped torture to death. With the complicity of authorities abroad, he then placed stories in the Argentine and Brazilian press claiming that the 119 had been killed during attempted guerrilla raids in those countries.[47]

Survivors portray Krassnoff as cold and calculating. Like Astiz in Argentina, Krassnoff stands out as a professional, a convinced ideologue determined to wipe out political activists and social reformers of every kind. Unrepentant and still admired by his superiors in the military, Krassnoff had gone on to become the commander of the Tucapel Regiment in the southern province of Temuco. Apparently unaware of any ethical standard about the preservation of human life, Krassnoff wrote to the local press defending one of his officers who had murdered a truck driver who had the misfortune to be blocking his way.[48] Krassnoff seemed like the perfect subject for the sixth *funa,* which would be held in conjunction with similar mobilizations elsewhere in Latin America and in Europe.

In a joint press release on the internet in May 2000, HIJOS members from Argentina, Chile, Uruguay, and Spain called for coordinated demonstrations on two continents. They invited students, labor unions, human rights organizations, and sympathetic citizens to hold *funas* and *escraches* of their own. The call suggested that people choose a site, such as the U.S. embassy, a military depot, the headquarters of a multinational corporation, an important political building, or a religious center. Describing Operation Condor as an organization dedicated to "the systematic repression and extermination of an entire generation of people of different nationalities who were struggling for social change," HIJOS asked the demonstrators to "shine a light on assassins and their accomplices." Since those guilty of violence had escaped trial and punishment, the announcement said, demonstrators should bring the force of social condemnation to bear on them by "converting their neighborhoods, their countries, and the entire world into their prison cells."[49]

Close to one thousand people in Santiago agreed that it was time to call Krassnoff to task. Since he had just been appointed director of a military hotel near avenida Providencia, Santiago's Fifth Avenue, the protesters decided to hold their *funa* there. Despite a large police presence, the dancing, music, and denunciations went on for twenty minutes. They distributed a flyer that included a thumbnail biography of Krassnoff's life, beginning with his participation in the assault on the presidential palace on 11 September 1973, and moving down his curriculum vitae to the torture centers he had run and the people he had assassinated.[50] Once the activists had finished near the hotel, they moved on to the center of the city. At Salvador Street, they stopped to give an update on other demonstrations against Operation Condor that were taking place that same day around the world.

With their noise-makers, the activists engaged in *escraches* and *funas* attempt to open up the kind of public debate that has been largely impossible elsewhere in society. Using the weapons of direct democracy, and largely depending on shaming rather than punishing those thought to be guilty of heinous crimes, the people who take part in *funas* and *escraches* also wish to open debate about the broader politics of their countries. Whether performed in person or on the web, *escraches* and *funas* seek justice. In fact, the motto of the *escraches* and *funas* is "If there is no justice, there are *escraches/funas.*" Those explaining *escraches* and *funas* say that they are concerned with justice, but they are also concerned with democracy. Those promoting *escraches* and *funas* do not want to limit the word *democracy* to questions of representative institutions; they also want to promote direct democracy, in which citizens overcome passivity to actively participate in the public arena, in which public opinion combines with public action. As one proponent of *escraches* has argued, "*Escraches* oppose the idea of action to the idea of representation; against political impunity, they shout *escrache.*"[51] The anonymous author of an article explaining the *escrache* is careful to point out that proponents do not view *escraches* as an alternative system of politics; they simply have developed the *escrache*—in the same way the Madres de Plaza de Mayo call for the disappeared to be brought back alive—as a strategy for highlighting the problems of impunity and the tendency to treat the atrocities of the dictatorship as if they simply happened and now should be forgotten. Those staging the *escraches* call for "trials and punishment," but they do not expect either.[52] Taking great pains to explain the symbolism at work in the *escrache,* they try to replace passivity with activity, chronicles with history. They want the military officers who say they didn't kill "people," but simply wiped out "subversives," to face the derision they deserve in the full glare of public opinion.

Although the HIJOS members and other young people never claim to be imitating their parents—only to be restoring the memory of them as fighters for social change—the practitioners of *escraches* and *funas* do attempt to enter the realm of guerrilla theater, albeit peacefully and at a symbolic level. Arriving late for a meeting in a noisy café in La Plata one wintry afternoon in June 2000, HIJOS member Margarita Merbilhaá giggled: "Our parents, who were highly disciplined, would have arrived on time; they would have regarded us as anarchists."[53] Many of those detained and disappeared by the Triple-A or the dictatorship were revolutionaries who were willing to take up arms in order to fight for a better society. Similar groups in Italy, Germany, and Uruguay believed that the time had come for world revolution. Other groups of young idealists in France, the United States, and the Netherlands, for example, used ridicule and collective jokes to shame those in power. One member of HIJOS called his group "an influence, an idea, something intangible, invulnerable, without an advance or a rear guard, expanding...like a gas."[54] The HIJOS branch in Argentina and the young people carrying out *funas* in Chile are deadly serious about making fun of those who still refuse to debate them. Unable to use the courts except, as at Astiz's trial, to make their presence felt, large numbers of young people have taken to the streets, where everyone is equal, to carry out participatory democracy through *escraches* and *funas*.

The young demonstrators practice the art of farce rather than melodrama; thus they caricature those they regard as grossly misusing power, those who robbed their parents of their lives and human dignity. But they refuse to see their parents as victims. Through their songs and shouts, they try to establish their own version of the truth by casting the perpetrators as ridiculous figures. By taking over public spaces for festivals, demonstrators redefine what they want through song, tambourine, or dance.[55] Repeatedly, in their actions and writings, HIJOS has argued that the goal of the *escrache* is to wake people from the passivity they developed during the dictatorship.

HIJOS wants to establish a stronger voice in the court of public opinion through their shaming rituals. Pursuing popular justice can sometimes end in vigilantism if directed against those lacking power. Gangs, such as those organized by the Triple-A or by the so called Work Group 3.3.2 of ESMA or the Hawk Brigade in Chile, used violence and prevented victims from contacting their families, having lawyers, or appearing in court. Those engaged in shaming authorities substitute shame for violence.[56] They shame them by making them confront their accusers and announcing to a larger public just what they have done. Those who want to debate their accusers in public are welcome to do so.

The carnivalesque *escraches* and *funas* replace official silences with narratives about what happened when government violence created state terror, when abductions, torture, and murder were so widespread that no one was safe. Virginia, an HIJOS member from Tucumán, recalls how her group was among the first to carry out public activity. They joined with other human rights groups and held a public funeral, symbolic of the funerals and burials that their parents were denied.

They also had a public "trial" of Bussi. Although they are children of activists, few of them had ever before taken part in public demonstrations. Virginia recalled, "This was the first time we saw so many people united around the same goal. It was a great vindication for us. And what's more, I felt myself grow calm."[57]

Of the junta members, Jorge Rafael Videla and Emilio Eduardo Massera are most frequently held responsible for the violence. From the point of view of most human rights groups, Videla, who served as head of the junta until 1981, had ultimate authority. Unable to bring him to trial after he was pardoned by Menem in 1990, human rights organizations, particularly the Abuelas de Plaza de Mayo, found another way. Documenting some 259 children of the approximately 400 said to have been taken as infants or born while their mothers were held captive, the Abuelas were able by October 2000 to match 70 with their biological families.[58] Their ingenious strategy was to charge Videla and Massera in 1998 for specific acts of trafficking in children, a charge not covered by any of the amnesties. By 2001, at least thirty more members of the armed forces and the police, including Jorge Acosta, had been indicted for kidnapping babies.[59]

The pursuit of democracy through the courts and in the streets has not been accepted by those who defend the regimes of Pinochet and the Argentine juntas. Attempts to shame those who still wield power have met with resistance. Massera lodged a complaint against HIJOS, accusing them of attempted robbery, assault, and resisting arrest during an *escrache* carried out against him on 5 June 2000. And on 19 August 2000, a right-wing deputy in Chile, Maximiano Errázuriz Talavera, formally accused the *funa* demonstrators of belonging to an "illegal organization." In Argentina, Hijos were severely beaten.[60]

JUSTICE AND REMEMBERING

Antjie Krog, the South African poet and radio commentator who covered the Truth and Reconciliation hearings in her country, has given a great deal of thought to the way one's interpretation of the truth is related to identity. She argues that "what you believe to be true depends on who you believe yourself to be."[61] Those who tortured do not want to be considered torturers. Those who survived the torture camps want to recall fighting for social justice rather than think of themselves as victims. Denigrated as subversives, they had to restore their sense of purpose or lose their identities. They had to freeze their fury in the ice of memory. Once thawed, their memory leads them to bear witness for those whose stories they lived to tell.

But memory and memorializing is not enough: the question remains of what kind of activity can most effectively democratize Chile and Argentina. When I spoke in June 2000 with Mariano Tealdi, a member of HIJOS's governing board, he was on his way to Rio de Janeiro for a conference on performance and politics.[62] Although he had never thought about the category of shaming rituals, he was fascinated by the concept, since he and the other Hijos had frequently discussed how to get public debate underway. When Argentina tried the commanders of the juntas in 1985, only eighty people a day were permitted into the courtroom. To save the former military leaders humiliation, there was no radio coverage and the trial was televised without sound. Frequently, defendants were missing, represented only by their attorneys. Although summaries of the testimonies were printed in the *Diario de juicio,* which was distributed widely, only the lawyers, defendants, and witnesses actually heard the accused. The symbolism of seeing but not hearing reversed the pattern of being blindfolded in detention, with only sound to maintain a connection to the outside world.

The procedure of the trials proved to those who wanted justice that acting in public was more necessary than ever. Realizing that news cameras respond to spectacles more than they do to "talking heads," every popular democratic or civil rights movement since the 1960s has had to consider how they should represent their struggle visually. Although shaming rituals occurred long before the existence of cameras, they are particularly well suited to substituting images for words, the visual for the verbal. Shaming rites make public the ethical failures of those in power. Acting in public engages those who prefer to stay aloof from conflict, to remain outside of the public eye. During shaming rituals, everyone must choose sides, whether they wish to or not. To force an unwilling audience to pay attention, demonstrators must act things out. Making visible what is invisible is the crux of incorporating memory of the atrocities into the collective consciousness. Even more importantly, it is in the streets, turned into open arenas for debate, that the possibilities for participatory democracy can really take hold.

Demonstrating to Remember in Spain

As HIJOS well knows, there is no time limit on seeking justice through public spectacles. Those mistreated in the past want to bear witness to what happened, and public demonstrations are an appropriate way to tell stories that have been overlooked or deliberately forgotten. So, when Augusto Pinochet was arrested in London on 16 October 1998 and held for human rights abuses, many people in Spain, as well as Chile, rejoiced. My Spanish friends embraced, drank toasts, held parties, and organized public demonstrations. For Spaniards, justice entailed not just telling the stories of how thousands of people suffered torture and death in Chile, but also telling about those who had died in prison or been executed following the Spanish Civil War. Without a reckoning of its own, Spain could finally look back on the post–Civil War period, the social movements against Franco, and the violent repression that preceded the transition to constitutional rule. In street demonstrations in 1998 and 1999, I heard youth and women, as well as men, denounce Pinochet, who ruled as dictator of Chile for seventeen years. But they also attacked Francisco Franco, who had been dead since 1975. The defenders of Franco and Pinochet, better dressed and older, also demonstrated. For many on both sides of the political divide, Pinochet did not simply represent Franco; he *was* Franco.

In the Mediterranean, where some form of fascism had once dominated Italy, France, Greece, Portugal, and Spain, only the French and the Italians were able to delve into the past. Spaniards were spared the plight of East Germans, who gained access to the records of secret police only to discover that their best friends, even their spouses, had spied on them.[1] But Spaniards, for whom the past remained largely unexamined, were also cut off from any continuity with their history, and thus from any sense of collective identity. Some countries underwent ruptures with their authoritarian pasts: Hitler committed suicide in his bunker, and Mussolini was hung by his heels in Rome. Franco, on the other hand, died peacefully in his bed after ruling Spain for thirty-seven years.

Nearly two years after Franco died, as the country slouched toward democracy, David and Martell Montgomery came to visit me in Spain. Longtime political activists, as young people they had raised money for Lincoln Brigaders fighting in Spain. As a married couple, they refused to visit Spain as long as the dictator Francisco Franco was alive. Now, in early June 1977, just before the first free elections in nearly forty years, they joined me in Barcelona. That spring Spain celebrated the legalization of political parties. Everyone went to every festival, just to hear the chants and have the opportunity to be with other people welcoming democracy.

I had been coming to Spain since 1964 to do historical research. My involvement in the country, where I spent nearly three years between 1967 and 1977, supplemented my participation in the Civil Rights, New Left, and feminist movements in the United States. In Spain, I joined furtive demonstrations in the late sixties and attended women's meetings in the early seventies. With the death of Franco and the eruption of politics, I too luxuriated in the growing sense of freedom that swept the country in the spring of 1977. The night David and Marty arrived, the Partit Socialista Unificat de Cataluña (United Socialist Party of Catalonia, PSUC) had scheduled a rally, and we decided to go. I didn't know where to get out of the subway, so I joked that we would just follow the red flags. The subway was jammed with people carrying banners and wearing baseball caps in the party's red and white colors. After a few stops, virtually everyone crowded out of the subway cars. The station echoed "Pay-Sook," the pronunciation of PSUC.

At least seventy thousand people milled around the huge municipal bull ring. The music gave way to boring speeches, but no one seemed to mind. The group that was least affected was made up of eight or nine burly guys with a grizzled old woman in the center. While everyone else wore the new insignias, she had on the black-and-white PSUC bandanna worn in the 1930s during the Spanish Civil War. When the speakers droned on too long, that group and others would interrupt and call, "Long live this" and "Down with that." The old woman joined the chants, and everyone cheered. She seemed to doze off for a while and then joined another round of chants. Finally, she initiated her own chant: "Viva el Frente Popular" (Long live the Popular Front). Everyone looked away and pretended she was not there.

The aged woman's chant recalled the Civil War, reviving unpleasant memories about how shaky alliances on the left had split apart, resulting in armed conflict followed by defeat and years of extraordinary repression. Her black-and-white scarf symbolized her commitment to the principles she had embraced in her youth. She must have hidden the scarf when Franco's Nationalist troops entered Barcelona in January 1939. I wondered who would listen to her chants and stories, when the Spanish Civil War was the elephant in the living room—a hovering presence no one wanted to discuss—during that democratic spring.

Forgetting became a sign of patriotism in Spain of the 1970s. Franco never had to answer for the violence his Nationalist coalition committed during and after the war, and neither he nor his advisers ever had to admit to their use of state terror during the long transition to constitutional rule. Historian Sebastian Balfour has argued that "a kind of collective amnesia descended on Spain...[as] part of the price of the peaceful transition to democracy."[2] Political theorist Paloma Aguilar Fernández claims that pretending to forget became a way to avoid reviving the bloody animosity of the Spanish Civil War and its aftermath.[3] Just before the country voted in the June 1977 elections, I remarked to a Spanish political scientist that hammering out a constitution and holding municipal and regional elections should have preceded national elections to the Cortes (parliament). He blanched and angrily responded: "Yes, and then we'd have had another Civil War." Certainly the Spanish Civil War was with us daily. When a woman dropped an egg in my neighborhood grocery store in Barcelona in 1968, the storekeeper reassured her that her accident "was not as bad as the Civil War." Where I lived, in the Gothic Quarter, the church of San Felipe Neri was still riddled with mortar shells, as were buildings near the port. When I tried to get brown sugar to make cookies, the storekeeper said he didn't keep brown sugar because it reminded his customers of the 1940s and 1950s, when brown bread and brown sugar were all people could get. The sense of tragedy pervaded ordinary conversations, leaving little space for individual stories.

The disappearance of women's stories is particularly striking, because so many women participated in the Civil War. The *milicianas* had fought as soldiers; Dolores Ibarruri, widely known as La Pasionaria, had been a leader of the Communist Party; anarchist women had an organization called Mujeres Libres, which was devoted to extending the meaning of the war to include winning a place for women as full participants in society.[4] Following the Spanish Civil War, hundreds of thousands of supporters of the former government, including thousands of women, faced firing squads, and hundreds of thousands more found themselves in French concentration camps and in prisons. Squeezed into cells meant for a single person, women lived close to death, which they irreverently referred to with a diminutive, "la Pepa." Mothers were frequently jailed with their babies, hidden from the public where no one could find them. Each afternoon at 5 P.M., the fascists came with their lists. Most prisoners had until late afternoon to discover their fate; mothers of infants knew earlier because officials came around midday to take their babies from them. Cellmates could only stop their hearts from beating long enough to hear whether their own name was being called. Even forty years later, women such as Angeles García-Madrid remembered the deathwatch as if reliving it each day.[5] Though the threat of imminent death diminished in the late 1940s and 1950s, as Franco courted Europe and the United States, political activists such as the young Puig Antich were executed well into the 1970s.

The obliteration of all these stories became part of the culture of forgetting that overtook Spain. In María Dolors Calvet's introduction to Giuliana Di Febo's book on women in the Spanish resistance, Calvet claimed that it was necessary "not only to retrieve the past to understand the present, but also in order to recognize that...women, contrary to what has been presumed over the years, have been historical actors."[6]

Even if some understood how gender helped shape politics in the past, few took women's public mobilizations into account. In fact, the social history of the last twenty-five years of the Franco dictatorship, especially the history of its last five years, has hardly been studied. Most historians and political scientists have focused on the negotiations among men representing different political and economic interests.[7] Analyzing how the ribbons are cut at the opening ceremonies for a bridge provides little insight about construction work. Similarly, by truncating the history of the last decade of Francoism, critics overlook the importance of public mobilizations in bringing negotiators to the table.

Franco's regime, which began with massive executions following secret detentions, ended with more refined, slightly modernized versions of the same practice. Members of clandestine parties and unions were routinely rounded up, tortured, and raped, as Constantina Pérez and her daughter were during a strike in the coal mining region of Asturias in 1963. But when Pérez died two years later, the funeral became an occasion for people to resist authority while mobilizing in her honor, despite the government's prohibition of public demonstrations.[8]

The protracted struggle for democracy in Spain entailed long periods of clandestinity, as well as campaigns against fascism and authoritarianism. Activists, who were unable at the time to document what they were doing, remembered and later recorded their stories, some of which appeared in narratives recounting how large numbers of working-class homemakers and young cultural rebels risked their lives in decentralized women's movements to fight against the regime. Without consideration of the networks that these women created to transform the country and their own lives, it is impossible to explain the seemingly rapid resurgence of democratic movements immediately following the death of Franco.

Lack of clarity about what *democracy* would mean after nearly forty years of authoritarian rule turned the word into a matter of contention. If the term *democracy* at first simply meant freedom from repression, it quickly shifted to incorporate political and social justice. For some, democracy meant the right to unionize and to give workers—generally thought of as male—increased political power. Others hoped to regain rights as citizens who could vote for the political party of their choice. The parties would in turn define political and social goals.

For at least a decade before the death of Franco, women throughout Spain developed associations to deal with social goals widely thought to be synonymous with democracy. In Asociaciones de Amas de Casa (Homemakers Associations), women's divisions of Asociaciones de Vecinos (Neighborhood Associations), and groups such as the Movimiento Democrático de Mujeres (Democratic Movement of Women, MDM), as well as women's professional societies, select groups of Spanish women confronted problems that affected them as wives and mothers. Other groups, concerned with providing women access to an expanded political sphere, worked to ensure them full rights as citizens. Both groups increasingly spoke about birth control, including abortion, and legal changes to decriminalize adultery and prostitution. For many women, the word *democracy* became a catchall for the right to a good and just life for women as well as men.

Relatively ignorant about the roles women had played in the long, secret struggles against Franco, many women in the 1970s welcomed an introduction to their own history. I remember bringing the autobiography of La Pasionaria, which had been re-released in English in 1977, to friends in Spain, who knew it existed but could not find it.[9] I also remember my thrill in discovering three issues of the journal *Mujeres Libres* (Free Women) at the Hoover Institution of War, Revolution, and Peace at Stanford University.[10] As with other women's movements in the 1970s, Spanish women began to search for their foremothers and tried to imagine a public history that included women. One of the most important books of that period, *Resistencia y movimiento de mujeres en España 1936–1976* (Resistance and the Women's Movement in Spain, 1936–1976), was by an Italian scholar, Giuliana Di Febo, who became a professor at the University of Rome. Influenced by the emergence of feminism in Italy in the 1970s, she also recognized the importance for Spain of the memoirs and oral histories that were just beginning to appear in Italy by women who had participated in the resistance against fascism.[11] Di Febo's book on women in the Spanish resistance was itself a time warp. The testimonies, gathered mostly in 1976–77, begin with memories of the period 1939–49, the decade after the end of the Spanish Civil War. But the women she interviewed were participants in the eruption of public political life that accompanied Spain's move toward a new form of constitutional democracy in the mid-1970s.

Many of us in the field of oral history have been sensitive to the fact that memories shift and change, depending on what the person hopes to achieve by telling his or her story. We want the story, but the storyteller needs to tell it to an audience and get validation. The relationship is intimate and may go on for a long time. The historian often has the benefit of academic titles and freedom, not to speak of money. But the narrator has had a glimpse into history. What she remembers depends on how her story fits her individual or collective identity.[12] She may need to remember because she is proud of something she achieved in the past. She may need to bear witness to atrocities she survived but others didn't. She may want to establish some connection between the person she was and the person she is now. In some cases, the narrative tells more about the intervening time than about the past or the present.

Most critics agree that memoirs and oral histories represent attempts to impose a certain logic on the past. The past is reshaped not only in relation to current circumstances, but also in relationship to the process of becoming. Activities or actions about which the subject is ashamed get repressed; experiences, not really noted at the time, take on significance because of present conditions. The testimonies and written material of the women with whom Di Febo spoke in 1977 seem to refer at least in part to their hopes for post-Franco Spain. Twenty years later, in 2000, when Di Febo reflected on her book in the Spanish women's historical journal *Arenal,* she had entirely different insights, which help explain the rebirth of public life and democratic movements in the 1960s and 1970s.[13]

By 2000 Di Febo realized that the women she interviewed had created a myth of leftist solidarity, a collective identity, to supercede the sectarianism of the Civil War. During the war, Anarchists, Socialists, Republicans, and Communists fought internecine struggles and called each other fascists. They even engaged in pitched battles with one another behind the lines in Barcelona and Málaga in May 1937. The women Di Febo interviewed, by beginning their narratives after the end of the war, bypassed their animosities to focus on the united struggle against Franco.

One of Di Febo's first informants was Manolita del Arco, a Communist militant who served eighteen years in prison and then waited for her husband, who spent an additional eight years behind bars.[14] She retained her identity as a political activist involved in public demonstrations. She suggested other militants whom Di Febo could interview, thereby skewing the testimonies toward people she liked and respected, presumably those who shared her views. The first person plural employed by most of the women indicated to Di Febo the strength of these women's sense of collective identity and their trust in Di Febo as one of them. The narrators told about how they survived as political prisoners, committed activists, and women who constituted a community.[15] Like Nieves Ayress, most of the women maintained a fierce loyalty to those women who had made personal sacrifices for the good of their comrades. Like the woman with the black-and-white bandanna, many of those who talked to Di Febo constructed a past that linked the present to the future.

Surrounding herself with male comrades, the old woman at the PSUC rally may never have experienced the female solidarity that became such an important part of the story Di Febo's colleagues wanted to tell. One image that appears frequently is the mother as prisoner: a woman whose nursing child is ripped away from her before her execution, or who gives birth in prison or in one of the concentration camps France set up on its southern border to prevent Spanish refugees from passing over the frontier. Other mother-prisoners were women whose children were outside prison, living with friends or relatives or on their own. The women who gave their stories to Di Febo in 1977 took the issue of a triple obligation—as mother, political militant, and citizen—into their accounts of triumph over suffering. To a degree not found in the usual political hagiographies—the one on Dolores Ibarruri, "La Pasionaria," for example—the women remembered their guilt as well as their pride in committing themselves to causes larger than themselves.

Di Febo was struck by the degree to which women who had suffered the worst retribution Franco could exact lacked rancor or desire for vengeance. In fact, their main goal in speaking to her, she thought, was to enhance the memory of a community of men and women who had shared strong political commitments. Since authoritarian governments generally lack any universal vision—committing themselves instead to idealizing a specific race or nationality or to negating the social aspirations of others—even the mere idea of a collective goal can sometimes help undermine authoritarian states. Many of the people with whom Di Febo spoke wanted to contribute to the historical record in the hope that their sacrifices and achievements would gain recognition. To that end, they gave Di Febo copies of letters that had been preserved and notebooks and journals that they, like male political prisoners, had written while they were in prison. Many hid these recollections during the years of repression; the Communist writer Carlotta O'Neill, for example, destroyed and rewrote her memoir four times. The women were finally ready to take their places in a history they had helped to create.

Janus-faced, many of the women Di Febo interviewed also had their eye on the future. Their interest in imposing certain interpretations of the past figured in their determination to help shape democratic politics once Francoism had ended. But they needed to adapt their identities to new political exigencies. For example, many of those giving testimony had belonged to centralized political parties in which there was very little debate. Their time in prison and afterward introduced them to new kinds of democratic practices. By 1976 and 1977, their experiences organizing themselves in independent associations and groups that sometimes engaged in street demonstrations gave them a sense of authority they had never before enjoyed. The stories they told about their experiences enhanced their position as political actors capable of defining the terms of debate in a democratized Spain.

The so-called transition to democracy in Spain is usually considered to have occurred between 1973, when the Basque guerrilla group known as ETA (Euskadi Ta Askatasuna, Basque Homeland and Freedom) blew up the car of the prime minister, Admiral Luis Carrero Blanco, Franco's designated successor, and 1982, when Socialist Felipe González was elected president. Actually, the transition can be said to have begun during the early 1950s and 1960s. In the Spanish case, at

least, contradictions in gender brought about by the authoritarian, patriarchal state helped define democracy for women. Roughly speaking,
paternalist policies attempted to wed women of all classes to the state.
A governmental policy promoted domesticity but at the same time
forced women into state service.[16] And discriminatory laws interfered
with mothers' ability to protect their children. Taken together, these im-
pelled women of various classes to oppose Francoism. Their antagonism took the form of campaigns to reduce the high cost of living, win
amnesty for political prisoners, and transform the adultery law, which
discriminated against women seeking custody of their children. In fact,
it was in defense of their families that women in Asturias, the Basque
Country, and Cataluña organized the first acts of resistance against the
government, when the cost of living rose too high in 1947.[17]

COLLECTIVE ACTION AND MASS MOBILIZATIONS
OF SPANISH WOMEN

After the Spanish Civil War ended in 1939, Franco's Nationalist forces
extended the reign of terror to the whole country. My friend Enric
Fuster's father had been the mayor of an anarchist pueblo outside of Valencia. His mother participated in village meetings in which local adults
discussed how to spend scarce resources. In 1936, Enric's mother and
her women friends were generally thrifty: they knew they had to put together meals out of the fruits, vegetables, and meat they could produce
or butcher in the village. But as poor women, they also had hopes for
how the Republic might transform their lives: none of the women had
ever had silk stockings, and each wanted a pair. The men ridiculed them
and reasoned with them. The women insisted: they wanted bread and
roses too.[18] Throughout the period after the fascist conquest of her village in 1938, which brought the arrest of her husband for being mayor,
she held on to her stockings. She brought her husband food in prison
and managed to support the family by herself during his three years of
incarceration. But as late as 1968, she proudly showed me her stockings.[19] She had also, without being "political," kept up her interest in
popular democracy. Not until the 1960s did women like her again insist
that democracy might hold special as well as equal promise for women.

   To some extent, the Franco government created the networks through
which many women mobilized in the 1960s and 1970s. Franco—who,
like many authoritarian nationalists, fascists, protofascists, or corpo-
ratists, wanted to dissolve any institution that mediated between indi-

viduals and the state—radically transformed the lives of Spanish women. While his government sought to return women to domestic life, it also wanted to overcome family and even church control over women. At the same time as the Franco government prohibited divorce and contraception and criminalized abortion and adultery, it forced all single, upwardly mobile women into the Sección femenina de la Falange (Women's Division of the Falange), drawing them away from church and family.

While women were drawn into participation in public service, the country remained a pariah: having sent the Blue Division to aid Hitler on the eastern front, Franco's Spain was barred from joining the United Nations, and it was not included in the Marshall Plan. Out of choice and necessity, in the immediate postwar period Spain pursued a policy of isolationism—called autarchy--in politics and economics. But during the early 1950s, the United States began to view Spain as a bulwark against communism and the ideal place for strategic air command and nuclear bases for the Cold War. Following a loan in 1951 and a military pact with the United States in 1953, Spain emerged from its economic isolation and entered a period of development paid for by the super-exploitation of the working class. Without the protection of democratic unions or the right to strike, male and female workers labored for long hours at low wages. According to Sebastian Balfour, many people were reduced to subsistence levels: "In 1950 meat consumption in Spanish cities reached only *half* the levels urbanites had consumed in the period from 1922–26, and the working-class population ate half the amount of bread it had consumed in 1936."[20]

The economic situation of women was particularly bad. Women's wages were generally half those of men. Balfour has calculated that "a semi-skilled male textile worker had to work a whole eight-hour day to purchase a dozen eggs, while an unskilled woman worker could barely earn enough to buy a loaf of bread."[21] Undoubtedly, the trolley boycott in Barcelona during the first week in March 1951 grew in response to the indignation fare hikes caused the working-class population of the city.[22] Working-class women, who were active in the boycott, found support among middle-class women. Many middle-class women lived in genteel poverty because their fathers, brothers, and husbands in Cataluña were considered traitors for defending the legally elected Spanish Republic and resisting the ultimately victorious Nationalists during the Spanish Civil War.

At a time when bread, sugar, and other foods were still being rationed, the national government squeezed Barcelona even more when it announced in late January 1951 that trolley fares in that city alone would go up 30 percent on the first of March. Throughout the month of February, men and women passed around clandestine announcements on small pieces of tissue paper telling about the proposed fare hike and asking people to boycott the trolleys.[23] The notes, which circulated especially freely in the big markets where women shopped daily, told people to make eight copies and pass them on. As February proceeded, the number of trolley passengers diminished substantially. Isabel Vicente, an activist who had been tried by Franco's Special Tribunal Against Masonry and Communism, had spent seven years in prison, regaining her freedom only in 1948.[24] On her release, she got a job as a worker in the Sadeta textile factory in Gracia, Barcelona's hand-manufacturing center. Throughout February she and her coworkers promoted the trolley strike by distributing messages clandestinely. Then on the first day "at five in the morning along with my coworkers on the first shift, we...seal[ed] off the street in front of a factory and closed it down. And then we ran to the other factories so that the other women factory workers would see us and be encouraged to follow our example. It was a complete success," she later boasted to Giuliana Di Febo.[25]

Calling for "Bread, peace, and freedom" and shouting "Death to Franco," crowds gathered all over the city. Even though public assemblies were illegal, groups of young people marched down Las Ramblas on 1 March and threw rocks at the almost empty trolleys that were passing. Men and women walked to work despite icy rain. Women of all classes took over downtown streets, as the police arrested or attacked any men they found in groups. Using the cover of a soccer game on 4 March, men, women, and children joined a large demonstration, which the police and soldiers brutally repressed. The crowd retaliated by overturning a trolley and setting it on fire. Even though the minister of public works issued a temporary fare reduction on 6 March, the local population was outraged that the authorities had killed one demonstrator, wounded twenty, and arrested ninety-eight, among them Isabel Vicente.[26]

On Sunday, 12 March, the newspapers ended their news blackout, claiming repeatedly that the boycott had ceased. They also reported a mobilization of almost 300,000 men, women, and children, who were marching toward the civic and commercial center in downtown from all the working-class and lower-middle-class districts of the city, singing their defiance. With such numbers and so many women and children, the authorities were intimidated, but later that night, police and soldiers arrested men found in small groups. The conservative newspaper, *La*

Vanguardia, wrote that at 11 A.M. on 13 March 1951, large numbers of "communist agitators"—presumed to be men—were shielded by women and children. The newspaper accused the women of following a timeless tradition of putting their own and their children's bodies between the police and the demonstrators.[27] Authorities were caught in a bind: although they arrested some women militants, such as Isabel Vicente, attacking women and children could be considered a massacre at a time when Spain was trying to regain its standing among European countries and was negotiating for loans from the United States. Viewing the boycott as a consumer rebellion at a time when the population was close to starvation, the government backed off to save face. Recognizing defeat, Franco ordered a return to the earlier trolley fares and replaced the mayor and governor of the province with other military men. Women had established a pattern for publicly shaming the authoritarian state and setting the stage for democratization.

Women have periodically engaged in street demonstrations in Spain, as they have throughout the world, especially when food, fuel, housing, or other quality of life issues were at stake. The trolley boycott was tied to other hardships.[28] Government corruption contributed to the black market, causing prices for basic foodstuffs to go sky-high. Taking matters into their own hands, some women attacked food sellers in the markets, contributing to a rumor that "housewives will refuse to renew their ration cards (on the ground that they are useless anyway), and will wreck shops that refuse to sell at ration prices without cards."[29] The movement against the increased trolley fares seemed to engage women as a group, without reference to class, race, or religion. In fact, though seeming to act only as women, wives, or perhaps as mothers, longtime political activists such as Isabel Vicente fought alongside less politically conscious women for the needs of the entire community. By demonstrating, they brought a new kind of public into existence and changed the terms of the debate. Men resisting the fare hikes would have appeared as political adversaries, communists trying to discredit the government, but the addition of women and children to street demonstrations transformed the rhetoric of resistance.

HOMEMAKERS, NEIGHBORS, AND DEMOCRATIC WOMEN

The Franco government was well aware of the need to win women over to its side, if only to indoctrinate future generations. To a degree seldom acknowledged, Spanish fascist programs ripped women from their families and drew them into relationships with the state. In an effort to gain support even from the least politicized women, the government launched the Asociaciones de Amas de Casa (Homemakers Associations) in 1963, under the auspices of the Sección Femenina (Women's Division) of the Falange. These organizations, which brought housewives under the control of middle-class women, helped some women gain social and political skills that they could put to other purposes. Struggling to help their families survive in burgeoning cities that lacked social services and fighting against the rising cost of living, some women took their identity as housewives as a license to clean up the mess in their neighborhoods and their country by joining Asociaciones de Vecinos (Neighborhood Associations) organized by workers from the clandestine unions. With the increased repression of those active in the underground union movement, formerly apolitical women campaigned for amnesty. In the course of fighting to free their relatives, they began to struggle for themselves and other women as well.

The Falange was a fascist party founded by José Antonio Primo de Rivera, son of Spain's former dictator, Miguel Primo de Rivera (1923–30). After the Civil War, Franco transformed the Falange into a corporate body, a state-dominated union in which workers were forced to submit to compulsory arbitration with their employers. In effect, all conflicts were resolved by fiat of Falange officials. Lacking the right to strike, workers had little leverage against abusive conditions. Nonetheless, beginning in 1947, in a dangerous but ultimately successful strategy, leftist workers began to infiltrate the fascist structure, disseminating ideas about workers' rights and struggling for dignity on the job.

Along with managing all workers, the Falange had another face: directing social services through the Auxilio Social, founded in 1937 to do support work behind Nationalist lines. After 1939, that social work passed to the Sección Femenina, which organized women of all classes. From 1940 on, all single women between the ages of seventeen and thirty-five had to participate for six months in the social service section of the Sección Femenina. Designed to reach women who did not voluntarily support the Falange, this service included three months of indoctrination into fascist ideas and three months of volunteer work in orphanages, hospitals, and other public institutions.[30] Those requiring certification from the state—a driver's license, passport, diploma, or a job in the civil service—had to show proof that they had served the party. All of the women college students I knew in the early 1970s had served their time, and most resented the indoctrination they received.

According to Giuliana Di Febo, "Only married women, nuns, widows,...war orphans, and, significantly, those women with eight unmarried siblings" were exempt.[31] The Sección Femenina became a vast feminine domestic army ensuring that Franco's cultural messages would be spread to women in every region of Spain. Efforts to get beneath the surface to see what this service meant in the lives of ordinary women have just begun,[32] but anecdotal evidence indicates that, for some women at least, contact with other women provided them with social skills that they later put to other political purposes. Trying to cement women's loyalty to the state, the Francoist government helped draw Spanish women into public life, where ideas of democracy could incubate.

The Falange also became involved in indoctrinating housewives. As early as 1940, the Falange created schools for homemakers *(escuelas de hogar)* to train women to be good wives and mothers according to middle-class values. Ostensibly intending to improve household hygiene and reduce infant mortality, the officials of the Sección Femenina also tried to inculcate piety and respect for authority.[33] In addition, as in liberal democracies well into the 1960s, every female student had to take a full complement of courses in home economics before receiving her high school diploma.

Enhancing women's commitment to maintaining hearth, household, and order assumed even greater political importance as urbanization accelerated. In 1956, in the wake of urban revolts in Madrid and the Basque Country, the government created a Ministry of Housing and placed it under the control of the Falange. Fearing a connection between social struggle and urbanization, which brought 440,000 additional people to Madrid alone between 1950 and 1960,[34] the government put its faith in housewives. To counteract housewives' attempts to pursue their own interests, the Homemakers Associations attached a patriotic purpose to women's domestic skills. By providing raw materials, training, and places for women to meet, the associations inculcated a collective identity that tied women to the regime. Since only about 13 percent of Spanish women worked outside the home in 1960 and women were usually forced to give up their job when they married, the Homemakers Associations provided a bulwark against reform by honoring women who deferred to patriarchy and wed themselves to the fatherland.

In actuality, in some cases the opposite occurred. With the formation of the Homemakers Associations, the government unwittingly initiated the development of social networks outside the home for lower-middle-class and working-class women. By participating in these Falange-run organizations starting in 1963, small groups of women acquired skills for working collectively that they could apply to other goals. Like the Housewives Associations launched by the Chilean Radical Party in 1947 (see Chapter 2), the Homemakers Associations in Spain created a terrain where party leaders could shape the views of lower-middle-class and working-class women. But in the Chilean Housewives Associations, and subsequently the Chilean Christian Democratic Mothers Centers, women also learned to use networks established for other purposes to fight for their own demands.

By 1970, official associations in Spain incorporated eight million homemakers, with thirty groups in Madrid alone.[35] With official sanction, housewives who were distressed about the increasing cost of living and the miserable conditions in the new working-class neighborhoods ringing Spanish cities formed their own networks. Independent groups of homemakers mobilized, building upon connections to neighbors and a growing familiarity with police practices to express dissatisfaction with their miserable standard of living. Women activists were able to fight back. For example, when prices began to rise rapidly in 1975 and inflation reached 18 percent, homemakers associations in Madrid boycotted the markets. To reprimand them, the government outlawed all such associations for three months.[36]

On the labor front, in 1964 factory workers engaged in clandestine organizing drives for Comisiones Obreras (Workers' Commissions) around auto plants in Barcelona and metallurgical plants in Madrid.[37] Beginning in 1965, men and women from the underground unions formed Asociaciones de Vecinos (Neighborhood Associations) in the new working-class districts all over Spain. At first, the majority of leaders were men, although women constituted most of the members. Since the main activity of the Neighborhood Associations was to resist increases in the cost of food and rent—precisely the kind of issues that preoccupied homemakers—and because women spent more time at home, they quickly shaped the local issues with which the Asociaciones de Vecinos were concerned. Over the decade, women in public housing and squatter communities began to take an active part in making decisions that affected their own lives. Their confidence in direct democracy grew accordingly.[38] By 1977, when I spoke to women in Asociaciones de Vecinos in Carabanchel, near Madrid, they referred to the need to reduce the costs of food, but they also demanded childcare and schools for their children.[39]

As workers of both sexes organized clandestinely, they faced intense repression. Illegal strikes followed a rapid increase in the cost of living in 1967 and 1968. Those whom police suspected of being leaders faced repeated arrest, frequently accompanied by torture. Many of the under-ground working-class leaders belonged to the clandestine Spanish Communist Party (Partido Comunista de España, PCE), which encouraged women to contact local bishops to beg for amnesty for all political prisoners, including their family members.

Some women began to venture out of their neighborhoods to visit imprisoned relatives, and they met others in the same situation. Groups in Barcelona, including some from the clandestine PSUC, Catholic organizations, and members of the underground Catalan Socialist Party, began to recognize one another. Often alone and lonely, some of the women began meeting on Saturday afternoons.[40] After a while, they began to call themselves Mujeres Democráticas to link the idea of liberating their relatives from prison with the democratization of Spain.

With the increasing arrests of sons, daughters, and husbands involved with the underground Workers Commissions in Madrid, women there formed the Movimiento Democrático de Mujeres (Democratic Movement of Women, MDM).[41] They too started to meet to talk about issues of common interest. Beginning with general discussions of how to survive when the chief breadwinner was in prison, the women quickly moved to general questions of democracy and specific problems they faced as women. Some groups linked their needs with an imperative for social change. Marisa Castro worked around the mines and metallurgical plants of Asturias with women who, though not themselves members of clandestine political parties, had mobilized against the police during the strikes of 1962 and 1964. Their husbands and children were members of clandestine unions, especially the Communist Party's Workers' Commissions. As the women worked with the political parties to liberate their relatives, they opened up space to express their heightened sense of themselves as participants in public decision-making. Castro believed that "many of the women of the PCE [were] conscious that although the struggle against the dictatorship [was] fundamental, they did not want the struggle for the rights of women to be overlooked."[42] The women of MDM included an improved personal life among these goals. Maruja Cazcarra and other clandestine Communist members of MDM in Zaragoza learned about Esperanza Martínez, who had been a guerrilla in Castellón in the early 1950s. She was arrested in 1952 and spent over a decade in prison without any gifts or letters from relatives until the local MDM chapter adopted her. They persuaded an older sympathizer, Victoria Martínez, to claim to be Esperanza's aunt. Since only blood relatives could visit or provide gifts to prisoners, the local MDM became Esperanza's surrogate family, bringing her back into the community of women. After her release from prison in 1965, Esperanza settled in Zaragoza and joined the MDM.[43]

Without really questioning why they had decided to help a woman, these largely left-wing women increasingly viewed women's emancipation as part of a united struggle for the democratization of Spain. They were not alone. Left-wing parties led campaigns to overthrow the dictatorship, and leftist Lucía González argued that "women must participate in political struggle in order to examine the special conditions of women; I do not consider it possible to have feminism without politics."[44] As social conditions worsened in the 1970s, many women inside and outside the political parties mobilized to get their needs met.

Just as the underground workers' movement had infiltrated the labor syndicates of the Falange, MDM began to infiltrate the official Homemakers Associations. MDM set up debates and meetings to discuss health care, education, and social conditions in working-class neighborhoods, such as Ventas, Carabanchel, and Chamartín around Madrid. Within a short time, the same activities spread to Valencia, Málaga, Alicante, and Castellón, until the movement swept as far as Valladolid in the north and Albacete in the south.[45] Although the government was surely aware of the growing cohesion of MDM groups all over Spain in the late 1960s, apparently authorities did not at first regard them as a sufficient threat to warrant repression.

An autonomous feminist movement began to develop alongside the social movement of women led by the MDM. Though obviously concerned with repression and the increasing cost of living, many women also began to emphasize the need to decriminalize contraceptives, abortion, and extramarital sex.[46] According to Amparo Moreno, one of the leading historians of the early Spanish women's movement, as early as 1967, women had organized a drive that secured 1,500 signatures on a letter to the government calling for reform of the civil and criminal codes. They particularly wanted to change laws that made adultery a criminal act and prohibited divorce and the dissemination of birth control. The signatories called for equal opportunity in work and education, the creation of free, high-quality childcare centers, and equal wages for equal work.[47] For many participants in Spain's social movements, there was no need to distinguish between democratization of the health, legal, economic, and social systems and the call for full citizenship for women.

MDM TAKES TO THE STREETS

In the late 1960s and early 1970s, while citizens groups grew in strength, repression intensified. Traveling by car in 1971 with some friends and their teenaged children to Santander, in the Basque Country, I personally witnessed police searches. As in Argentina and Chile at that time, youth was suspect in Euskadi (the Basque Country). Young people were considered guilty until proven innocent whether or not they belonged to ETA and whether or not there was evidence that an alleged ETA member had participated in a crime. Authorities sought to make an example of ETA, which claimed responsibility in 1968 for assassinating Melitón Manzanas, the reviled director of the Brigada Política Social (Political Police) in the Basque Country. Manzanas was widely reputed to be a torturer who was especially interested in women activists, according to the *New York Times*.[48] Following the assassination, the military police arrested fifteen ETA members, including Juana Dorronsoro Ceberio, age fifty-two, and Iziar Aizpura, a girl of fifteen,[49] and kept them in prison, where they underwent torture for two years. The government alleged that six of the accused had planned the assassination. The fifteen, accused of "banditry and terrorism," were to be judged in a military court in Burgos on 2 December 1970.[50] The symbolic center of fascism in Spain, Burgos had been the seat of Franco's government during the Spanish Civil War. It regained its reputation for repression when prosecutors called for death sentences for six of the conspirators and a total of five hundred years incarceration for the remaining nine.

The lack of due process, the years of prison and torture, and the summary military trials in which the prisoners were charged on the basis of confessions made under torture were reminiscent of the proceedings that followed the Nationalist victory in 1939. Viewing democratization as its principal goal, MDM led popular mobilizations throughout Spain to save the victims of the Burgos trial. On 3 November 1970, moving quickly to reach the maximum number of people before the police arrived, three hundred women from MDM marched into traffic in Madrid and called for freedom, democracy, and an end to the death penalty. A month later, another group of women silently marched with signs calling for commutation of the death sentences against the six alleged terrorists. Because of pressure from within Spain and abroad, Franco mobilized huge demonstrations to support his regime. Crowds of workers bused in from their factories and dignitaries from various Nationalist and Falangist organizations marched down the Paseo del Prado, Madrid's main thoroughfare, with signs saying, "Who cares about foreign opinion" and "Throw Europe in the garbage." But Franco did, in fact, care about foreign opinion, and, in a dramatic pre–New Year's announcement on 30 December 1970, he commuted the sentences of the ETA defendants. That day, women from MDM organized an impromptu demonstration, heartened by the victory they had helped achieve. While they were celebrating, they beat empty casserole dishes to protest the high cost of living.[51]

A year before right-wing women in Chile took up this symbolic practice, MDM women had beaten pots and pans for a very different purpose. Through their actions, MDM and its supporters argued for a connection among the reforms they desired: the right to unionize, to gather in public, and to elect their own political representatives. Building upon a vision of social transformation, MDM also demanded the free, high-quality childcare centers and social services they required as mothers.

MDM began to change from within. With close ties to the underground Communist Party and to the Brotherhood of Workers of Catholic Action (Hermandades Obreras de Acción Católica, HOAC), a Christian social welfare group, MDM was caught between two movements that applauded women's commitment to social change but penalized women who delved too deeply into issues of sexual liberation or the struggle between the sexes. Marisa Castro recruited for MDM: "I began to organize in the working-class neighborhoods, with the wives of workers, and also with rural women. Everything was illegal. Normally when I called a meeting of women it was to speak of "women's things": birth control, sexuality, [and] children."[52] While pursuing changes in the legal system, including the decriminalization of prostitution, birth control became a topic of interest. Causing a rift that would gradually drive the women from Catholic Action out of the organization, the majority of MDM members called for free distribution of birth control information and devices. Couching their proposals in the language of reform, MDM eventually proclaimed the emancipation of women as part of their vision of a democratic society.

Fearful of losing their hard-won place in the movement for democracy and committed to amnesty for their imprisoned relatives, MDM was reluctant to raise cultural questions about the relationship between the sexes. The program for the third MDM conference, held clandestinely in October 1971, revealed fissures dividing MDM from the feminists. As the meeting opened, MDM's statement of purpose declared that "in contrast with other feminine movements in America and Europe, the

Democratic Movement of Women does not propose a separate women's movement but [supports] activities tied to other democratic sectors of the country that are fighting against the dictatorship."[53] Confident that women could eventually overcome the machismo of the men in the unions and the leftist political parties, these women fervently hoped that they could transform their situation as women from within the left.

PROTESTS AGAINST THE ADULTERY LAWS

Democratic public opinion grew like mushrooms around the Francoist state, and MDM coordinated the democratic women's organizations in Spain in the period just before Franco's death on 20 November 1975. Calling on women from the various Homemakers Associations, the Neighborhood Associations, and disparate independent groups of students and professionals, MDM mobilized to fight for social justice and women's rights. When the Franco government chose Sección Femenina to gather information about Spanish women for the United Nations Decade of Women in 1975, MDM protested and organized clandestine women's groups in demonstrations designed to raise issues about education, working conditions, and the quality of life. In an effort to have women tell a more accurate story about the condition of women in Spain, they scheduled the first nationwide women's conference to take place clandestinely in a convent just outside Madrid on 8–10 December 1975. By chance, Franco died three weeks before the feminists met.

The conference split between those fighting against patriarchy and for expanding options for women's sexuality—that is, fighting for fundamental cultural transformations associated with feminism—and those committed, as the MDM was, to improving the conditions of working-class women on the job and compelling the left to grant women as a group a place in the democratic struggle.[54] Antedating feminist battles about equality and difference that would be waged in Europe and the Americas in the 1980s,[55] the Spanish women's movement divided over what issues to emphasize. In 1975, MDM came down firmly on the side of equal rights, especially equal pay for equal work, and an end to sexual harassment on the job. It called for childcare centers and the distribution of birth control through the public health service. Feminists called for abortion rights, sexual equality, and increased punishment of rapists. They emphasized that sexual freedom—including freedom from violence of every kind—was necessary before any woman could become a political subject.[56]

Although MDM never regained the leadership of a diverse women's movement, it became increasingly feminist. By 1976, it was calling itself the MDM/MLM, the second acronym standing for Movimiento de Liberación de la Mujer (Movement for Women's Liberation).[57] Linking the vindication of women to the general struggle for amnesty around which MDM was born in 1965, MDM/MLM led the women's movement in calling for amnesty for women accused of moral crimes, such as prostitution or having abortions. It also joined with other feminists to support the institution of a divorce law and abolition of the adultery law.[58]

Opposition to the adultery law and other so-called sexual laws that discriminated against women linked many branches of the Spanish women's movement after the death of Franco.[59] At the end of the Civil War in 1939, Franco had repealed the divorce and abortion laws and reinstituted the Civil Code of 1889, which incorporated elements of the Napoleonic Code. Although divorce was forbidden, people could sometimes get a legal separation. In general, young children remained with their mothers if parents went their separate ways. But if the paternal family or the husband wanted custody of the child, they could threaten to take the woman to court and charge her with adultery. Since adultery was considered a crime punishable by up to six years in jail and a fine of up to a thousand dollars, generally women gave up the custody of their children rather than go to prison.

The definition of adultery varied by gender. For the husband to be considered an adulterer required that he attempt to bring his mistress into the conjugal home or that he carry on with her outside the home in a scandalous way; that is, he had to repeatedly engage in sexual relations with her in public. However, a married woman could be considered an adulterer if she traveled with a man to whom she was not married. Her lover also faced charges of adultery if he knew she was married. Despite the law, though, Spanish mores were changing. In the late sixties, many of the people I knew were married and living with other people.

During the first transitional government between 1976 and 1977, the hypocrisy of the double standard, the lack of divorce, and the injustice of the civil code provided an opportunity for women of all classes to unite in a citizens' struggle for democracy, greatly expanding the limits of ordinary democratic discourse. Although women might have different rationales for their opposition, emphasizing either equality or women's right to sexual freedom, they agreed that the adultery law must be abolished. Middle-class university-educated women and working-class women viewed women's liberation from discriminatory legislation as an intrinsic part of any campaign to democratize Spain. Some believed that the parties of the left would include women in a generalized struggle for freedom. Others argued that liberals and leftists resembled fascists and nationalists in their attitudes toward women. Working-class women, supportive of amnesty struggles for the liberation of husbands and children jailed as members of the clandestine unions, allied with feminists to overcome the shame associated with adultery charges. Among the cases of adultery brought against women in the year after Franco's death, two that attracted particular attention were those of María Inmaculada Benito and María Angeles Muñoz.

Both cases reveal the degree to which social mores, especially sexual relations, had changed during the last days of Franco, but they also point to the continued power of patriarchy tied to authoritarianism, enforced in part through shame. In 1976, twenty-five-year-old Timoteo Carmelo Caneiro charged his twenty-two-year-old wife, María Inmaculada Benito, with adultery and held her up to public humiliation "because he could."[60] A year after Franco's death, as the political leaders negotiated a settlement that would lead to free elections in the spring of 1977, the civil code and the political system Franco had created remained unchanged. Benito and Caneiro had married in 1973, and their son was born seven months later. They both continued having affairs. Although Caneiro's father was a conservative military officer, he and his wife seemingly accepted the life led by Benito and Caneiro, a *gauchist* artist who specialized in antigovernmental themes. When Benito decided to go away for two weeks with a friend, Alberto Carasol, she left her son with her in-laws.[61]

Benito's faith that her in-laws accepted the younger couple's bohemian life changed when Benito returned to Zaragoza and Caneiro's parents refused to give back her son. Within a few days, the young couple signed a separation agreement giving Benito custody and providing visiting privileges to Caneiro.[62] Their parting was quite common in Spain, where, unable to divorce, many Spanish couples simply separated and began new households. Had Benito never married, she would have been required by law, as a woman under twenty-five years old, to live with her parents.

We might ask why, after signing the custody agreement, Caneiro then charged his wife and friend with adultery. And the answer would probably include wounded pride and a misplaced sense of honor. Benito, who now lives in Barcelona, thinks that her father-in-law wanted to assert his patriarchal authority, and the law provided a means for doing just that.[63] Caneiro's parents seem to have felt ashamed and furious that their daughter-in-law was leading an independent life. Benito believes that they decided they would raise their grandson to follow their more conservative practices. Francisco Ibáñez, the Caneiro family attorney, claimed that the separation would have humiliated the young husband.[64] While honor now seems an archaic emotion, the family's standing in the larger community depended on it. Zaragoza is a small town in which most of the middle class would have been aware of the separation.[65]

Benito's lawyer, Gloria Labarta, a twenty-six-year-old feminist and a founder of the Democratic Association of Aragonese Women (ADMA, Asociación Democrática de Mujeres Aragonesas), viewed the adultery charge as part of the systematic sexual intimidation she associated with Spanish authoritarianism. Looking back from the perspective of 2001, Labarta thought Benito was extraordinarily courageous.[66] After all, she was willing to stand in the public spotlight and risk going to prison in order to confront injustice, with only the nascent feminist movement in Zaragoza to support her. ADMA, formed shortly before Benito was brought up on charges, was a cross-class alliance dedicated to waging an ideological struggle against a legal system that discriminated against women, and it viewed the law that shamed women as an intrinsic part of the antidemocratic, patriarchal system that continued to govern the lives of Spanish women. In pursuit of the kind of democracy craved by the women of ADMA, they wanted to reform the entire civil and criminal code to end distinctions between legitimate and illegitimate children, establish rights for single mothers, and win equality in the workplace.[67]

Trials are frequently accompanied by public relations campaigns, and the Zaragoza trial was no exception. ADMA began with an open letter to the minister of justice signed by over a thousand people. In the letter, they demanded equality and an end to what they called "moral duplicity." They claimed that "while [the law] recognizes men's sporadic extramarital relations as normal, [the law] severely castigates the same acts by women and can impose a punishment of up to six years of prison" for those women.[68] They appealed to the minister of justice, who was helping to launch the first free elections in Spain in nearly forty years, to recognize moral equality as a right of citizenship.

María Inmaculada Benito was exonerated after opposing groups used the campaign to reverse the shame she suffered by being brought to trial and having her personal life exposed to public view. Feminists from all over Spain embraced Benito's cause as their own and came to

Zaragoza for the trial, though the hearing took place behind closed doors. Even the Association of Women Jurists, a conservative and very proper women's professional organization that refused to directly support Labarta and ADMA, wanted to change the law.[69] The Women Jurists in fact chose to reexamine all aspects of marital law, including domestic finances, custody rights, and domestic violence. They called for more modern legislation governing women's rights on the job and rights for women prisoners.[70] Some feminists used historical arguments to shame Spain for holding women to different moral standards than men, and claimed that the Benito trial reminded them of the Spanish Inquisition.[71] Feminists wanted to help shape the future of democratic Spain and reverse its history of injustice. Facing down accusations of adultery became a principal way of achieving their goals.

While masses of people made democracy their slogan, feminists wanted to construct it brick by brick. Changing the law was the mortar, and eighteen cases of adultery were pled before Spain's Supreme Court in 1976. Women of all classes were willing to bear the shame and notoriety that came from fighting their husband in court. The movement for democracy through abolition of the adultery law took great care not to differentiate among women attacked as adulterers. Whatever their class and whatever the situation, those defending the adultery cases put the criminal code, not individual women, on trial. One case remained relatively anonymous in Madrid. Only using initials, a husband asked for a six-year prison sentence and a fifty-million-*peseta* fine for his wife and her lover. Clearly from the working class, this woman, known as C. G. F., had taken a job at a hotel. She may or may not have been a victim of sexual harassment when she became the lover of her boss. It is not clear how long the relationship had been going on when the police surprised them in bed. During the trial, Madrid's feminists filled the halls of the courthouse, carrying signs calling for repeal of the adultery law. Refusing to confine their demonstration to the courthouse, the women marched through the surrounding streets, although public demonstrations were still prohibited in Spain. Because they were women—and perhaps because authorities viewed the question of adultery as one of lascivious interest—the police stood by as the women marched. One observer reported that a letter signed by twelve thousand women demanded that the minister of justice repeal the adultery law.[72]

At the same time in Barcelona, masses of women of all classes and political persuasions united in support of María Angeles Muñoz, a thirty-year-old domestic servant. Her case raises questions about class as well as gender in the transitional period. In her early twenties, Muñoz married Ramón Soto Gómez in 1970. After the couple had been together for fourteen months, the husband ran off to Mayorca, abandoning her and their two-month-old daughter, Yolanda. To support her child, María Angeles Muñoz took jobs cleaning apartments. In order to pay her expenses, she admitted two boarders, a single man and an old woman, who cared for the child in exchange for free rent. With no legal possibility of divorce, María Angeles Muñoz went to court in 1973 to try to get her husband, who visited from time to time, to pay child support. When Soto visited Barcelona in 1974, he realized that his estranged wife was pregnant. Before the birth of her second daughter, who may also have been his child, she accused him of abandonment. After another two-year absence, he returned to Barcelona in 1976. At that time, his parents demanded custody of six-year-old Yolanda, and when Muñoz refused to relinquish her older daughter, Soto denounced her as an adulterer.[73]

Barcelona, where I lived in the fall of 1976, was filled with rumors and covered with flyers prepared by the Asociación de Vecinos of San Andrés of Besós, where Muñoz made her home. Feminists from the recently formed Asociació Catalana de la Dona (Catalan Women's Association) found Muñoz a lawyer and contacted women's groups of every description. Women from the independent homemakers associations and other women's groups that were springing up all over the city to fight the rising cost of living portrayed Muñoz as a traditional wife and mother who had been deprived of her husband's support and now risked losing her child. At another time, Muñoz, despite her pain, might have handed over her daughter. At another time, local women, careful of their respectability, might have scorned Muñoz, who had put her boarder's name on her second child's birth certificate. Feminists might have viewed the law simply as an example of the double standard that prevailed in all social classes and in all political groups. But during the transition to democracy, when discrimination against women seemed to be a part of Spain's fascist legacy, women in the demonstrations in which I participated chanted, "Machismo es fachismo." If machismo was fascist, then motherhood had become democratic, and women of all classes came together to support Muñoz's rights as a mother.

In November 1976, Muñoz was summoned to court, ordered to give up her child, cited for contempt, and finally imprisoned. In various demonstrations, culminating in one on 12 November that I attended along with over five thousand women of all ages, Muñoz's supporters called for rights of divorce and repeal of all laws that discriminated against women.[74] The November demonstration was notable because it included many elderly women, as well as representatives of almost all the Neighborhood and Homemakers Associations of the city. The homemakers of Sants and Hostafrancs called for "Equal rights for women and men." Others held signs saying, "We are not our husband's property" or "Down with the discriminatory laws!" To the other chants was added, "Amnesty for everyone! Amnesty for all women!" an improvisation on the demand the clandestine unions and MDM had been making for amnesty for all political prisoners. Despite continued support, Muñoz was convicted. Only in 1978 were Articles 450 and 452 of the Penal Code repealed. Only then did women gain freedom from being jailed and fined because of laws defining them as adulterers.[75]

REMEMBERING FOR JUSTICE'S SAKE

Demonstrating against the Spanish regime always took enormous courage. In the last years of Franco's rule, as he balanced desire for foreign investment and tourism against his wish to dominate society, those who opposed him lived in a dangerous and contradictory world in which they sometimes could gather freely, and at other times faced brutal repression. Male and female workers, activists, and those accused of terrorism were routinely arrested, tortured, and raped in secret detention centers all over Spain. In the winter of 1968, an impromptu demonstration against a military crackdown was met with tanks in Atocha, near the main railroad station in Madrid. The film school in Madrid, known as a hotbed of intellectuals critical of the government, was repeatedly closed down and students arrested, because the regime hated and feared its young *gauchist* critics. Spanish demonstrations in September 1973 protesting the coup in faraway Chile led Franco to issue a decree forbidding comparisons between Chile and the Spanish Civil War.[76] And we should never forget the military trials and execution for "terrorism" of five young activists in September 1975, two months before Franco's death and two years after his prime minister, Arías Navarro, had announced an *apertura,* or opening, to democratic politics.

Many of those who demonstrated to achieve their version of democracy also had to deal with the past. Gathering the testimonies of those who overcame pain, shame, and the fear of death in order to fight against sexual and political repression was part of the way women contributed to creating a new political regime. Writing in 1998 about the transition to democracy in South Africa, poet and radio commentator Antjie Krog spoke about her hopes for the Truth and Reconciliation Commission, in which survivors could tell their stories and demand the truth from those seeking amnesty for their crimes. Krog pondered what such a process could achieve if it were concerned with "the widest possible compilation of people's perceptions, stories, myths and experiences, [so that it would] have chosen to restore memory and foster a new humanity." She presumed that it would thus achieve "justice in its deepest sense."[77] Spain never had a formal reckoning with its past, but those seeking justice continue to tell their stories.

Mobilizing for Democracy

This book ends where it began, with idealistic women and young people seeking justice and overcoming fear through direct action and storytelling. Despite over three decades of work on social movements, transitions to democracy, and popular struggles for human rights, few people concerned with social justice and democracy view demonstrations by women and young people as more than episodic, a strategy to be used as a last resort when it is impossible to impede government action by any other means. But many organizers, including Hebe de Bonafini, leader of the Asociación de Madres de Plaza de Mayo, are beginning to think that the ability to move into the streets quickly is the only way societies can protect themselves against government abuses and even state terrorism.[1] Imagining a separate political sphere, a fifth estate in which ordinary citizens can put pressure on their government regarding major issues, large numbers of women and young people have voted with their feet in the public squares of their countries.

The idea of public spaces in which democracy can be enacted develops from debates that critics, including feminists, have carried out with social theorist Jürgen Habermas.[2] Applying his theory to conditions beyond the eighteenth-century bourgeois public sphere he described has led feminists and other critics to think about the variability and multiplicity of public spheres.[3] Some observers have recognized the streets, mass meetings, and holiday celebrations as places and gatherings where people act out alternative visions of society. Historian Elsa Barkley

Brown, writing about Afro-American women in Richmond, Virginia, examines their decision to "vote" with their songs, voices, and activities in Black churches, and then in mass meetings where they assumed responsibility for governing their communities.[4] Mary Ryan, writing about civic rituals and parades in Jacksonian America, has highlighted how certain women, interested in social change but barred from the franchise, nevertheless expressed their opinions in the streets as well as in moral reform societies.[5] And Nancy A. Hewitt, examining the development of multiracial politics in Tampa, Florida, has shown how Latina, Black, and white working-class women forged alternative communities in which they could register their opposition to repression, exploitation, and segregation.[6] All three instances indicate efforts to use words, signs, music, ritual objects, and costumes to show participants' dissatisfaction with particular social or political processes or with the direction their government was taking. But few have examined street demonstrations in light of theories of direct democracy.

An important exception is Nancy Fraser, who argues that because of Habermas's particular notion of "rationality" and "reasoned public debate" as a precondition for democratic public discourse, he automatically discounted popular mobilizations—and whole categories of activists.[7] Like many other contemporary social theorists, he viewed crowds and demonstrators as erratic and subject to the manipulation of demagogues. Having rejected direct action as a form of democracy, Habermas certainly underestimated the potential of public demonstrations to fundamentally alter the terms of politics. Flipping the focus to view youthful demonstrators of both sexes and women of all ages reveals the important place in political change played by those ordinarily overlooked as participants in public life.

This analysis and older arguments such as those developed by Rosa Luxemburg, the early-twentieth-century communist theoretician and activist, make possible a reconsideration of the impact of mass movements on politics. Luxemburg was concerned with how to balance popular mobilizations, which tend to run their course, with political parties and trade unions, which tend to become bureaucratic. As she saw it, through periodic massive demonstrations, decentralized groups could revitalize hierarchical organizations. Although she ridiculed those who thought that they could harness this power and promote such uprisings or revolutions on demand, she wrote about what she called the "mass strike" and admired what workers could accomplish once mobilized.[8] Without idealizing demonstrators, she recognized that mass mobilizations presented alternative visions of social relations and could destabilize and even topple authoritarian governments. From a Habermasian perspective, mass mobilizations create spaces where participants argue for worlds quite different from the ones they inhabit. Focus on youthful demonstrators of both sexes and women of all ages reveals the significant role women and young people have increasingly played. But these struggles are seldom considered in the context of the phenomenon known as the "transition to democracy."

"Transition to democracy" is a term developed to explain a process by which authoritarian governments gave way to legislative democracies without armed struggle, civil war, or dramatic ruptures at the end of repressive regimes.[9] With no preparation, seemingly invulnerable military regimes in Greece, Portugal, and Spain suddenly collapsed in the 1970s.[10] To some degree, all the transitions were negotiated settlements between authoritarian leaders and members of an opposition with whom the transfer of power was worked out. The regimes changed, but most social relations, including relations between the sexes, remained essentially the same. The transitions were bridges between systems that ruled by decree, enforced by the military, and democracies in which civil law and an independent judiciary theoretically prevailed. Because transitions permitted outgoing rulers to retain many of their powers, judges who had collaborated with authoritarian regimes, police, and even members of the military continued to run their departments for decades after the transition. And critics generally underestimate the degree to which the transitions followed particularly bloody periods of repression, as the old leaders attempted to hold on to their power.

Getting the dictators to step down was far more difficult than it appears in retrospect. In the 1970s and 1980s, right-wing governments intensified their hold over the population they hoped to keep in check. For example, Francisco Franco, fearing the changes popular agitation was bringing in Spain, carried out widespread repression against workers and activists, particularly young radicals. In 1982, a disastrous defeat in the Malvinas War discredited the Argentine military government and forced it to hold general elections in October 1983. The Radical Party's Raúl Alfonsín was elected and sworn in as president in December 1983, but the Argentine military neither accounted for the political prisoners who had been alive when the military agreed to leave office nor respected the democratically elected government. They attempted six uprisings between 1985 and 1989. On the other side of the Andes, in Chile, on Corpus Christi Day in June 1987, during Augusto Pinochet's last days, the secret police carried out a military assault on twelve young alleged terrorists believed to be members of the revolutionary group Frente Patriótico Manuel Rodríguez (Manuel Rodríguez Patriotic Front). Instead of arresting those they suspected of plotting against the government, the police murdered them in cold blood, according to a plan called Operation Albania, which others call the Corpus Christi massacres.[11] A 1988 referendum in Chile, engineered by Pinochet to justify remaining in power for another decade, ended in defeat. A civilian was elected as president and a transitional democratic government came to power in 1990. Nevertheless, Pinochet engineered his continuation as commander-in-chief of the armed forces until 1997, hobbling Chile's progress toward any meaningful democracy. The Chilean military held the balance of power until Judge Baltasar Garzón of Spain attempted in 1998–99 to try Pinochet for crimes against humanity.

Another frequently overlooked aspect of the transitions is the degree to which they took place in the streets as well as the conference rooms.[12] Mobilizations and other forms of direct action did not in themselves bring down the authoritarian regimes, but they weakened them. They demonstrated the vulnerability of the dictators and the military and forced them to the bargaining table. And then popular mobilizations seemed to diminish. It may at first seem obvious that once formal democratic institutions reappeared, movements in the streets would stop. In the 1970s, sociologist Elsa M. Chaney noted that women frequently take center stage and demonstrate during periods of crisis, but that they quickly demobilize and go home once the crisis is over.[13] Political scientist Jane S. Jaquette, studying women's protest movements, has argued that the women's resistance movements throughout Latin America in the 1970s and 1980s actually may have contributed to their exclusion from power after the transitions.[14] She and others have claimed that the separatism—organizing as women—that protected women from the authorities later prevented women as a group from vying for power during the democratization process. Without ignoring the undoubted sexism of the opposition, Jaquette merely underscores an additional reason for the failure of male political leaders to recognize the political abilities of women—or, by implication, young people—or their contributions to challenging the authority of the governments against which they had demonstrated so ardently.

However, popular pressure seems to diminish during transitions both because the image of a common enemy begins to blur and because the leaders of opposition groups frequently quash their supporters' public activity. Since mass movements traditionally represent what Argentine sociologist Elizabeth Jelin calls "a new means by which to relate the political and social..., in which the everyday social practices are included alongside and in direct connection with ideological and institutional politics,"[15] their disappearance is one reason that transitional governments have not fulfilled the hopes for social change that many of those engaging in direct action tried to achieve. Without citizens willing and able to pressure their elected representatives to act in accordance with popular wishes once in office, it may be impossible to keep elected officials from acceding to the pressure of those who dominate the political system. Decentralized movements, such as the women's associations and youth groups that existed during the transition, tend to lose their access to public attention once dictatorships are replaced by representative bodies. The absence of an institutional way for women's and other citizens' groups to function in democracies—perhaps through confederations—remains a problem for those who believe in the power of direct democracy to help shape more socially emancipatory forms of government in the future. But the leaders of transitional governments also deliberately demobilize the social movements of women and young people that helped bring them to power.

Few theorists have really considered what the demobilization of women, youth, workers, citizen's groups, peasants, or indigenous people has meant for democracy. Chilean political scientist Manuel Antonio Garretón, speaking in advance of the 1988 plebiscite in Chile, warned that the demonstrations (which he and others had originally supported as part of the opposition's strategy of destabilizing the dictatorship of Augusto Pinochet) had to stop. He worried that any further direct action would alarm the larger population and give credence to the military's argument that social chaos would ensue if they stepped down. In fact, all the new governments struggled for stability and legitimacy and feared the crowd's use of extralegal methods of shaming, their recourse to arguments about morality and ethics, and their demands that the government publicly explain its policies.[16] It has therefore been a common practice of revolutionary, liberal, and reactionary governments to demobilize mass movements once the new government comes to power.[17] Demobilization of the popular forces has been part of the reason that women and young people, as well as workers, agriculturalists, and citizens groups, which played such a significant part in the transitions to democracy in the Mediterranean, Central Europe,

South Africa, and Latin America, largely disappeared in the period after the authoritarian governments fell.

Of course, leaders of popular demonstrations sometimes are invited to work for the new government in an official capacity. They also run for office. But whether appointed or elected, they serve as individuals and are usually cut off from the people with whom they demonstrated and the spaces they previously occupied. As a woman from a shanty-town told me shortly after the democratic government had been installed in Chile, the same people with whom she had demonstrated against the dictatorship for better medical services were now telling her that she was exaggerating about a meningitis epidemic that was sweeping her community. Even officials who continue to uphold the popular democratic principles that they held as demonstrators are powerless unless they have a mass movement to back them. Without the threat of street protests and recourse to public shaming, those who continue to support alternative visions of democracy lose their power. Ordinary women and young people who speak collectively may be perennial irritants, but mobilizations are necessary to keep the channels of democratic debate open.

The challenge participatory democracy poses for future governments lies in the possibility of periodically exercising rights of assembly and free speech. Under repressive conditions, merely getting the story out is a means of fighting back. Nieves Ayress, her mother, Virginia Moreno, and Ayress's fellow prisoner Inés Antúnez created public spaces in which to tell their story. So too, Chile's Mujeres por la Vida took their arguments about Pinochet and his supporters to the streets and the subway, the supermarkets and the courts. Spanish women, dissatisfied with a mere change of government, promoted cultural and legal changes to gain control over their sexuality while continuing to exercise their rights as mothers. Both groups of Madres de Plaza de Mayo continue to act as tribunes, holding meetings and marches to reshape government policies in Argentina.

Although few will make the same choices as the women and young people discussed here, increasing numbers of people will find themselves in the streets, protesting against their government. Despite access to public communication through the internet, mobilization in streets and plazas and public meetings still provides a prominent way to affect decision-making. Viewing street demonstrations as part of the democratic process, critic John Berger argued just after the French uprising of May 1968 that "mass demonstration[s] can be interpreted as the symbolic capturing of a capital.... The demonstrators interrupt the regular life of the streets they march through or the open spaces they fill. They 'cut off' these areas, and...they transform them into a temporary stage on which they dramatise the[ir] power."[18] Such symbolic seizures of space can take place under any kind of government. Dramatic, peaceful assemblies can enact direct democracy. Mobilization in street demonstrations and public commemorations through holidays also evoke deep memories of personal as well as collective commitments, losses, and regeneration, which are revealed in testimonies and oral histories that attempt through narration to cleanse the shame torturers and victors tried to instill.

Histories such as this one are intent on monitoring public meetings and street demonstrations for what they tell about democratic activities, but they are also concerned with the transformative power of remembering and telling stories. In fact, recounting these stories simulates direct action by enabling actors and speakers to recall how they dealt with loss, defeat, bewilderment, shame, and righteous anger by expressing their feelings collectively. More than assessments of trauma and survival, these stories constitute expressions of shared political histories. Remembering these women and young people—admirable or hateful as some of them are—underscores the good and bad qualities of decentralized associations that mobilize in the streets. Such women and young people pose tempting alternatives to the quiescence so many associate with contemporary democratic politics.

Notes

PROLOGUE

1. In his discussion of Michel Foucault's ideas about the panopticon replacing the prison cell as a way of establishing discipline after the French Revolution, historian Martin Jay speaks about the "sadistic gaze of a diffuse and anonymous power whose actual existence soon becomes superfluous to the process of discipline." See Martin Jay, *Downcast Eyes: The Denigration of Vision in Twentieth-Century French Thought* (Berkeley: University of California Press, 1994), p. 410.

2. Maurice Halbwach, *On Collective Memory,* ed. Lewis A. Coser (Chicago: University of Chicago Press, 1992), pp. 174–75. Those engaging in participatory democracy through direct action seldom justify themselves in written arguments, but make political arguments through their action, a phenomenon that has been studied in depth by social movement theorists. These theorists roughly divide into two groups according to the emphasis they place on identity. In confronting older theories that any collective behavior was largely irrational, one group has emphasized the rational choices that participants in social movements make. As an antidote to the subsequent idea that people make choices purely out of self-interest, the other group has attempted to demonstrate that passions and commitments galvanize participants to take action and sustain them in their struggles. See, for example, Jeff Goodwin, James M. Jasper, and Francesca Polletta, eds., *Passionate Politics: Emotions and Social Movements* (Chicago: University of Chicago Press, 2001). I am grateful to Erich Goode for introducing me to this volume.

While trying to account for the motivations of activists, however, these theories have not considered the place of visual images in projecting certain views of democracy and justice, the way reestablishing solidarity and a sense of group cohesion requires overcoming shame, the means by which self-identified groups have reclaimed certain public spaces, the nature of participatory democracy, or the manner in which gender identity fuels all of these. That is the goal of this book.

3. All contemporary theories about shame derive from Mary Douglas's *Purity and Danger* (London: Routledge and Kegan Paul, 1966). Her analysis of boundaries and the dangers of pollution to both individuals and societies has made it possible to investigate how metaphors of the body work in the cultural realm and how threats to one are interpreted as threats to the other.

4. Agnes Heller, *The Power of Shame: A Rational Perspective* (London: Routledge and Kegan Paul, 1985), p. 5. I am grateful to Beth Goldblatt and Sheila Meintjies for introducing me to this work and for showing the applicability of Heller's theories to consideration of the gendered nature of torture. See Beth Goldblatt and Sheila Meintjes, *Gender and the Truth and Reconciliation Commission: A Submission to the Truth and Reconciliation Commission* (Johannesburg: Gender Research Project, Centre for Applied Legal Studies, University of Witswatersrand, 1996). This submission appears in *Truth and Reconciliation Commission of South Africa* (Cape Town: Truth and Reconciliation Commission and the Department of Justice, 1998), pp. 282–316.

5. Heller, *The Power of Shame*, p. 40.

6. Victor Toro, a survivor of the Chilean torture centers, became the person in whom other prisoners were asked to confide so that the group would know what the authorities had learned. Working with actors and psychiatrists from the International Trauma Studies Program at New York University, Toro and other survivors commented on the dramatization of their testimonies. International Trauma Studies Program, New York University, videotape no. 5, 15 January 1999. I am grateful to Dr. Jack M. Saul for allowing me to view the tapes.

7. June Price Tangney and Ronda L. Dearing, *Shame and Guilt* (New York and London: Guilford Press, 2002), p. 83.

8. Inger Agger, *The Blue Room: Trauma and Testimony among Refugee Women: A Psycho-Social Exploration* (London and Atlantic Highlands, N.J.: ZED Books, 1992), p. 8.

9. Pilar Calveiro, *Poder y desaparición: Los campos de concentración en Argentina* (Buenos Aires: Colihue, 1995), p. 94.

10. Even when individual mothers and grandmothers do not remind their children about social rules, others in society do. I am not blaming female relatives, since they are themselves tied to culture by these same mechanisms. But the daughters and sons who became political activists and revolutionaries have generally defied these rules, as did the Madres de Plaza de Mayo and other women considered here.

11. Agger, *The Blue Room*, pp. 94–95; Antjie Krog, *Country of My Skull* (Johannesburg: Random House, 1998), p. 179.

12. Jean Franco, "Gender, Death, and Resistance: Facing the Ethical Vacuum," in *Fear at the Edge: State Terror and Resistance in Latin America*, ed. Juan E. Corradi, Patricia Weiss Fagen, and Manuel Antonio Garretón (Berkeley: University of California Press, 1992), p. 104.

13. Agger, *The Blue Room*, p. 313; Goldblatt and Meintjes, *Gender and the Truth and Reconciliation Commission*, p. 33.

14. Agger, *The Blue Room*, p. 95.

15. Nieves Ayress, International Trauma Studies Program, New York University, videotape no. 5, 15 January 1999.

16. For a brief discussion of what democracy meant in connection with U.S. foreign policy, see Abraham F. Lowenthal, "The United States and Latin American Democracy: Learning from History," in *Exporting Democracy: The United States and Latin America,* ed. Abraham F. Lowenthal (Baltimore, Md.: The Johns Hopkins University Press, 1991), pp. 261–83.

17. Robert Viola and Leopoldo Galtieri of the Argentine military juntas were among the Latin American dictators trained in the School of the Americas. For a brief historical survey, see George Monbiot, "Backyard Terrorism," *The Guardian* (London), 30 October 2001, p. 17.

18. In a judgment in Palm Springs, Florida, the U.S. civil court recognized that so-called democrats such as Carlos Eugenio Vides Casanova and José Guillermo Garcia were responsible for the slaughter of civilians in El Salvador. When they were ordered to pay $54.6 million to three victims of their repression, they provided an occasion for the *New York Times* to offer a consideration of U.S. foreign policy in Central America. See Stephen Kinzer, "U.S. and Central America: Too Close for Comfort?" *New York Times,* 28 July 2002, p. 14.

19. Jean L. Cohen, "The Public and the Private Sphere: A Feminist Reconsideration," in *Feminists Read Habermas: Gendering the Subject of Discourse,* ed. Johannna Meehan (New York: Routledge, 1995), p. 60.

20. The most extensive literature on shaming rituals comes from anthropologists. See esp. the articles in Sharon MacDonald, Pat Holden, and Shirley Ardner, eds., *Images of Women in Peace and War: Cross-Cultural and Historical Perspectives* (Madison: University of Wisconsin Press, 1988). I have written about shaming rituals among the Igbo-Ibibio women of Nigeria in "Naked Mothers and Maternal Sexuality: Some Reactions to the Aba Women's War," in *The Politics of Motherhood: Activist Voices from Left to Right,* ed. Alexis Jetter, Annelise Orleck, and Diana Taylor (Hanover, N.H.: University Press of New England, 1997), pp. 209–24.

21. The most important contemporary reappraisal of Emile Durkheim's work can be found in David Kertzer, *Ritual, Politics and Power* (New Haven, Conn.: Yale University Press, 1988). Kertzer shows that rituals do not just reinforce shared values but create solidarity in the absence of consensus (p. 61).

An older but still valuable contribution to recognizing how rituals operate to create new political opportunities can be found in Sally Falk Moore, "Political Meanings and the Simulation of Unanimity: Kilimanjaro 1973," in *Secular Ritual,* ed. Sally F. Moore and Barbara G. Myerhoff (Assen/Amsterdam: Van Gorcum, 1977), pp. 151–72.

CHAPTER 1

1. Enrique Soria, "Crónicas de la Guerra Sucia: El furtivo olor de los naranjos," *El diario* (New York), 25 November 1998, p. 5; Carlos Villalón, "Una historia de amor al estilo del Bronx," *La información* (New York), 15–30 November 1998, pp. 9–14; Jorge Ramos, "Así me torturó Pinochet," *El diario,* 14

January 1999, p. 16; Joyce Wadler, "Years after Torture, a Cry against Pinochet," *New York Times,* 3 February 1999, p. B2.

2. Personal interview with Amalia Moreno, Nieves Ayress's maternal aunt, Santiago, Chile, 13 June 2000.

3. Quoted in Francesca Miller, *Latin American Women and the Search for Social Justice* (Hanover, N.H.: University Press of New England, 1991), p. 147.

4. Personal interview with Nieves Ayress, New York City, 9 January 1999. A variety of interviews with women revolutionaries appear in Marta Diana, *Mujeres guerrilleras: La militancia de los setenta en el testimonio de sus protagonistas femeninas* (Buenos Aires: Planeta, 1996). The volume includes an especially important section by Graciela Daleo of Argentina, who refused a pardon from President Carlos Saúl Menem because she rejected the idea that radicals who fought for social change had provoked the military, which was occasionally overzealous in its attempts to repress them. The theory that the radicals and the military were equally guilty is known as the theory of the Two Devils. A former Montonero, Daleo insists that she was a revolutionary militant, not a guerrilla. See pp. 243–73.

5. Marc Cooper, who knew Charles Horman Jr. and Frank Teruggi, another American journalist who disappeared after the coup, writes movingly about what it was like to be a young American leftist in Chile under the Popular Unity government and during the first hours of the coup. See *Pinochet and Me: A Chilean Anti-Memoir* (London and New York: Verso, 2001). Evidence about U.S. complicity in the deaths of Horman and Teruggi appears in Diana Jean Schemo, "U.S. Victims of Chile's Coup: The Uncensored File," *New York Times,* 13 February 2000, pp. 1, 6; and Ralph R. Ortega, "CIA Papers May Solve Old Puzzle," *Daily News* (New York), 13 February 2000, p. 26.

6. Different groups quantify state terror in different ways, but all estimates are open to dispute, because many disappearances and deaths remained unreported. Chile's Comisión Nacional de Verdad y Reconcilación (Truth and Reconciliation Commission), appointed in 1990, was authorized to consider only those who died violently between 11 September 1973 and 11 March 1990. These are the official numbers:

Commission's figures on numbers killed	
Victims of human rights violations	2,115
Victims of political violence	164
Total	2,279

Cases classified by cause of death	
Disappeared	957
Executed or died under torture	815
Shot while fleeing	101
Killed during protests	93
Victims of personal fights presented as political disputes	90
Victims of political violence during 1973	87

Died during protest demonstrations	38	
Killed during gun battles	39	
Total	2,279	

Sex of victims		
Women	126	5.5%
Men	2,153	94.5%

Age of victims		
Under 16	49	2.1%
16–20	269	11.8%
21–25	557	24.4%
26–30	512	22.4%
31–35	287	12.6%
36–40	152	6.7%
41–45	164	7.2%
46–50	97	4.3%
51–55	53	2.3%
56–60	34	1.5%
61–65	15	0.7%
66–70	8	0.4%
71–75	3	0.1%
Over 75	2	0.1%
Of unknown age	77	3.4%
Total	2,279	100%

Although the commission placed the total number killed at 2,279, the actual count is 3,236, which includes 957 whose deaths were not attributed to political causes or for whom the committee found insufficient information. *Informe de la Comisión Nacional de Verdad y Reconciliación 2* (Santiago: Comisión Nacional de Verdad y Reconciliación, 1991), pp. 883–85 (subsequently cited as *Informe Rettig*). An English edition of the report appeared as *Report of the Chilean National Commission on Truth and Reconciliation,* 2 vols., trans. Phillip E. Berryman, with an introduction by José Zalaquett (Notre Dame, Ind.: University of Notre Dame Press, 1993); for the statistics, see 2: 899–904.

Survivors, including the Association of Families of the Detained and Disappeared, claim that 10,000 people were killed. Others believe that 50,000 to 150,000 were detained and tortured, and that 6,000 to 15,000 were abducted and never heard from again. Lecture by Pedro Alejandro Matta, a torture survivor, to the Council for International Exchange Seminar, Santiago, June 19, 2000.

7. Nieves Ayress, quoted in Jacques Res, "La mujer mas torturada en Chile," handwritten Spanish translation in the collection of Amalia Moreno, in Santiago, Chile, p. 2 (Amalia Moreno's collection is subsequently referred to as CAM); originally published in *Panorama* (Haarlem, The Netherlands), 18 February 1977.

8. The intelligence forces of the army, navy, and air force targeted known leftists even before the special intelligence agency, DINA, began working informally around November 1973 under the direction of General Manuel Contreras Sepúlveda, who reported directly to Augusto Pinochet. The most notorious torture center, Villa Grimaldi, established May 1974, focused on members of the MIR. Personal interview with Nieves Ayress, New York City, 9 July 2000.

9. Personal interview with Alejandra López, Santiago, Chile, 23 June 2000. López, who is working on an oral history of the working-class community of La Legua, is something of an urban archeologist whose work promises to reveal how a neighborhood that was once viewed as a center of revolutionary commitment has been turned into a drug-ridden center of crime and social degradation.

10. Quoted in A. Pinochet U[garte], *El día decisivo: 11 de Septiembre de 1973*, 3d ed. (Santiago: Editorial Andres Bello, n.d.), n.p.

11. This narrative comes from the judicial declaration that Margarita del Carmen Durán gave on 20 November 1990 after returning from exile. The *Declaración jurada* is in the Fundación de Documentación y Archivo de la Vicaría de Solidaridad, Arzobispado de Santiago, Chile (subsequently referred to as Vicaría). At the request of the archivist, I describe the documents rather than identify them by catalogue number.

12. Ibid.

13. In a personal discussion with me and Nora de Cortiñas, who is a member of the Argentine Madres de Plaza de Mayo, Línea Fundadora (Founding-Line Mothers of the Plaza de Mayo), Nieves Ayress explained that she thought intelligence forces seemed to be developing their practices during the first months after the coup. Personal interview with Nieves Ayress, New York City, 16 December 2000. Later Nieves discovered on the Internet that two of her torturers were Osvaldo Pincetti, known as "Doctor Mortis," and Ciro Torres. See Mercedes Castro, "Tejas Verdes: Ex agente identifica al Alcalde Labbé y a Krassnoff como instructores de la Dina," http://www.primeralínea.cl/modulos/noticias/constructor/detalle_noticias.asp?id_noticia=40952 (26 December 2001).

14. Personal interview with Nieves Ayress, New York City, 9 July 2000.

15. Luz Arce Sandoval, who began working for DINA to save herself and her brother, wrote about her collaboration in *El infierno* (Santiago: Planeta, 1993). The other well-known woman collaborator was Marcia Alejandra Merino Vega, whom the Association of Families of the Detained and Disappeared tried to have indicted for the murder of five former comrades. Her appeal for understanding appears in *Mi verdad: "Mas allá del horror, yo acuso…"* (Santiago: A.T.G., 1993).

16. Merino, *Mi verdad*. See also the case against Osvaldo Romo Mena, nicknamed "El Guatón Romo," in Juzgado del crimen: Osvaldo Romo Mena, Marcelo L. Móren Brito, Corte de Apelaciones de Santiago, Secretaria Criminal, 12–07–94, Plaintiff Alejandro Hoya Hernández, in Vicaría, pp. 267–68.

17. Osvaldo Romo Mena, one of the few torturers actually tried and imprisoned for his crimes, seems to have been fascinated by Lumi Videla and blames Marcia Alejandra Merino Vega for her apprehension and death. He claims that Merino was zealous in her efforts to aid the security forces when

they were cruising the street looking for leftists. When they inadvertently passed Videla, Merino frantically pointed her out, ensuring that she fell into their net. Nancy Guzmán, *Romo: Confesiones de un torturador* (Santiago, Chile: Planeta, 2000), pp. 84, 88, 91.

18. Guzmán, *Romo*, pp. 84–86.

19. Inger Agger, *La pieza azul: Testimonio feminino del exilio*, trans. Patricia Salinas and Victoria Olivares (Santiago: Editorial Cuarto Propio, 1993), pp. 92–93. The book appeared in English as *The Blue Room: Trauma and Testimony among Refugee Women, A Psycho-Social Exploration*, trans. Mary Bille (London and Atlantic Highlands, N.J.: Zed Books, 1994), pp. 71–72.

20. Margarita Durán, Declaración jurada, in Vicaría.

21. Ibid.

22. Ibid.

23. Personal interview with Nieves Ayress, New York City, 9 July 2000.

24. Personal interview with Margarita Romano, Santiago, Chile, 23 June 2000. Romano, a philosophy professor, was in her forties in 1973. She agreed to hide a package for an unknown student, and the authorities arrested her and held her in a concentration camp with Nieves Ayress. When Romano's grandson asked us why the torturers were especially brutal to Ayress, Romano speculated that they found Ayress attractive because she was young and pretty, and that the security forces wanted to track down her Cuban boyfriend.

25. Pilar Calveiro, *Poder y desaparición: Los campos de concentración en Argentina* (Buenos Aires: Ediciones Colihue, SRL, 2000), pp. 37–38.

26. In 1995, Samuel Blixen published the first comprehensive study of Operation Condor in the Uruguayan newspaper *Brecha*. An expanded study appears in Samuel Blixen, *Operación Condor: Del archivo del Terror y el asesinato de Letelier al caso Berrios* (Barcelona: Virus Editorial, 1998). *Condor* was a code word for gathering and storing intelligence concerning union activists, leftist students, intellectuals, and dissident generals. Special agents assassinated their opponents wherever they found them in Latin America, Europe, and the United States. Before the Oklahoma City bombing, the most important terrorist act that took place on American soil occurred on 21 September 1976, when former Chilean ambassador Orlando Letelier and his colleague Ronni Moffitt were blown up as their car passed Embassy Row, near Dupont Circle, in Washington, D.C. The American-born DINA agent Michael Townley, who had grown up in Chile, worked with a Chilean chemist, Eugenio Berríos, to make the bomb. According to Daniel Brandt, Pinochet turned Townley over to the U.S. government for prosecution in 1978 with the proviso that other secrets would be kept confidential. See Daniel Brandt, "Operation Condor: Ask the DEA," 10 December 1998, in www.pir.org/condor.html (19 July 2001).

27. Virginia Moreno, in Vicaría. The account in the text depends on the first letter from Virginia Moreno to the general director of the *carabineros*. The declaration was made on 31 January 1974, the day after the detention and disappearance of her husband, daughter, and sixteen-year-old son.

28. Ibid.

29. Ibid.

30. Ibid.

31. Nieves Ayress seldom mentions Antúnez by name. Personal interview with Nieves Ayress, Washington, D.C., 20 January 2001.

32. Res, "La mujer mas torturada en América Latina," back of p. 2, CAM.

33. This description comes from the letter Virginia Moreno wrote to Raquel Lois, Visitadora Social, National Executive Secretary of the Detained, Ministry of National Defense, dated Santiago, 14 March 1974, in Vicaría. Additional details appear in Res, "La mujer mas torturada en América Latina," back of p. 2, CAM.

34. Ayress is quoted in Res, "La mujer mas torturada en América Latina," back of p. 2, CAM.

35. Res, "La mujer mas torturada en América Latina," front of p. 3, CAM.

36. The communiqué of February 1975 was issued by the Women's International Democratic Federation, p. 2. Descriptions of the physical and psychological abuse that Nieves Ayress, her father, and her brother suffered, including the threat that the father and brother would be forced to engage in sexual relations with Nieves, appears in a letter to the Commission on Human Rights of the United Nations written by Carlos José Ayress Moreno, Nieves's brother, who escaped to Rome. "A los señores miembros del comité investigador de los derechos humanos en Chile: Comisión Derechos Humanos de la O.N.U.," 23 June 1975, CAM.

37. Villalón, "Una historia de amor al estilo del Bronx," p. 12.

38. The reminiscence comes from a militant working-class leader in La Victoria widely known as Olga. La Victoria, like La Legua, was a center of Popular Unity support before the coup and a target of government repression afterward. See Jo Fisher, *Out of the Shadows: Women, Resistance, and Politics in South America* (London: Latin American Bureau, 1993), p. 21. Journalist Marc Cooper refers to "Red Olga," whom he describes as "the obstreperous, square-shouldered, white-haired Communist matriarch of La Victoria." Cooper, *Pinochet and Me,* p. 90.

39. Res, "La mujer mas torturada en América Latina," front of p. 3, CAM.

40. Ibid.

41. Fanny Edelman, secretary general of the International Democratic Federation of Women, "Report to the Third Session of the International Commission for Research [on] Crimes Committed by the Military Junta of Chile," 18–21 February 1975, four typed pages, redistributed in 1998, photocopied and in the possession of the author, p. 4. Carlos José Ayress Moreno repeated the charge to the Human Rights Commission of the United Nations on 23 June 1975, CAM.

42. Pilar Calveiro explains in *Poder y desaparición,* p. 84, how in Argentina a torturer who had murdered Graciela Geuna's husband earnestly reassured her that he had placed the family's dog and cat in good hands. Nieves Ayress recalled how the physician examined the fetus in Res, "La mujer mas torturada en América Latina," front of p. 3, CAM.

43. Pedro Alejandro Matta, lecture the Council for International Exchange Seminar, 19 June 2000, Santiago, Chile. Journalist Gladys Díaz suffered several heart attacks and was revived so that she could submit to further torture. See "Mit verklebten Augen auf dem Grill," *Der Spiegel* (Hanover), 31 January–February 1977, pp. 92, 94–95.

44. Personal interview with Nieves Ayress, New York City, 9 July 2000. Postcard entitled "Buscados por la Justicia Internacional: Asesinos, Torturadores, Complices," published by María Roja, 2000, CAM.

45. Moreno, "Copia exacta del original manuscrito entregado el 11 de marzo de 1974 a las 16:00 horas, en el primer juzgado del crimen de San Miguel," CAM and Vicaría.

46. Ibid.

47. Joseph Novitski, "Chile Finds Tense Peace under the Junta," *Washington Post*, 27 May 1974, p. A16.

48. Ibid., pp. A1, A16.

49. Ibid.

50. Rafael Otero, "Los rivales del 'Playboy,'" *La Segunda*, 4 June 1974, 2d ed., n.p., CAM; the column itself is dated 27 May 1974.

51. Paz Alegría, "Perfecto estado de salud," *La Segunda*, 4 June 1974, p. 3, CAM.

52. Moreno, "Copia exacta del original manuscrito entregado el 11 de marzo de 1974," CAM and Vicaría.

53. Novitski, "Chile Finds Tense Peace under the Junta," p. A16.

54. Alegría, "Perfecto estado de salud," p. 3, CAM.

55. Otero, "Los rivales del 'Playboy,'" n.p., CAM.

56. Letter from Virginia M. de Ayress, dated 5 June 1974, and addressed to the director of *La Segunda*, CAM. This letter was never published.

57. Personal interview with Amalia Moreno, Santiago, Chile, 13 June 2000.

58. Personal interview with Nieves Ayress, New York, 16 December 2000.

59. In late October 1998, when Pinochet was detained in London, Nieves Ayress distributed copies of the 1975 document that appeared as Edelman, "Women's International Democratic Federation."

60. Edelman, "Women's International Democratic Federation," p 1.

61. Ibid., p. 4.

62. Beth Goldblatt and Sheila Meintjes fought to have the Commission on Human Rights Abuses of the South African Truth and Reconciliation Commission consider the ways in which gender affected women's lives under apartheid and why it was so difficult for women to tell their own stories. Goldblatt and Meintjes helped organize a special closed meeting of the commission at which women could feel free to talk about themselves. Beth Goldblatt and Sheila Meintjes, *Gender and the Truth and Reconciliation Commission: A Submission to the Truth and Reconciliation Commission* (Johannesburg: Gender Research Project: Centre for Applied Legal Studies, University of Witswatersrand, 1996), p. 4.

63. Calveiro, *Poder y desaparición*, p. 106.

64. Philip Jacobson, "Bid to Free Chile Junta's Top Victim: Luz Tells Her Terrible Tale," *Sunday Times* (London), 19 December 1976, p. 6.

65. Ibid.

66. Ibid.

67. See Ayress's statement quoted in Soria, "Crónicas de la Guerra Sucia," p. 5.

68. Ibid.

69. Ayress, quoted in Ramos, "Así me torturó Pinochet," p. 16.

CHAPTER 2

1. Joan Garcés, *Revolución, congreso, y constitución: El caso Tohá* (Santiago, Chile: Quimantú, 1972); and *Allende y la experiencia chilena: Las armas de la política* (Barcelona: Ariel, 1976). More than anyone else, Joan Garcés gathered the evidence that led to the attempt by Spanish judge Baltasar Garzón to extradite Augusto Pinochet to Spain in 1998 to stand trial for his crimes against humanity.

2. María Correa Morandé, *La guerra de las mujeres* (Santiago, Chile: Editorial Universidad Técnica del Estado, 1974); Teresa Donoso Loero, *La epopeya de las ollas vacías* (Santiago, Chile: Editora Nacional Gabriela Mistral, 1974).

3. Carol Andreas, *Nothing Is As It Should Be: A North American Woman in Chile* (Cambridge, Mass.: Schenkman Publishing Company, 1976).

4. Marc Cooper, *Pinochet and Me: A Chilean Anti-Memoir* (London and New York: Verso, 2001); and Ariel Dorfman, *Heading South, Looking North: A Bilingual Journey* (New York: Penguin Books, 1999).

5. I have changed the names of some women with whom I spoke in order to protect their privacy. Those names are always identified in the text as pseudonyms.

6. Alejandro Portelli, *The Death of Luigi Trastulli and Other Stories: Form and Meaning in Oral History* (Albany: State University of New York Press, 1991), opens with an engaging introduction explaining the development of the practice of oral history. Careful to avoid the romanticizing of oral sources as compared to written texts, Portelli tried to contextualize the stories the speakers told. The dialogue among workers, housewives, and historians and scholars, such as Portelli and Luisa Passerini, about what fascism, the postwar period, and the ascendency of the Christian Democrats had meant to them, has provided an entirely new perspective on the past. See especially Passerini's *Fascism in Popular Memory: The Cultural Experience of the Turin Working Class* (Cambridge, Eng.: Cambridge University Press, 1997).

Oral history also became one of the research areas of a group of British scholars, among whom Anna Davin, Paul Thompson, Sally Alexander, Sheila Rowbotham, and the late Raphael Samuels are only some of the best known. Worried that the generations of political activists before them, especially women organizers, sexual reformers, and members of the social movements of the 1920s and 1930s, would be lost forever, many set out to record their stories about race, class, and gender. There was a great deal of self-examination by feminist scholars who worried about class as well as racial and ethnic differences between those holding the tape recorders and writing down the texts and those speaking. Feminist scholars were desperately afraid that in trying to document the lives of people very different from themselves, they had been guilty of another kind of expropriation. The best collection of feminist reflections on this subject can be found in Sherna Gluck and Daphne Patai, eds., *Women's Words: The Feminist Practice of Oral History* (New York: Routledge, 1991). In consideration of how women carved out gendered spaces for themselves in the Nazi Party, Claudia Koonz interviewed some of the former women leaders in her *Mothers in the Fatherland* (New York: St. Martin's Press, 1981). And Lisa Baldez and Margaret

Power each have written about the women from conservative and right-wing parties who created a movement called Poder Femenino (Feminine Power), which grew into a mass movement that helped destabilize the Popular Unity government in Chile. See Lisa Baldez, *Why Women Protest: Women's Movements in Chile* (New York: Cambridge University Press, 2002); Margaret Power, *Right-Wing Women in Chile: Feminine Power and the Struggle against Allende, 1964–1973* (University Park: Pennsylvania State University Press, 2002).

Other practitioners of oral history worried about the differences gender might make for memory. Luisa Passerini and Polymeris Vogus, among others, explored the question of what gets recorded and what becomes part of the collective memory. See especially Luisa Passerini and Polymeris Vogus, eds., *Gender in the Production of History* (Fiesole, Italy: Department of History and Civilization, European University Institute, 1999); and Selma Leydesdorff, Luisa Passerini, and Paul Thompson, eds., *Gender and Memory,* vol. 4 of the *International Yearbook of Oral History and Life Stories* (Oxford, Eng.: Oxford University Press, 1996).

South Africa too became a fertile ground for oral historians. A controversial work, part oral memoir, part compilation, called *The Long Journey of Poppie Nongena* (Johannesburg: Jonathan Ball Publishers, 1980), written by Elsa Joubert, documented the life of a Black African maid in Cape Town. A bestseller, the book caused speculation about who the author really was and about what its largely white audience wanted when they read this book during the last decade of apartheid. See especially Anne McClintock, *Imperial Leather: Race, Gender and Sexuality in the Colonial Contest* (New York and London: Routledge, 1995). On the other hand, it remains an important narrative about the life of a woman whose identity pass determined her life. From another perspective, a truly remarkable collaborative work can be found in Josette Cole's *Crossroads: The Politics of Reform and Repression 1976–1986* (Johannesburg: Ravan Press, 1987), written by a participant observer and historian who was engaged with Regina N'Tongana and the Women's Committee of the Crossroads squatter settlement as they resisted attempts to forcibly remove them from their shacks near the airport in Cape Town. Cole's book is a fine example of how a historian can achieve direct action in writing.

7. Personal interview with Alicia Cabrini [pseud.], Rancagua, Chile, 19 January 1994.

8. When women are raised to secure provisions for their families, they frequently engage in collective action when there are shortages or high prices for basic commodities. The literature on women's consumer rebellions is vast. A cross-section can be found in David Barry, *Women and Political Insurgency: France in the Mid-Nineteenth Century* (New York: St. Martin's Press, 1986); John Bohstedt, "Gender, Household and Community Politics: Women in English Riots, 1790–1810," *Past and Present* 12 (August 1988): 88–122; Barry, "The Myth of the Feminine Food Riot: Women as Proto-Citizens in English Community Politics, 1790–1810," in *Women and Politics in the Age of Democratic Revolution,* ed. Harriet Applewhite and Darlene Levy (Ann Arbor: University of Michigan Press, 1990); Cynthia A. Bouton, "Gendered Behavior in Subsistence Riots: The French Flour War of 1775," *Journal of Social History* 23 (summer

1990): 735–54; Frank Dana, "Housewives, Socialists, and the Politics of Food: The 1917 New York Cost-of-Living Protests," *Feminist Studies* 11 (summer 1985): 255–85; Belinda Davis, "Food Scarcity and the Empowerment of the Female Consumer in World War I Germany," in *The Sex of Things: Gender and Consumption in Historical Perspective,* ed. Victoria de Grazia (Berkeley: University of California Press, 1996): 287–310, and her *Home Fires Burning: Food, Politics, and Everyday Life in World War I Berlin* (Chapel Hill: University of North Carolina Press, 2000); Barbara Alpern Engel, "Not by Bread Alone: Subsistence Riots in Russia during World War I," *Journal of Modern History* 69, no. 4 (December 1997): 696–721; Ruth A. Frager, "Politicized Housewives in the Jewish Communist Movement of Toronto, 1923–1933," in *Beyond the Vote: Canadian Women and Politics,* ed. Linda Kealey and John Sangster (Toronto: University of Toronto Press, 1989); Temma Kaplan, "Women's Communal Strikes in the Crisis of 1917–22" (in Russia, Italy, Spain, and Veracruz, Mexico), in *Becoming Visible: Women in European History,* ed. Renate Bridenthal, Claudia Koonz, and Susan Mosher Stuard, 2d ed. (Boston: Houghton Mifflin, 1987), pp. 429–49; Paul R. Hanson, "The 'Vie Chère' Riots of 1911: Traditional Protests in Modern Garb," *Journal of Social History* 21 no. 3 (spring 1988): 463–81; Paula E. Hyman, "Immigrant Women and Consumer Protest: The New York City Kosher Meat Boycott of 1902," *American Jewish History* 70, no. 1 (1980): 91–105; Iain J.M. Robertson, "The Role of Women in Social Protest in the Highlands of Scotland, c.1880–1939," *Journal of Historical Geography* (Great Britain) 23, no. 2 (1997): 187–200; Donna F. Ryan, "Ordinary Acts and Resistance: Women in Street Demonstrations and Food Riots in Vichy France," *Proceedings of the Annual Meeting of the Western Society for French History* 16 (1989): 400–407; Judith Smart, "Feminists, Food and the Fair Price: The Cost of Living Demonstrations in Melbourne, August-September 1917," *Labour History* (Australia) 50 (1986): 113–31; Lynne Taylor, "Food Riots Revisited," *Journal of Social History* 30 (winter 1996): 483–96.

9. Lisa Baldez says estimates of the crowd's size varied from twenty thousand to one million. Baldez, *Why Women Protest,* p.113.

10. "Emplazamiento al presidente hacen mujeres DC," *El Mercurio,* 4 September 1973, p. 19.

11. "Impresionante demostración de las mujeres en provincias," *El Mercurio,* 7 September 1973, p. 23.

12. "Millares de mujeres democráticas se reunieron en la Alameda: Repudio femenino al gobierno," *El Mercurio,* 6 September 1973, pp. 1, 10.

13. "Millares de mujeres democráticas se reunieron en la Alameda," *El Mercurio,* 6 September 1973, pp. 1, 10.

14. The same mistake is visible in recent theories of civil society and public discourse that follow the line of analysis developed by Jürgen Habermas. For consideration of the refusal of theorists like Jürgen Habermas to include popular mobilizations in their discussions of public discourse, see Belinda Davis, "Reconsidering Habermas, Gender, and the Public Sphere: The Case of Wilhelmine Germany," in *Society, Culture, and the State in Germany, 1870–1930,* ed. Geoff Eley (Ann Arbor: University of Michigan Press, 1994), p. 409. Although Camilla Townsend is sympathetic to the Popular Unity government, she

is cognizant of the ways in which the government's focus on the interests of male workers and peasants weakened their cause. See Camilla Townsend, "Refusing to Travel *La Via Chilena*: Working-Class Women in Allende's Chile," *Journal of Women's History* 4, no. 3 (winter 1993): 43–63. Heidi Tinsman also examines the dwindling support rural women gave to Allende. She argues that the Popular Unity's provision of family wages enhanced the economic power and authority of rural men, some of whom used their increased authority and public freedom against their wives and children. See Tinsman, *Partners in Protest: The Politics of Gender, Sexuality, and Labor in the Chilean Agrarian Reform, 1950–1973* (Durham, N.C.: Duke University Press, 2002).

15. Temma Kaplan, "Female Consciousness and Collective Action: The Case of Barcelona, 1910–1918," *Signs: Journal of Women in Culture and Society* 7, no. 3 (spring 1982): 545–66; reprinted in *Rethinking the Political: Gender, Resistance and the State*, ed. Barbara Laslett, Johanna Brenner, and Yesim Arat (Chicago: University of Chicago Press, 1995), pp. 145–66. It goes without saying that such ideas are socialized and have nothing to do with biological instincts.

16. For statistical breakdowns of the election returns, see Townsend, "Refusing to Travel *La Via Chilena*," 47. Because women's suffrage had been granted incrementally, women were segregated from men when they voted. Women gained the right to vote in municipal elections in 1935, but they could not vote in presidential elections until 1952, following changes in the law in 1949. When women gained equal suffrage, their votes continued to be counted separately.

17. Although Allende never gained more than 44 percent of women's votes in any neighborhood in Santiago, he won as much as 54 percent of men's votes in two neighborhoods. See figures in Margaret Power, *Right-Wing Women in Chile*, p. 140.

18. María de los Angeles Crummett, "El Poder Femenino: The Mobilization of Women against Socialism in Chile," *Latin American Perspectives* 4, no. 4 (fall 1977): 110.

19. A fictionalized account of right-wing women's efforts to prevent Allende from coming to power appears in Correa Morande, *La guerra de las mujeres*, pp. 12, 21–22. See also Crummett, "El Poder Femenino," 104. I am grateful to María Crummet for allowing me to see the notes from her interviews. Please consult Michèle Mattelart, "Chile: The Feminine Version of the Coup d'Etat," in *Sex and Class in Latin America: Women's Perspectives on Politics, Economics and the Family in the Third World*, ed. June Nash and Helen Icken Safa (New York: J.F. Bergin, 1980), pp. 279–301. See p. 282 for a discussion of the women mourning outside La Moneda presidential palace in 1970.

20. Edy Kaufman, *Crisis in Allende's Chile: New Perspectives* (New York: Praeger, 1988), p. 125, considers the involvement of the United States in the plot to kidnap General Schneider, a subject that also appears in *Hearings before the Select Committee to Study Governmental Operations with Respect to Intelligence Activities of the United States*, 94th Cong., 1st sess., 1975; published in vol. 7 of *Covert Action* (Washington, D.C.: Government Printing Office, 1976), p. 157 [subsequently cited as *Covert Action*].

21. *Appendix to Select Committee Interrogatories for Former President Richard M. Nixon throughout December 1975 and January 1976*, p. 68, in

http://www.arclibrary.org/publib/Church/reports/pdf/ChurchB4-7-Appendixpdf
15 (15 April 2003). The Senate committee found that "the CIA spent $1.5 mil-
lion in support of *El Mercurio,* the country's largest newspaper and the most
important channel for anti-Allende propaganda. According to CIA documents,
these efforts played a significant role in setting the stage for the military coup of
September 11, 1973." *Covert Action,* p. 176.

    22. Lisa Baldez, following the *New York Times,* estimates that the crowd
may have been as small as five thousand. See Baldez, *Why Women Protest,* p.78.
Writing right after the coup in 1973, Michèle Mattelart recognized that the
March of the Empty Pots revealed highly sophisticated planning and execution.
See Mattelart, "Chile." When María Angeles Crummet interviewed women on
the right, they proudly spoke about their own skills in organizing women as
mothers and housewives. See her "El Poder Femenino."

    23. "Protesta femenina por las ollas vacías," *El Mercurio,* 2 December
1971, p. 1.

    24. Margaret Power, *Right-Wing Women in Chile,* pp. 147–68; Baldez,
Why Women Protest, pp. 76–97.

    25. Mattelart, "Chile," p. 282.

    26. "Marcha de las mujeres se realiza a las 18 horas," *El Mercurio,* 1 De-
cember 1971, p. 17.

    27. Mattelart, "Chile," p. 282. I am grateful to Margaret Power for sending
me the article by Carmen Mereno entitled "Cómo es la mujer chilena actual?"
which appeared in *Eva* (Santiago, Chile), 5 July 1968, pp. 8–11. There Mattelart and her husband, Armand, discuss their recently published book, *La mujer
Chilena en una nueva sociedad: Un estudio exploratorio acerca de la situación
e imagen de la mujer en Chile* (Santiago, Chile: Editorial del Pacifico, 1968).

    28. Even if it seemed inconceivable to the left, the right-wing women were
highly skilled political agents and increasingly won support among women of
all classes. For example, the secretary general of the Chilean Communist Party,
Luis Corvalan, commented that the march should have been called "the march
of the full stomachs"; he entirely failed to understand that some of the working-
class and lower-middle-class women mobilized by the right had been convinced
by scare tactics that their families would soon lack necessities. Corvalan, "No
Empty Frying Pans in Chile: Only the Rich Are Protesting," reprinted in *Atlas*
(Santiago, Chile), 21 (February 1972): 25–26.

    29. Power, *Right-Wing Women in Chile,* p. 158.

    30. Quoted in Power, *Right-Wing Women in Chile,* p 160. Power's book,
which is the first full-scale study of women's organizations on the right in Chile,
provides a detailed analysis of how extremely astute right-wing women organizers manipulated symbols and enhanced traditional stereotypes to attract a
mass following that helped overthrow the Popular Unity government. Lisa
Baldez, who has studied Chilean women across the political spectrum and collaborated with Margaret Power in many of the interviews with right-wing
women, shares Power's appreciation for their skill in casting themselves as
"apolitical." See Lisa Baldez, "Nonpartisanship As Political Strategy: Women
Left, Right, and Center in Chile," in *Radical Women in Latin America: Left and*

Right, ed. Victoria González and Karen Kampwirth (University Park: Pennsylvania State University Press, 2001), pp. 273–98.

31. A right-wing account can be found in "Gran número de heridos: Graves incidents," *El Mercurio,* 2 December 1971, pp. 1, 12.

32. Ibid.; Knudson, *The Chilean Press,* p. 51. Power attributes the fighting to male youth brigades, each claiming that the other side provoked the violence. Power, *Right-Wing Women,* p. 157 n. 73. Baldez, who also attributes the fighting to the young men, says the violence forced Allende to declare a state of siege and discredited José Tohá, minister of the interior and one of Allende's most trusted advisers. This eruption set the stage for a pact between the National Party and the Christian Democrats. See Baldez, "Nonpartisanship As a Political Strategy," p. 278.

33. "Sectores políticos repudian agresión a las mujeres," *El Mercurio,* 3 December 1971, p. 25.

34. Here I am borrowing from Alison Brysk's treatment of what she calls the "politics of persuasion." In discussing human rights activists, especially the Madres de Plaza de Mayo in Argentina, she thinks that the junta's perception of them as powerless women initially protected them from attacks. Most scholars—including myself—have considered women's social movements under repressive governments rather than under progressive ones. Studies of right-wing women in Chile demonstrate the ways symbolic protests can also be used to discredit democratic governments. See Brysk, *The Politics of Human Rights in Argentina: Protest, Change, and Democratization* (Stanford, Calif.: Stanford University Press, 1994), p. 10.

35. Personal interview with Teresa Valdés, Santiago, Chile, 17 January 1994.

36. Crummett, "El Poder Femenino," pp. 104, 107.

37. These attempts have been well documented. Contemporary evidence appeared in the report of the Senate select committee known popularly as the Church Committee, which was chaired by Frank Church. See *Covert Action.* In the 1990s, Peter Kornbluh of the National Security Archives, a nonprofit human rights organization, sued under the Freedom of Information Act to get the CIA and the State Department to release eighty thousand documents dealing with political relations between the United States and Chile in the 1970s. The National Security Archives can be reached at www.gwu.edu or www.nsa.gwu.edu.

38. Heidi Tinsman points out that "the UP incorporated more land... in less than three years than the Christian Democrats did in six." *Partners in Protest,* p. 210.

39. This account of agrarian reform comes from a speech that Pedro Vuskovic, the minister of economy, development, and reconstruction, made to several thousand women at the National Stadium in Santiago on 29 July 1971. Vuskovic, "Conversation with the Women of Chile," trans. and ed. Dale L. Johnson, in *The Chilean Road to Socialism* (Garden City, N.Y.: Anchor Press, 1973), p. 464.

40. Paul W. Drake, *Socialism and Populism in Chile, 1932–1952* (Urbana: University of Illinois Press, 1978), pp. 319–20.

41. Peter Winn (producer), "In Women's Hands: The Changing Roles of Women," *Américas,* no. 5 (1993), available through Annenberg Educational Videos.

42. Nina Donoso, "Las mujeres protestamos!" *El Mercurio,* 5 December 1971, p. 41.

43. For a discussion of the shortages, see Videla de Plankey, "Las mujeres pobladores de Chile en el proceso revolutionario," in *Perspectivas femeninas,* ed. María del Carmen Elu de Leñero (Mexico City: Dirección General de Divulgación SepSetentas, 1976), p. 206.

44. Mattelart, "Chile," pp. 289–90.

45. Crummet, "El Poder Femenino," p. 110.

46. Vuskovic, "Conversation with the Women of Chile," p. 463.

47. Ibid., pp. 471–73.

48. Videla de Plankey, "Las mujeres pobladores de Chile en el proceso revolucionario," p. 206.

49. Kaufman, *Crisis in Allende's Chile,* p. 65.

50. Paz Covarrubias, "El movimiento feminista Chileno," in *Chile: Mujer y sociedad,* ed. Paz Covarrubias and R. Franco (Santiago, Chile: UNESCO, 1978), p. 639, cited in Teresa Valdés and Marisa Weinstein, "Organizaciones de pobladoras y construcción democrática en Chile: Notas para un debate," in *La mujeres y la vida de las ciudades,* ed. María del Carmen Feijoó and Hilda María Herzer (Buenos Aires: Grupo Editor Latinoamericano Iled-América Latina, 1991), pp. 113, 116. A more comprehensive study of how the Mothers Centers functioned after the coup can be found in Teresa Valdés and Marisa Weinstein, *Mujeres que sueñan: Las organizaciones de pobladoras 1973–1989* (Santiago, Chile: Facultad Latinoamericana de Ciencias Sociales [Flasco], 1993), esp. pp. 46–70. For the role middle-class women played in the Mothers Centers and Neighborhood Associations, see Mattelart, "Chile," pp. 293–94. To place the Mothers Centers in the context of the development of women's movements in the history of Chile, consult Catalina Palma, *Chilean Women* (Birmingham, Eng.: Trojan Press, 1984), p. 5.

51. Valdés and Weinstein, "Organizaciones de pobladoras," p. 114; Mattelart, "Chile," 293–94. In Brazil, according to Barbara Weinstein, government social workers also attempted to shape the habits and opinions of working-class housewives through the Serviço Social da Indústria (Industrial Social Services, SESI). See Weinstein, *For Social Peace in Brazil: Industrialists and the Remaking of the Working Class in São Paulo, 1920–1964* (Chapel Hill: University of North Carolina Press, 1996), pp. 239–47.

52. Kaufman, *Crisis in Allende's Chile,* p. 64.

53. Ibid.

54. Mattelart, "Chile," p. 292; Knudson, *The Chilean Press,* p. 63; Videla, "Las mujeres pobladoras," p. 204.

55. Videla, "Las mujeres pobladoras," pp. 204, 206.

56. Crummet, "El Poder Femenino," p. 106.

57. This figure comes from Valdés and Weinstein, "Organizaciones de pobladoras," p. 116; and their subsequent *Mujeres que sueñan,* p. 69, where they point out that the Mothers Centers that continued to give their principal

support to the Christian Democrats may have remained aloof from COCEMA, the government coordinating body. Videla, whose research was done right after the coup, estimated that there were only half a million women in twelve thousand centers in 1973 ("Las mujeres pobladores," p. 205)

58. Neves-Xavier de Brito, "Brazilian Women in Exile," p. 65, cited in Francesca Miller, *Latin American Women and the Search for Social Justice* (Hanover, N.H.: University Press of New England, 1991), p. 182.

59. Allende was quoted in the *New York Times,* 21 February 1973, and cited in Kaufman, *Crisis in Allende's Chile,* p. 65.

60. The material on inflation and wages appear in "La papelera en TV: Terminada la papelera. Se acaba libertad del pensamiento escrito en nuestro pais," *El Mercurio,* 28 June 1973, p. 27.

61. Kaufman, *Crisis in Allende's Chile,* pp. 77–78.

62. Ibid., p. 78.

63. Women's creation of a sense of community in mining enclaves has been observed around the world. The isolation of the mines has contributed to an extraordinary sense of solidarity among those who live around them, sometimes including the truckers, small shopkeepers, and surrounding farmers. For descriptions of women's activities in a variety of mining communities, see Agnes Smedley, *Daughter of Earth* (New York: Feminist Press, 1976); Domitila Barrios de Chungara, *Let Me Speak! The Story of a Woman around the Bolivian Mines* (New York: Monthly Review Press, 1978); and Temma Kaplan, "Redressing the Balance: Gendered Acts of Justice around the Mining Community of Río Tinto in 1913," in *Constructing Spanish Womanhood: Female Identity in Modern Spain,* ed. Victoria Lorée Enders and Pamela Beth Radcliff (Albany: State University of New York Press, 1999), pp. 283–300. The most sophisticated study of the place of gender in a mining area appears in Thomas Miller Klubock, *Contested Communities: Class, Gender, and Politics in Chile's El Teniente Copper Mine, 1904–1951* (Durham, N.C.: Duke University Press, 1998).

64. This was according to the congressional investigation by Senator Frank Church recorded in *Covert Action,* p. 8. For a further discussion of the role of the media in undermining the Popular Unity government, see Jerry W. Knudson, "The Chilean Press during the Allende Years, 1970–1973," unpublished lecture delivered at Temple University, n.d., copy in possession of the author, p. 82.

65. Jerry W. Knudson, "The Chilean Press," p. 23.

66. *Punto Final,* 19 December 1972, p. 27, cited in Knudson, "The Chilean Press," p. 8.

67. Crummett, "El Poder Femenino," p. 106.

68. María Teresa Alamos, "Carmen Miranda," *El Mercurio,* 24 June 1973, p. 22.

69. "Marcha preparan mujeres de los mineros," *El Mercurio,* 25 June 1973, p. 1; "Marcha inician mujeres de los mineros," *El Mercurio,* 26 June 1973, pp. 1, 8; "Entusiasta apoyo a esposas de mineros," *El Mercurio,* 27 June 1973, pp. 1, 12.

70. "Entusiasta apoyo a esposas de mineros," *El Mercurio,* 27 June 1973, pp. 1, 12.

71. "Marcha preparan mujeres de los mineros," p. 1; "Marcha inician mujeres de los mineros," pp. 1, 8.

72. Ibid.

73. "Delegación fue recibida por S.E.," *El Mercurio*, 27 June 1973, pp. 1, 12.

74. "Entusiasta apoyo a esposas de mineros," pp. 1, 12.

75. "Marcha preparan mujeres de los mineros," p. 1.

76. "Entusiasta apoyo a esposas de mineros," pp. 1, 12.

77. "Esposas de mineros visitaron a Allende," *El Mercurio*, 28 June 1973, p. 20. Articles about women who aided Allende by supporting their husbands' refusal to strike appeared in leftist papers such as *Seminar* and *El Teniente*. In the article from 29 June 1973 entitled "Allende Gains Women's Support," an old woman, Teresa Rojas, is quoted as chastising miners, including members of her own family, for "forgetting that this government is the government of the working class." Another woman who opposed the strike at El Teniente was shot at three times. Despite these and other efforts to publicize certain women's opposition to the strike, the paper never wrote about shortages, limiting mentions of how women were struggling to support their families to articles on the woman's page saying that good housewives use leftovers creatively (10 August 1973).

78. "Mujeres organizan Cabildo del Hambre," *El Mercurio*, 26 June 1973, p. 23.

79. "Santiago puede quedar sin pan," *El Mercurio*, 28 June 1973, p. 22.

80. "General Prats comandó Tropas a las que se rindieron los sublevados," and "Allende pidió estado de Sitio," *El Mercurio*, 30 June 1973, pp. 1, 12.

81. *Washington Post*, 14 August 1973, cited in Kaufman, *Crisis in Allende's Chile*, p. 67.

82. *El Mercurio*, 16 and 18 August 1973, cited in Kaufman, *Crisis in Allende's Chile*, p. 67.

83. Crummet, "El Poder Femenino," p. 107; *El Mercurio*, 19, 26, and 23 August 1973; and *Washington Post*, 23 August 1973, cited in Kaufman, *Crisis in Allende's Chile*, p. 67.

84. "Chile en el filo de la Navaja" (translated from the Frankfurt *Allgemeine Zeitung*), *El Mercurio*, 5 September 1973, p. 2.

85. "Mujeres Gremialistas piden inhabilidad de S. Allende," *El Mercurio*, 7 September 1973, pp. 1, 10.

86. "Dramático anuncio: Allende: 'Hay harina sólo para tres o cuatro días,'" *El Mercurio*, 7 September 1973, p. 17.

87. "Angustioso escasez de pan," *El Mercurio*, 8 September 1973, pp. 1, 12; "Revista Noticiosa," *El Mercurio*, 9 September 1973, p. 11.

88. "Angustioso escasez de pan," pp. 1, 12. Here and elsewhere, *El Mercurio* may have promoted articles dealing with the dissatisfaction of working-class and poor people in order to demonstrate that they too were turning against Allende.

89. "El drama en la cola del pan," *El Mercurio*, 10 September 1973, pp. 21, 26.

90. "Casi mitad de panaderías cerró en Valparaíso," *El Mercurio*, 10 September 1973, p. 26.

91. Personal interview with María Prada [pseud.], Chicago, 25 September 1998.

92. Mattelart, "Chile," p. 179.

93. My translation of a statement by Clara de Sierra from Antofagasta quoted in "Mujeres desesperadas piden leche para dar a sus hijos," *El Mercurio*, 8 September 1973, p. 11.

94. Crummett, "El Poder Femenino," pp. 104, 107.

95. Quoted in Tomás G. Sanders, "Military Government in Chile," in *The Politics of Anti-politics*, ed. Brian Loveman and Thomas M. Davies Jr. (Lincoln: University of Nebraska Press, 1978), p. 272, cited in Kaufman, *Crisis in Allende's Chile*, p. 68.

96. Power, *Right-Wing Women in Chile*, p. 229.

97. "Manifestación femenina frente a Ministerio de Defensa," *El Mercurio*, 11 September 1973, p. 10.

98. Both women were quoted in an anonymous article in the *Los Angeles Times*, 31 January 1974, probably written by David Belnap, cited in Kaufman, *Crisis in Allende's Chile*, pp. 68–69; see also Crummet, "El Poder Femenino," p. 103.

99. Miller, *Latin American Women*, p. 185.

100. Morande, *La guerra de las mujeres*, p. 32; Crummet's sources claim that within three months of the March of the Empty Pots, El Poder Femenino had formed and was in control of the women's movement. See Crummet, "El Poder Femenino," p. 104.

101. Morande, *La guerra de las mujeres*, p. 32.

102. Margaret Power and Lisa Baldez interviewed some of the remaining three hundred members of SOL in 1993. See Baldez, *Why Women Protest*, p. 116; Power, *Right-Wing Women*, pp. 229, 230.

103. Personal interview with María Prada [pseud.], New York, 25 February 1994.

104. Mattelart, "Chile," pp. 284–85.

105. Ibid., p. 287.

106. Ibid., pp. 287–88.

107. Vuskovic, "Conversation with the Women of Chile," pp. 458, 473.

108. Patricia M. Chuchryk, "Feminist Anti-authoritarian Politics: The Role of Women's Organizations in the Chilean Transition to Democracy," in *The Women's Movement in Latin America: Feminism and the Transition to Democracy*, ed. Jane S. Jaquette (Boston: Unwin Hyman, 1989), p. 160.

109. See esp. Correa Morandé, *La guerra de las mujeres;* and Loero, *El epopeya de los ollas vacias*.

110. Salvador A. Allende Gossens, *El pueblo debe organizarse y actuar: El presidente Allende en Concepción* (Santiago, Chile: Consejeria de Difusión de la Presidencia de la Republica, 1972), pp. 196–97. Translated by and quoted in Elsa M. Chaney, "The Mobilization of Women in Allende's Chile," in *Women in Politics*, ed. Jane S. Jaquette (New York: John Wiley & Sons, 1974), p. 269. For a lively and comprehensive study of what the Popular Unity government was able to achieve, see Peter Winn, *Weavers of the Revolution: The Yarur Workers and Chile's Road to Socialism* (New York: Oxford University Press, 1986).

CHAPTER 3

1. The ways in which women, using the language of rights, have demanded equality with men by forming separate movements of women is one of the insights Joan Wallach Scott presents in *Only Paradoxes to Offer: French Feminists and the Rights of Man* (Cambridge: Harvard University Press, 1996).

2. Teresa Valdés and I met in the fall of 1986 when she taught at the Columbia University Center for Iberian and Latin American Studies. From that time on, in Santiago, New York, Miami, and Washington, D.C., we have spoken informally and held taped interviews about Mujeres por la Vida. In 1986, along with Chilean poet and human rights activist Marjorie Agosín, we wrote a short article about the situation of women in Chile. See Temma Kaplan, Marjorie Agosín, and Teresa Valdés, "Women and the Politics of Spectacle in Chile," *Barnard Occasional Papers on Women's Issues* 3, no. 2 (1986): 1–8.

3. Marjorie Agosín was the first to write about the *arpilleristas* as a social movement dedicated to human rights, and she has written extensively about the *arpilleras* as testimonials and works of art. See her *Scraps of Life: Chilean Arpilleras: Chilean Women and the Pinochet Dictatorship*, trans. Cola Franzen (Toronto: Williams-Wallace Publishers, 1987–88), and *Tapestries of Hope, Threads of Love: The Arpillera Movement in Chile, 1974–1994* (Albuquerque: University of New Mexico Press, 1996).

4. A good introduction to the work of the Vicaría can be found in Hugo Fruhling, "Resistance to Fear in Chile: The Experience of the Vicaría de la Solidaridad," in *Fear at the Edge: State Terror and Resistance in Latin America*, ed. Juan E. Corradi, Patricia Weiss Fagen, and Manuel Antonio Garretón (Berkeley: University of California Press, 1992), pp. 124–25.

5. Working through FLACSO, the Latin American Organization for Faculty in the Social Sciences, an independent research agency, Valdés has published numerous works on demography and women's social movements in Chile. See, for example, *Chile: Mujeres latinoamericanas en Cifras* (Santiago, Chile: Instituto de la Mujer, Ministerio de Asuntos Sociales de España y Facultad Latinoamericana de Ciencias Sociales, FLACSO, 1992); *Documentos de Trabajo: El movimiento social de mujeres y la producción de conicimientos sobre la condicion de la mujer*, vol. 43 of Serie Estudios Sociales (Santiago: FLACSO, 1993). The informal archivist of Mujeres por la Vida, Teresa Valdés seems to have kept most of the flyers, stickers, posters, pictures, and notes about organizing demonstrations and making women's political demands explicit to the opposition. Those files, which she has made available to me, are organized by year. They are cited as CTV (Colección Teresa Valdés) with the year.

6. Personal interview with Juanita Álvarado, Santiago, Chile, 18 January 1994.

7. See Chapter 1, n. 6 for a statistical breakdown of those who disappeared.

8. Francesca Miller, *Latin American Women and the Search for Social Justice* (Hanover, N.H.: University Press of New England, 1990), p. 184.

9. Patricia M. Chuchryk, "Feminist Anti-authoritarian Politics: The Role of Women's Organizations in the Chilean Transition to Democracy," in *The Women's Movement in Latin America: Feminism and the Transition to Democracy*, ed. Jane S. Jaquette (Boston: Unwin Hyman, 1989), p. 160; Teresa Valdés and Alicia Frohmann, *Documentos de trabajo: "Democracy in the Country and in the Home," The Women's Movement in Chile*, vol. 55 of Serie Estudios Sociales (Santiago: FLACSO, 1993); and Edda Gaviola, Eliana Largo, and Sandra Palestro, *Una historia necesaria: Mujeres en Chile 1973–1990* (Santiago, Chile: Akí & Aora, 1994).

10. The most comprehensive study of working-class women's participation in the opposition movement is Teresa Valdés, *Venid, benditas de mi Padre: Las pobladoras, sus rutinas y sus sueños* (Santiago: FLACSO, 1988). Detailed analyses of how Chile's working-class and poor women created a social movement of resistance can be found in Veronica Ingrid Shild, "Gender, Class and Politics: Poor Neighborhood Organizing in Authoritarian Chile," Ph.D. diss., University of Toronto, 1991; and Marieke Heemskerk, " 'I Believe I Grew a Lot…': An Oral History of Women's Participation in Popular Organizations in the Poblaciones of Santiago de Chile since the Pinochet Dictatorship, 1973–present," master's thesis, University of Utrecht, the Netherlands, 1995.

11. Naomi Rosenthal and Michael Schwartz, "Spontaneity and Democracy in Social Movements," *International Social Movement Research* 2 (1989): 47.

12. Irene Rojas spoke to anthropologist Marieke Heemskerk, as quoted in "I Believe I Grew a Lot," p. 79.

13. Cáceras quoted in Heemskerk, "I Believe I Grew a Lot," p. 79.

14. Rojas in an interview with Heemskerk, in "I Believe I Grew a Lot," p. 118.

15. Frans J. Schuurman and Ellen Heer, *Social Movements and NGOs in Latin America: A Case-Study of the Women's Movement in Chile*, vol. 2 of Nijmegen Studies in Development and Cultural Change (Saarbrücken and Fort Lauderdale: Verlag Breitenbach, 1992), pp. 32–33. See also Cathy Lisa Schneider, *Shantytown Protest in Pinochet's Chile* (Philadelphia: Temple University Press, 1995).

16. The reminiscences of Violeta Morales, a leader of the Folkloric Group, appear in Marjorie Agosín, *Tapestries of Hope*, p. 110.

17. Viviana Díaz Caro, Sola Sierra Henríquez, Gustavo Adolfo Becerra, and Mireya García Ramírez, *Un camino de imágenes: 20 años de historia de la Agrupación de Familiares de Detenidos Desaparecidos de Chile* (Santiago, Chile: Corporación Agrupación de Familiares de Detenidos Desaparecidos, 1997), p. 29.

18. *Chilean Resistance Courier No. 9: Bulletin of the Movement of the Revolutionary Left (MIR) Outside Chile (Oakland, California)*, no. 18 (May–June 1978), pp. 16, 52.

19. Olga Poblete, *Día Internacional de la Mujer en Chile: Otro capítulo de una historia invisible* (Santiago, Chile: Ediciones MEMCH "83," 1987), pp. 68–72.

20. Tomás Moulian, "A Time of Forgetting: The Myths of the Chilean Transition," trans. Margot Olvarria; and Priscilla Hayner, "Truth Commissions: Exhuming the Past," *NACLA: Report on the Americas* 32, no. 2 (September–October 1998): 16–22, 30–32.

21. "¡Cinco Años!" *Vamos Mujer* 2 (March–April 1985), p. 5, available in *Chilean Women's Organizations and Protest Activities, 1985–1987*, in Special Collections, Firestone Library, Princeton University (subsequently referred to as *Chilean Women's Organizations*), folder 2. The *Informe de la Comisión Nacional de Verdad y Reconciliación* (Report of the National Commission on Truth and Reconciliation, informally called the Informe Rettig, or Rettig Report) (Santiago: Comisión Nacional de Verdad y Reconciliación, 1991), 2: 701–26: discusses what is known about the 141 people who died in the repres-

sion of the Days of National Protest that took place between 1983 and 1985 (subsequently referred to as *Informe Rettig*).

22. *Informe Rettig*, 2: 702. Teresa Valdés recalls that labor leaders and women activists promoted this strategy. Phone interview, 23 June 2002.

23. *Informe Rettig*, 2: 706.

24. *Informe Rettig*, 2: 713–14.

25. Account in a letter coordinated by Mujeres por la Vida and distributed to various foreign embassies in Santiago on 22 March 1984. Letter addressed "De nuestra mayor consideración," CTV 1984–85, photocopied and in the possession of the author. Julieta Kirkwood, who died of breast cancer in 1986, wrote *Ser Politica en Chile: Los nudos de la sabiduria feminista* (Santiago, Chile: Editorial Cuarto Propio, 1990), but her influence on the women's movement in Chile goes far beyond her writings.

26. Teresa Valdés, " 'Mujeres por la Vida:' Women's Struggle for Democracy in Chile," unpublished paper, p. 2; "Hoy y no mañana," two-page photocopied statement followed by nine pages of typed names of signatories, CTV, 1983. See also Liza Baldez, *Why Women Protest: Women's Movements in Chile* (New York: Cambridge University Press, 2002), pp. 154–60, for consideration of Mujeres por la Vida.

27. The events organized by Mujeres por la Vida are outlined in two pages of " 'Mujeres por la Vida': Itinerario de una lucha," CTV, 1983–87 (subsequently referred to as "Itinerario"; the pages are unnumbered in the manuscript; page numbers in brackets refer to the author's numbering).

28. For a discussion of the growing feminist commitment of the resistance movement in Chile, see Lylian Mires, "Las mujeres y su articulación con el sistema político," *Proposiciones 22: Actores Sociales y Democracia* (Santiago, Chile: Ediciones Sur, 1993) p. 99.

29. Personal interview with María Asunción Bustos, Santiago, Chile, 12 January 1994.

30. *Informe Rettig*, 2: 703.

31. In a different context, Nancy Fraser has discussed the creation of public spheres as repositories of democratic ideals. See Fraser, "Rethinking the Public Sphere: A Contribution to the Critique of Actually Existing Democracy," in *Habermas and the Public Sphere,* ed. Craig Calhoun (Cambridge, Mass.: MIT Press, 1999), p. 139 n. 14.

32. Olga Poblete, *Día Internacional de la Mujer en Chile*, pp. 16, 21; "Día Internacional de la mujer, 8 de marzo de 1987," Documento MEMCH "83," *Chilean Women's Organizations*, box 1, folder 8, item 1 (February 1987).

33. Poblete, *Día Internacional,* p. 26. Teresa Valdés recalls the fights Mujeres por la Vida had with trade union leaders, who refused to have the day called a celebration. They believed erroneously that the holiday commemorated the Triangle Shirtwaist Fire in New York in 1909, and insisted on tying the day exclusively to women factory workers. Bitter fights ensued between Mujeres por la Vida and the labor leaders over who had the right to organize the day's events. Phone interview with Teresa Valdés, 23 June 2002.

34. Poblete, *Día Internacional,* p. 32.

35. Ibid., p. 64.

36. Ibid., pp. 51–52, 66.

37. Typed flyer, "A la opinión pública," signed "Mujeres por la Vida, Santiago, 8 de Marzo de 1984," in CTV, 1984–85. See also "Itinerario" [p. 1].

38. Letter addressed to foreign ambassadors, dated Santiago de Chile, 22 March 1984, and signed by a variety of women's groups, including the Women's Department of the National Union Coordinating Committee, the Committee on the Rights of Women of the Chilean Commission on Human Rights, the Executive Committee of MEMCH "83," and Mujeres por la Vida, in CTV, 1984, pp. 1–3.

39. Letter addressed to foreign ambassadors, CTV, 1984, pp. 1–3.

40. *Informe Rettig*, 2: 726.

41. "Itinerario" [p. 2].

42. Personal interview with Paulina Weber, Santiago, Chile, 14 January 1994.

43. Poblete, *Día Internacional*, pp. 32, 72.

44. Personal interview with Teresa Valdés, Santiago, Chile, 18 January 1994.

45. "Itinerario" [p. 3].

46. *Informe Rettig*, 2: 730.

47. "Señor embajador de...," a photocopied form letter sent by Mujeres por la Vida, CTV, 1986.

48. "Declaración...Mujeres por la Vida," CTV, 1986.

49. "Sustentáculos para los manifestantes," one-page photocopied document in CTV, 1986.

50. "Instructivo," one-page map and instructions for the 7 March 1986 International Woman's Day March, CTV, 1986.

51. "Decimos 'NO+' porque 'Somos +': Libreto: Día Internacional de la Mujer," March 1986, one-page photocopied song sheet, CTV, 1986.

52. *Informe Rettig*, 2: 733.

53. Poblete, *Día Internacional*, pp. 74, 76; "Itinerario" [p. 4]; "Así ejercemos nuestros derechos democráticos," Santiago, Chile, 20 March 1986, one-page photocopied list of goals, CTV, 1986.

54. "¡Acción de propaganda de mujeres en supermercados! ¡No seremos complices de financiar la mentira!" two-page booklet, signed "Mujeres chilenas," photocopied, CTV, 1986; "¡Participemos en la desobediencia civilpatriótica!" one-page photocopied flyer, CTV, 1986.

55. Saa tells this story in "In Women's Hands: The Changing Roles of Women," *Américas,* which Peter Winn produced and Raúl Julia narrated. Available from Annenberg Educational Videos (1993).

56. "Pliego de las mujeres," four-page photocopied list of women's demands, with a handwritten note by Teresa Valdés explaining that the document was prepared by the women's organizations to be presented to the Civic Assembly and incorporated into the document called "Chile Demands," CTV, 1986.

57. Teresa Valdés, "Women for Life: Women's Struggle for Democracy in Chile," lecture given at the Center for Iberian and Latin American Studies, Columbia University, February 1987.

58. "Pliego de las mujeres," p. 2.

59. Ibid.

60. Ibid., pp. 3–4.

61. "Convocatoria," photocopied one-page list of goals and sponsors for the March 20 march, CTV, 1986; Valdés, " 'Women for Life': Women's Struggle for Democracy in Chile," CTV, 1986 [p. 4]; "Itinerario" [pp. 4–8].

62. "Sector mujeres: Evaluación crítica del funcionamiento de la Asamblea," CTV, two-page photocopied document, CTV, 1986, pp. 1–2.

63. "Sector mujeres," p. 2.

64. "Evaluación y propuesta de la comisión creativo de la Asamblea de la civilidad," 11 July 1986, eleven-page photocopied document, CTV, 1986, pp. 1–5.

65. "¡No mas dictadura! ¡Viveremos!" 24 July 1986, CTV, 1986.

66. "Itinerario" [p. 7].

67. "Señores, ministros, Corte Suprema, *presente,*" 30 July 30 1986, one-page photocopied document, CTV, 1986.

68. "Las mujeres al pueblo de Chile," 28 August 1986, one-page photocopied document, CTV, 1986; *Informe Rettig,* 2: 736.

69. "A la opinión pública," two-page photocopied document, signed by Mujeres por la Vida, dated August 28, 1986, CTV, 1986; "A la opinión pública," one-page photocopied document, dated Santiago, September 1986, CTV.

70. Fanny Pollarolo interview in Eugenia Hola and Babriela Pischedda, *Mujeres, Poder y Política: Nuevas tensiones para viejas estructuras* (Santiago, Chile: Educiones Centro de Estudios de la Mujer, 1993), p. 200; personal interview with Fanny Pollarolo, Santiago, Chile, 14 January 1994.

71. "Itinerario" [p. 9].

72. Ibid.

73. *Informe Rettig,* 2: 737.

74. One photocopied page, Mujeres por la vida, "Declaración pública," Santiago, 10 March 1987, CTV, 1987; "Itinerario" [p. 10].

75. "Itinerario" [p. 11]; interview with Graciela Bórquez, Santiago, Chile, 20 January 1994.

76. Photocopy of a letter to Señora Cármen Ramírez, National Director of the Women's Department of the Christian Democratic Party, dated 19 August 1987, CTV, 1987; photocopied eight-page plan for the meeting "Libreto gimnasio nacional," 25 August 1987, CTV, 1987.

77. "De luto en silencio mujeres recuerdan el 11," *Fortín mapocho,* 12 September 1987, clipping in CTV, 1987.

78. Valdés and Frohmann, "Democracy in the Country and in the Home, " pp. 16–17.

79. Five-page photocopied plan, analysis, and fundraising letter entitled "Campaña 'NO ME OLVIDES,'" signed "Mujeres por la vida" and dated Santiago, 15 November 1988; Sandra Radié, "Mujeres por la Vida: 'Para que no me olvides,'" *Raz y Justicia,* no. 57 (October 1988), pp. 23–24, clipping in CTV, 1988. I am grateful to Teresa Valdés for providing me with a video of the demonstration.

80. Phone interview with Teresa Valdés, 23 June 2002.

81. One-page photocopied sheet, "Convocatoria: Día internacional de la mujer," Santiago, 7 March 1989, CTV, 1988–89.

82. Ibid.

83. Frohmann and Valdés, "Democracy in the Country and in the Home," p. 17.

84. Ibid., pp. 18–20.

85. "Mujeres por la vida: Llenaron la Suprema con pescado podrido," *Fortín Mapoche,* 23 January 1990, p. 7, clipping in CTV, 1988–90.

86. Patricia Moscoso and Esteban Valenzuela, "Mujeres: Vamos a andar," *Revista APSI* (9–25 January 1986) [p. 1], CTV. One branch of U.S. feminism followed a similar trajectory. For a compelling account about how feminism emerged among women members of SNCC (Student Nonviolent Coordinating Committee) during the Civil Rights struggles in the American South, see Sara Evans, *Personal Politics* (New York: Vintage Books, 1979). For the role black women played in the Civil Rights movement, see Belinda Robnett, *How Long? How Long: African American Women in the Civil Rights Movement* (New York: Oxford University Press, 1997).

87. Moscoso and Valenzuela, "Mujeres: Vamos a andar" [p. 3].

88. Ibid.

89. Personal interview with Fanny Pollarolo, Santiago, Chile, 19 January 1994.

CHAPTER 4

1. A substantial number of books deal with the period from 1973 to 1983 in Argentina, covering the Peronist restoration, the period in which the right-wing Triple-A death squads operated, the coup, and the Dirty War. The report of the National Commission on the Detained and Disappeared, published as *Nunca Más: The Report of the Argentine National Commission on the Disappeared,* intro. Ronald Dworkin (New York: Farrar Strauss Giroux, 1986), is probably a good place to begin. I have carried out interviews with some of the Madres and with others who were in Argentina during the Dirty War, and they will be mentioned in the notes as they come up.

Among the variety of interviews with members of the Madres de Plaza de Mayo, see Marjorie Agosín, *The Mothers of Plaza de Mayo: The Story of Renée Epelbaum 1976–1985,* trans. Janice Molloy (Trenton, N.J.: Red Sea Press, 1990); Mabel Bellucci, "El movimiento de Madres de Plaza de Mayo," in *Historia de las mujeres en la Argentina,* ed. Fernanda Gil Lozano, Valeria Silvina Pita, and María Gabriela Ini (Buenos Aires: Taurus, 2000), 2: 267–87; Marguerite Guzman Bouvard, *Revolutionizing Motherhood: The Mothers of the Plaza de Mayo* (Wilmington, Del.: SR Books, 1994); Jean-Pierre Bousquet, *Las Locas de la Plaza de Mayo* (Buenos Aires: El Cid Editor, 1983); Alejandro Diago, *Conversando con las Madres de Plaza de Mayo: Hebe memoria y esperanza* (Buenos Aires: Ediciones Dialéctica, 1988); Jo Fisher, *Mothers of the Disappeared* (London and Boston: ZED and South End Press, 1989); Matilde Mellibovsky, *Círculo de amor sobre la muerte* (Buenos Aires: Ediciones del

Pensamiento Nacional, 1990); Marysa Navarro, "The Personal is Political: Las Madres de Plaza de Mayo," in *Power and Popular Protest: Latin American Social Movements,* ed. Susan Eckstein (Berkeley: University of California Press, 1989); Piera Paola Oria, *De la casa a la plaza* (Buenos Aires: Editorial Nueva América, n.d.); and John Simpson and Jana Bennett, *The Disappeared and the Mothers of the Plaza de Mayo: The Story of the 11,000 Argentinians Who Vanished* (New York: St. Martin's Press, 1985).

In contrast to a lot of oral history, where even the most thoughtful and committed writers come from outside the community, those collecting the Madres' testimonies are frequently Madres themselves. These works are unparalleled for the insights they provide about the Madres as activists and about their thoughts at the time they gave their testimony.

2. Personal interview with Nora Morales de Cortiñas, Buenos Aires, Argentina, 21 November 1991.

3. Bouvard refers to Jorge Bonafini's commitment to the Third World Church, under whose auspices he taught Sunday school and worked among the poor. *Revolutionizing Motherhood,* p. 102.

4. Evidence about the government's action in the Dirty War is quoted in Amos Elon, "Letter from Argentina," *New Yorker,* 21 July 1986, p. 86; my translation of Brailovsky as quoted in Mellibovsky, *Circulo de amor,* pp. 7–8. Following the report of the Argentine National Commission on the Disappeared (CONADEP) in September 1984 and the trials of the commanders of the Argentine juntas in 1985–87, vast amounts of information were released to the public.

5. Fisher, *Mothers of the Disappeared,* p. 66; Agosín, *The Mothers of Plaza,* p. 85.

6. Quoted in translation in Fisher, *Mothers of the Disappeared,* p. 143.

7. Ibid., p. 60.

8. My translation of her recollection in Mellibovsky, *Circulo de amor,* p. 55.

9. Ibid., pp. 55–56.

10. Inés Izaguirre, "Recapturing the Memory of Politics," *NACLA: Report on the Americas* 31, no. 6 (May–June 1998): 33 n. 17, where she provides a chart of the number of disappearances between 1971 and the coup on 24 March 1976. She shows that 1,058 people, or 9 percent of all those who disappeared before 1983, were abducted even before the coup on 24 March 1976. John Simpson and Jana Bennett of the BBC argued that 200 died at the hands of the Triple-A in 1974 and 850 in 1975. See *The Disappeared and the Mothers of the Plaza de Mayo,* p. 65. According to them, by the time of the coup, there was a political killing every five hours and a bomb every three hours.

Izaguirre's argument, developed more fully in *Violencia Social y Derechos Humanos* (Buenos Aires: EUDEBA, 1998), is that preceding their war of extermination against all those they opposed, they had defeated the Ejército Revolucionario del Pueblo (People's Revolutionary Army, ERP) and had decimated the leftist Peronist Montoneros, the largest guerrilla group. She claims that the government not only violated the human rights of those it tortured and murdered, but that the government also violated the rules of war.

11. Inés Izaguirre, citing Laura Bonaparte's *El mundo guarda silencio: La tragedia de Canuelas* (Buenos Aires: Editorial Catálogos, 1993), argues that

Seneildín was one of the most important people connecting the Triple-A to the military, and that he was even involved in helping right-wing military efforts in Central America in the 1980s. Izaguirre, "Recapturing the Memory of Politics," p. 33 n. 5.

12. Izaguirre, "Recapturing the Memory of Politics," p. 33 n. 17.

13. Ibid.; Piera Paola Oria claims that over 300 people disappeared at the hands of the Triple-A and of another right-wing group, the Comando Libertadores de América. See Oria, *De la casa a la plaza,* pp. 37–38. Carlos Santiago Nino (*Radical Evil on Trial* [New Haven, Conn.: Yale University Press, 1996], p. 53) argues that in the first three months of 1976, just before the military coup, 149 died violent political deaths. As with the numbers of those who disappeared during the dictatorship, all these numbers are open to dispute because no official records remain.

14. Cited in Rodríguez, "Un genocidio 'corajudo,'" *Madres de Plaza de Mayo,* May 1995, p. 3.

15. Simpson and Bennett, *The Disappeared,* p. 41; Nino, *Radical Evil on Trial,* p. 53.

16. Simpson and Bennett argue that the junta made a concentrated effort to appear judicious in the first days of the coup. Initially, although they suppressed what they considered "subversive material," suspended the unions, and announced that terrorists would be "shot on sight," they did not execute anyone from the previous government. *The Disappeared and the Mothers of the Plaza de Mayo,* p. 40; *Nunca Más,* p. 448, provide the following breakdown of those who were abducted and disappeared during the dictatorship:

Blue-collar workers	30.2
Students	21.0
White-collar workers	17.9
Professionals	10.7
Teachers	5.7
Self-employed and others	5.0
Housewives	3.8
Military conscripts and members of the security services	2.5
Journalists	1.6
Actors, performers	1.3
Nuns, priests	0.3

17. *Núnca Mas,* p. 285.

18. This quote, which may be the most frequently reproduced statement of the junta's beliefs, first appeared in an interview with the *International Herald Tribune* on 26 May 1977, one year after the Dirty War had begun. It clearly expresses what the junta viewed as subversion and the lengths to which they were willing to go to impose their "moral values" on the country.

19. Critic Diana Taylor argues that the junta turned every aspect of the terror into a spectacle and that to counteract the government, those who wanted to resist attempted to stage their responses and mount alternative performances.

See *Disappearing Acts: Spectacles of Gender and Nationalism in Argentina's "Dirty War"* (Durham, N.C.: Duke University Press, 1997).

20. Navarro, "The Personal Is Political," p. 246.

21. File no. 6974, quoted in *Nunca Más*, p. 57.

22. Elon, "Letter from Argentina," p. 75; *Nunca Más*, p. 10.

23. Miriam Lewin speaks about Massera in *Ese Infierno: Conversaciones de cinco mujeres sobrevivientes de la ESMA* (Buenos Aires: Editorial Sudamericana, 2001), p. 142. She co-authored the book with Manú Actis, Cristina Aldini, Liliana Gardella, and Elisa Tokar, who were also prisoners at ESMA.

24. There are many reports about the markers. See, for example, Elon, "Letter from Argentina," p. 75. In the mid-1980s, a woman who had lost her child went to the cemetery to bring flowers. Beyond tombs dated 19 November 1976, she saw wooden crosses with the inscription N.N. for "no name" or "anonymous." On one of her visits, a cemetery worker approached her and begged her not to report the crosses he was placing on the graves. Diago, *Conversando con las Madres*, p. 189.

25. Mellibovsky, *Circulo de amor*, pp. 59–60.

26. Simpson and Bennett, *The Disappeared and the Mothers of the Plaza de Mayo*, p. 133. As in Europe during the Holocaust, state terror seems to have worked to suppress a sense of solidarity in all but the most heroic people. The vast majority of the population of Argentina seems to have preferred to make themselves invisible rather than risk disappearing.

27. Élida de Galletti in Oria, *De la casa*, p. 142. See also the account in Navarro, "The Personal Is Political," p. 250.

28. María Adela Gard de Antokoletz is quoted in Mellibovsky (my translation), *Circulo de amor*, p. 40.

29. Quoted in Enrique Arrosagaray, *Biografía de Azucena Villaflor: Creadora del movimiento de Madres de Plaza de Mayo* (Buenos Aires: Privately printed, 1997), p. 122.

30. It would be interesting to compare Villaflor's background, gender identity, and commitment to Peronism to that of Doña María Roldán, the Peronist union activist, about whom historian Daniel James has written in *Doña María's Story: Life History, Memory, and Political Identity* (Durham, N.C.: Duke University Press, 2000).

31. One of the early Madres, María del Rosario Cerruti, claimed that Azucena Villaflor was such an avid Peronist that they almost came to blows, one of the reasons the Madres avoided talking about their own or their children's political views. Arrosagaray, *Biografía de Azucena Villaflor*, p. 172.

32. Juana de Pargament, quoted in Arrosagaray, *Biografía de Azucena Villaflor*, p. 116.

33. For the account by Antokoletz, see Mellibovsky, *Circulo de amor*, pp. 39–40. This story, with some variations, appears in a variety of sources. As late as 1981, Élida de Galletti, the honorary president of the Federación Latinoamericana de Asociaciones de Familiares de Detenidos y Desaparecidos (American Federation of Associations of Families of the Detained and Disappeared, FEDEFAM), told the same story. Speaking to the FEDEFAM meeting in Caracas, she attributed the decision to carry out an illegal assembly to Azucena

Villaflor. The lecture forms appendix 1 in Oria, *De la casa,* pp. 135–48, 141–42.

34. The account of the meeting in the offices of Monsignor Gracelli comes from María Adela Gard de Antokoletz, one of the first Madres and Azucena's close friend in the early days of the organization. Her reminiscence appears in Arrosagaray, *Biografía de Azucena Villaflor,* pp. 113–16. Azucena Villaflor's cousin, with whom she had grown up and with whom she was very close, recalled the story about the woman with the agenda (p. 117).

35. Mellibovsky, *Circulo de amor,* p. 40.

36. Ibid., p. 16.

37. By the end of May 1977, there was a core group of Madres, who included Azucena Villaflor, María del Rosario Cerruti, Juana de Pargament, María Adela Gard de Antokoletz, Beatriz de Neuhaus (known as Ketty), Kita de Chidíchimo, Chela Mignone, Élida de Galletti, Esther Careaga, Agustina Paz, Martha Vázquez, Nora Morales de Cortiñas, María Ponce de Bianco, Gloria Nolasco, Josefa de Noia, Renée Epelbaum, Raquel Arcuschín, Eva Castillo Obarrio, Carmen Lapacó, Dora Penelas, Carmen de Cobo, Raquel Mariscurrena, Haydée Garcia Buela, Susana Godano, Aída Sarti, Adela de Atencio, and Hébe Mascia. Within a short time, Hebe de Bonafini, from La Plata, joined them as a regular participant. Arrosagaray, *Biografía de Azucena Villaflor,* p. 187.

38. My translation of Élida de Galletti as quoted in Oria, *De la casa,* p. 143.

39. Quoted in Elon, "Letter from Argentina," p. 79.

40. My translation of de Bonafini as quoted in Diago, *Conversando con las Madres,* p. 122.

41. Quoted in Fisher, *Mothers of the Disappeared,* p. 149.

42. My translation of de Bonafini's statement in Diago, *Conversando con las Madres,* p. 122.

43. Quoted in Fisher, *Mothers of the Disappeared,* p. 91.

44. Quoted in Laura Beatriz Gingold and Inés Vásquez, "Madres de Plaza de Mayo: Madres de una nueva práctica política?" *Nueva Sociedad* (Mexico) 93 (January–February 1988): 115 n. 3.

45. My translation from Diago, *Conversando con las Madres,* p. 34.

46. Translated and quoted in Fisher, *Mothers of the Disappeared,* p. 158.

47. Amos Elon's paraphrase of Borges appears as a quotation taken from Elon, "Letter from Argentina," p. 79.

48. Translated and quoted in Fisher, *Mothers of the Disappeared,* p. 59.

49. Ibid.

50. De Bonafini cited in Diago, *Conversando con las Madres,* p. 184.

51. Personal interview with Nora de Cortiñas, New York, 15 December 2000.

52. Simpson and Bennett, *The Disappeared and the Mothers of the Plaza de Mayo,* pp. 156–57; María del Rosario has presented the most detailed memories of the incident in Arrosagaray, *Biografía de Azucena Villaflor,* pp. 134–35.

53. Her recollections, supported by later notes in her diary, appear in Arrosagaray, *Biografía de Azucena Villaflor,* pp. 135–36.

54. Oria, *De la casa,* p. 113; see another account in *Historia de las Madres de Plaza de Mayo* (Buenos Aires: Asociación Madres de Plaza de Mayo, 1989), p. 5; quotation translated in Fisher, *Mothers of the Disappeared,* p. 54.

55. This account appears in Arrosagaray, *Biografía de Azucena Villaflor*, p. 210.

56. Arrosagaray, *Biografía de Azucena Villaflor*, pp. 211–12.

57. Hebe de Bonafini, "Conferencia pronunciada el 6 de julio de 1988 en Liber/Arte por la presidenta de la Asociación [de] Madres de Plaza de Mayo," *Historia de las Madres de Plaza De Mayo* (Buenos Aires: Documentos Página/12, 1997), pp. 9, 19, 41.

58. The main documentation about the meeting at Pereyra Park to organize the cell structure comes from Arrosagaray, *Biografía de Azucena Villaflor*, pp. 197–201.

59. Arrosagaray, *Biografía de Azucena Villaflor*, pp. 197, 202.

60. Ibid., p. 214.

61. Fisher, *Mothers of the Disappeared*, pp. 66–67; Arrosagaray, *Biografía de Azucena Villaflor*, pp. 212–17.

62. Oria, *De la casa*, p. 115.

63. Luisa Valenzuela, "Making Love Visible: The Women of Buenos Aires," *Vogue* May 1984, pp. 344–45.

64. For a detailed near-contemporary account of the disappearances from the Santa Cruz Church on December 8, followed by the abductions of Azucena Villaflor and Sister Léonie Duquet on December 10, see Bousquet, *Las Locas de la Plaza de Mayo*, pp. 73–80; also see "Los rostros y los nombres de la memoria: 1977–8/10 December 1999" (Buenos Aires: Madres de Plaza de Mayo Línea Fundadora y Familiares de las Víctimas de la Santa Cruz, 1999).

65. Although Lila Pastoriza was struck by Azucena Villaflor de Vicenti's appearance, at the time she didn't know who Villaflor was. Many years later, after Pastoriza gained her freedom and gave testimony, like the hundred or so others who survived ESMA and the other clandestine prisons, she tried to recall every scrap of evidence she could. Because the guards who had worked at ESMA on Sundays were somewhat more lax, and those with whom they were familiar, like Pastoriza, sometimes got special treatment, the guard let her go around with him that Sunday, 11 December, and even left her alone for a short time with the prisoners. She first saw Villaflor before she was tortured, but Villaflor was manacled, hooded, and lying face down on a cot. Eager for information about her son, Villaflor gave Pastoriza his surname, Vicenti. Pastoriza did not immediately identify her as Azucena Villaflor. Moreover, although Azucena Villaflor seems to have told Pastoriza that she belonged to a group, Pastoriza, who had been at ESMA for a while, knew nothing about what was going on outside and had never heard of the Madres. See Arrosagaray, *Biografía de Azucena Villaflor*, pp. 278, 280.

Pastoriza's process of recollection raises many issues about memory. Pastoriza, like many others, had developed different categories by which to order her memories, and one category seems to have been political affiliation. As odd as it may have been for her to encounter a forty-five-year-old housewife, the anomaly only became meaningful after she learned about the Madres and put the time of Azucena's abduction within the time frame of her own incarceration. The literature about recovered memory has dealt largely with recalling personal trauma such as sexual abuse, and a lot remains to be discussed about how political identity may affect processes of recollection.

66. Arrosagaray, *Biografía de Azucena Villaflor*, pp. 268–69.

67. Ibid., pp. 272–73, 278.

68. Ibid., pp. 273, 278.

69. De Bonafini in Diago, *Conversando con las Madres*, pp. 122–23; Oria, *De la casa*, p. 115.

70. Bousquet, *Las Locas de la Plaza de Mayo*, pp. 97–98.

71. Quoted in Simpson and Bennett, *The Disappeared and the Mothers of the Plaza de Mayo*, p. 285.

72. Bousquet, *Las Locas de la Plaza de Mayo*, pp. 102–104.

73. Ibid., pp. 97–106; for Cecilia, see pp. 105–106, 183–90; Fisher, *Mothers of the Disappeared*, p. 73.

74. Fisher, *The Mothers of the Disappeared*, p. 90.

75. Quoted in ibid., p. 108.

76. My translation from Mellibovsky, *Circulo de amor*, p. 15.

77. Quoted in Fisher, *Mothers of the Disappeared*, pp. 91–92.

78. Juana de Pargament explained how she became the association's treasurer and how they had to buy an apartment because no one would rent to them. Fisher, *Mothers of the Disappeared*, pp. 92–93; de Bonafini, "Conferencia pronunciada el 6 de julio de 1988," p. 24.

79. Fisher, *Mothers of the Disappeared*, pp. 110, 114.

80. Quoted in ibid., p. 115.

81. Quoted in Agosín, *The Mothers*, pp. 95–96.

82. Fisher, *Mothers of the Disappeared*, pp. 117, 120–21.

83. Hebe de Bonafini, "Conferencia pronunciada el 6 de julio de 1988," p. 28.

84. "Madres en la calle: Novena Marcha de la Resistencia," *Madres de Plaza de Mayo* 5, no. 12 (December 1989): 21.

85. Fisher, *Mothers of the Disappeared*, pp. 118, 120–21.

86. Diago, *Conversando con las Madres*, pp. 154, 190.

87. Agosín, *The Mothers*, p. 21.

88. "Madres en la calle," 21.

89. Robert Cox, "Never Again?" *Index on Censorship* (March 1986), p. 8.

90. Bousquet, *Las Locas de la Plaza de Mayo*, pp. 7–8.

91. Diago, *Conversando con las Madres*, p. 29.

CHAPTER 5

1. Margerite Guzman Bouvard, *Revolutionizing Motherhood: The Mothers of the Plaza de Mayo* (Wilmington, Del.: Scholarly Resources, 1994), p. 94.

2. Quoted in "Los desaparecidos," *Boletín de Madres de Plaza de Mayo* (February 1984), p. 2.

3. Marguerite Feitlowitz, *A Lexicon of Terror: Argentina and the Legacies of Torture* (New York: Oxford University Press, 1998), pp. 41–46. For efforts to come to terms with state violence in Brazil and Uruguay, see Lawrence Weschler, *A Miracle, a Universe: Settling Accounts with Torturers* (Chicago: University of Chicago Press, 1998).

4. Jo Fisher, *Mothers of the Disappeared* (Boston: South End Press, 1989), pp. 82, 84.

5. Fisher, *Mothers of the Disappeared*, p. 82; personal reminiscences of Enrique Garguin and Ana Julia Ramírez, New York, 9 January 2002.

6. Bouvard, *Revolutionizing Motherhood*, p. 94.

7. See "Los desaparecidos," *Boletín de Madres de Plaza de Mayo* (February 1984) p. 2, for the Madres' assessment of the meaning of this law. They argue that the government wanted to put the disappearances behind them without assessing blame.

8. An anonymous Madre quoted in Alejandro Diago, *Conversando con las Madres de Plaza de Mayo: Hebe memoria y esperanza* (Buenos Aires: Ediciones Dialéctica, 1988), p. 186.

9. Quoted in Eduardo Martín de Pozuelo and Santiago Tarín, *España acusa: La represión y desaparición de cientos de españoles en Chile y Argentina, al descubierto en una estremecedora investigación histórica* (Barcelona: Plaza and Janés, 1999), p. 51.

10. Quoted in ibid., p. 51.

11. Quoted and translated in Fisher, *Mothers of the Disappeared*, p. 152.

12. Quoted in Fisher, *Mothers of the Disappeared*, p. 129.

13. The forms are reproduced in Amnesty International, *Témoignage sur les camps de détention secrets* (Paris: Editions EFAL, 1980), cited in Alfredo Martin, *Les mères "folles" de la Place de Mai, maternité, contre-institution et raison d'état* (Paris: Renaudot, 1989), pp. 51–52.

14. The case of Cecilia Marina Viñas and her son is one of the best documented of the cases the Spanish judge Baltasar Garzón brought against the junta for human rights abuses. Two survivors of ESMA, Amalia Larralde and Sara Solarz de Osatinsky, testified about the birth of a son Cecilia Viñas called Rodolfo Penino on 15 October 1978. The boy was taken by Jorge Vildoza, head of one of the so-called work groups at ESMA. He named him Javier Vildoza. Years later, while surfing the Internet, Javier saw a message from the Abuelas de Plaza de Mayo urging young people who thought they might have been abducted to have a DNA test. The twenty-one-year-old had the test, discovered his true identity, rejoined his birth family, and now calls himself Javier Penino Viñas. His abduction formed the basis of one of the charges of kidnapping minors and falsifying their identity that sent former junta member Admiral Emilio Eduardo Massera to prison in 1998. Unfortunately, all this occurred more than a decade after the phone calls from Javier's mother. The most detailed discussion of the case can be found in Martín de Pozuelo and Santiago Tarín, *España acusa*, pp. 105–10. A slightly different but equally compelling version appears in Rita Arditti, *Searching for Life: The Grandmothers of the Plaza de Mayo and the Disappeared Children of Argentina* (Berkeley: University of California Press, 1999), pp. 171–72.

15. Carlos Santiago Nino, one of Alfonsín's chief legal strategists, gives an inside view of how the government sought to establish the rule of law after the bloodbath of the military dictatorship. Since Nino was present at many of the meetings in which Alfonsín considered what legal action to take in the face of possible military uprisings, he provides a unique account of Alfonsín's reasoning. See *Radical Evil on Trial* (New Haven, Conn.: Yale University Press, 1996), esp. pp. 68–73 and 94–104.

I have translated Hebe de Bonafini's frequently repeated statement that there would be no public *revindicación* to mean "vindication" or "exoneration." Since the Madres frequently face charges of wanting vengeance rather than justice, I think it is especially important to stress their commitment to full disclosure, if not by the judicial officials then in the court of public opinion.

16. Marjorie Agosín, *The Mothers of the Plaza de Mayo (Línea Fundadora): The Story of Renée Epelbaum, 1976–1985*, trans. Janice Molloy (Trenton, N.J.: Red Sea Press, 1990), p. 79.

17. This represents the view of María Adela Gard de Antokoletz, called Marta, in Jean-Pierre Bousquet, *Las Locas de la Plaza de Mayo* (Buenos Aires: El Cid Editor, 1983), pp. 181–82. Rabossi and Alfonsín believed that the torturers and murderers would want to clear their consciences about what they had done. Later, in South Africa, the South African Truth and Reconciliation Commission granted amnesty on an individual basis to those who confessed before they were denounced. To save themselves from prison, many members of the police and the armed forces admitted to authorities and the families of those who had disappeared how the person had died and where the body was hidden. The family of Steve Biko, hoping to keep the killers in prison, sued and lost their attempt to have the amnesty declared unconstitutional. Although their suit failed, many perpetrators who concealed parts of the truth were denied amnesty. Unfortunately, others who simply remained silent eluded public scrutiny.

18. Gard de Antokoletz, *Las Locas*, pp. 181–82.

19. Agosín, *The Mothers of the Plaza*, pp. 79, 103; my translation from Piera Paola Oria, *De la casa a la plaza* (Buenos Aires: Editorial Nueva América, 1991), p. 100; de Bonafini in Diago, *Conversando con las Madres*, p. 122.

20. One example of the Madres' statements against CONADEP appears in de Bonafini, *Historia de las Madres de Plaza de Mayo* (Buenos Aires: Asociación Madres de Plaza de Mayo, 1989), p. 18.

21. Epelbaum wrote to the National House of Deputies in June 1986 saying, "It is also urgent to sanction a law that declares forced disappearance to be a crime against humanity. For such a crime, amnesty would not be permissible and those responsible would be subject to extradition." The letter is cited in Agosín, *The Mothers of the Plaza*, p. 103.

22. Quote from Hayden White, "The Value of Narrativity in the Representations of Reality," *Critical Inquiry* 7, no. 1 (autumn 1980): 14. For an expanded version of this argument, see *The Content of the Form: Narrative Discourse and Historical Representation* (Baltimore, Md.: The Johns Hopkins University Press, 1987).

23. De Bonafini, *Historia de las Madres de Plaza de Mayo*, p. 18.

24. Quoted in Fisher, *Mothers of the Disappeared*, pp. 142, 148, from *Madres de Plaza de Mayo*, no. 2 (January 1985) and no. 10 (September 1985).

25. Nino, *Radical Evil on Trial*, p. 69. Madre Graciela de Jeger discusses *Nunca Mas*'s theory of the Two Devils or two evils in Fisher, *Mothers of the Plaza de Mayo*, p. 131.

26. Translated and cited in Fisher, *Mothers of the Disappeared*, pp. 143, 148, from the editorial in *Madres de Plaza de Mayo*, no. 2 (January 1985).

27. Fisher, *The Mothers of the Disappeared*, pp. 130, 136. See Nino, *Radical Evil on Trial*, pp. 67–73, for Alfonsín's earliest efforts to establish the rule of law and gather evidence. In an interview with Amos Elon, Eduardo Rabossi admitted that he and Alfonsín had underestimated the fear of self-incrimination and the loyalty to the corps of lower-ranking members of the armed forces. Prosecutors had to rest their cases on evidence provided by prisoners who had been blindfolded through most of their captivity. See Amos Elon, "Letter from Argentina," *New Yorker*, 21 July 1986, p. 88.

28. De Bonafini, *Historia de las Madres de Plaza de Mayo*, p. 19.

29. Nino, *Radical Evil on Trial*, pp. 87–90.

30. Ibid., p. 93.

31. The Punto Final, or Full Stop Law, required that "all claims based on criminal activity as defined in Law 23,049 be sent to prosecutors within sixty days of Congress's passing the law." Arguing that activity of prosecutors all over Argentina intensified, Nino says, "When I returned to Argentina in the middle of March 1987, I learned that I had underestimated the law's effect: I had estimated the number of trials prompted by the law at 150, but in fact there were 400—twenty times the number of defendants tried to date." Nino, *Radical Evil on Trial*, pp. 93–94.

32. Ibid., p. 101.

33. Clearly differing with Alfonsín about how to deal with the military, Nino provides an analysis filled with admiration for Alfonsín's courage and determination to confront violence with law. Ibid., pp. 94–104.

34. De Bonafini, *Historia de las Madres de Plaza de Mayo*, p. 20.

35. It is unclear when the Madres first became aware of the Universal Declaration of Human Rights and the anniversary of its signing on 10 December 1948. But those Madres and members of the Families of the Detained and Disappeared who were abducted from Santa Cruz Church on 8 December 1977 were assembling signatures for a protest letter that was to appear on Human Rights Day. Bousquet says that the Families were associated with the League of the Rights of Man, an established human rights organization closely associated with the Communist Party. Members of the Families must have known about the holiday. A year after the abduction of the twelve people, including the three Madres, the United Nations delegate in Argentina joined others in laying a wreath on the statue of Argentina's independence leader, San Martín, in the Plaza de Mayo on 10 December 1978 in remembrance of those abducted the previous year. Diago, *Conversando con las Madres*, p. 123. On 10 December 1981, when the Madres felt strong enough to call for active resistance against the junta, they organized the first March of Resistance.

36. Bouvard, *Revolutionizing Motherhood*, p. 164.

37. Political scientist Bonnie N. Field even adopts the term "frozen democracy," first employed by Terry Lynn Karl in "Petroleum and Political Pacts," *Latin American Research Review* 22, no. 1 (January 1987): 63–94, to discuss how political pacts at the time of transitions from authoritarianism to democracy "tend to demobilize new social forces, circumscribe the participation of certain actors in the future, and 'may hinder future self-transformation of the society, economy, or polity thereby producing a sort of frozen democracy.'"

Quoted in Bonnie N. Field, "Frozen Democracy? Pacting and the Consolidation of Democracy: The Spanish and Argentine Democracies in Comparative Perspective," prepared for the 2000 meeting of the Latin American Studies Association, Miami, 16–18 March 2000, p. 2.

38. Beatriz Giobellina of the Institute of Habitat and Environment at the National University of Tucumán, Argentina, assembled data about the relationship between Argentina's financial crisis of late 2001 and 2002 and the governments that ruled the country after 1971. She calculated, in millions of dollars, how the national debt increased under the military junta from 1976 to 1983. Her findings follow:

1971 (Alejandro Lanusse)	4.800	(dictatorship)
1973 (Cámpora/Juan Perón)	4.890	
1974 (María Estela Martínez de Perón)	5.000	
1975 (Martínez de Perón)	7.800	
1976 (Jorge Videla)	9.700	(dictatorship)
1983 (Reynaldo Benito Bignone)	45.100	(dictatorship)
1983 (Raúl Alfonsín)	46.200	
1988 (Alfonsín)	58.700	
1989 (Saúl Menem)	65.300	
1990 (Menem)	62.200	
1991 (Menem)	61.334	
1994 (Menem)	85.656	
1995 (Menem)	98.547	
1999 (Menem)	146.219	
2000 (Fernando de la Rúa)	147.667	

Beatriz Giobellina, Institute of Habitat and Environment at the National University of Tucumán, Argentina. Reported by Antoni Marin, in http://espanol.groups.yahoo.com/group/politicaconosur (17 January 2002).

39. Martin Abregu, director of the human rights organization Center for Legal and Social Studies, criticized Hebe de Bonafini for being a leftist gadfly who used the same tactics in dealing with civilian government that she did with the junta. De Bonafini justified her support for the students' demonstrations against the introduction of tuition and entrance exams by explaining that she "came to the rally because many of these students were children of the disappeared who were being randomly arrested and taken to the same prisons where their parents were tortured and killed." See Calvin Sims, "The Rock, Unyielding of the Plaza de Mayo, *New York Times International,* 2 March 1996, p. 4.

40. Horacio Verbitsky, *The Flight: Confessions of an Argentine Dirty Warrior,* trans. Esther Allen (New York: New Press, 1996).

41. Translated and quoted in Fisher, *Mothers of the Disappeared,* p. 129.

42. Fisher, *Mothers of the Disappeared,* pp. 128–29; my translation of de Bonafini in Diago, *Conversando con las Madres,* p. 158.

43. De Bonafini in Diago, *Conversando con las Madres,* p. 157.

44. Dr. Laura Bonaparte, a psychologist, mother of Noni Bonaparte and one of the Founding-Line Madres, received word that all that was left of her

daughter was her hands in a glass bottle; then she learned that her child was buried in Avellaneda Cemetery, in what turned out to be a mass grave. For a contemporary account, see Paul Heath Hoeffel and Juan Montalvo [pseud.], "Missing or Dead in Argentina," *New York Times Magazine* 21 (October 1979), pp. 45–47, 51, 54, 58, 66, 68, 72–74, 76, 80. See the discussion of the reburial of Marcelo Gelman in Antonius C. G. M. Robben, "State Terror in the Netherworld: Disappearance and Reburial in Argentina," in *Death Squad: The Anthropology of State Terror,* ed. Jeffrey A. Sluka (Philadelphia: University of Pennsylvania Press, 2000), pp. 91–92. Rita Arditti provides a moving account of Berta Schubaroff's memories of her son in *Searching for Life*, p. 89.

45. Bouvard, *Revolutionizing Motherhood*, p. 150.

46. A truly humane and comprehensive study of the Abuelas de Plaza de Mayo can be found in Arditti, *Searching for Life*.

47. Ibid., pp. 65, 90.

48. Ibid., pp. 118–19.

49. Despite her clear regard for Hebe de Bonafini, critic Marguerite Bouvard has attempted to be scrupulously fair. Bouvard contacted Renée Epelbaum, then president of the Founding-Line Madres, the group most troubled by what they considered Hebe de Bonafini's increasingly authoritarian leadership. Bouvard explains that the Abuelas endorse the exhumations of those they think may be their daughters and daughters-in-law so that experts can determine from the pelvic bones whether or not the women delivered the infants with whom they were pregnant. All the groups respect the wishes of the families and only support those exhumations to which the families have consented. See Bouvard, *Revolutionizing Motherhood*, pp. 149–51.

50. My translation of Hebe de Bonafini's quotation in Diago, *Conversando con las Madres*, p. 193.

51. Rita Failbel and Irena Klepfisz, "An Interview with Renée Epelbaum: Still Struggling for Peace and Justice in Argentina," *Bridges* 1, no. 1 (spring 1990), reproduced online at http://www.pond.net/*ckinberg/bridges/backissues/epelbaum (10 January 2000).

52. In *Crazy for Democracy: Women in Grassroots Movements* (New York: Routledge, 1997), I refer to two leadership styles that seem to characterize activist women. One I call artisanal, by which I mean that the person works in a variety of positions in several different organizations. The artisan's goal is service to the cause, and she benefits from the *esprit* she shares with her colleagues.

I call the other role that of the conductor. She assumes the responsibility for one organization and generally coordinates all participants. Although conductors generally receive credit for the achievements of the organization and assume more traditional leadership patterns, they also bear the blame for anything that goes wrong, and they often seem to occupy a different place from those with whom they share an association. Responsible for keeping the group together, they seldom have anyone to share the burdens of leadership.

53. Renée Epelbaum as quoted in Failbel and Klepfisz, "An Interview with Renée Epelbaum," p. 5.

54. Diago, *Conversando con las Madres*, p. 195.

55. Bouvard, *Revolutionizing Motherhood*, p. 163.

56. Marguerite Feitlowitz, *A Lexicon of Terror*, p. 186.

57. Arditti, *Searching for Life*, p. 167; personal interview with María Elisa Lenci, La Plata, Argentina, 27 June 2000.

58. "Recent Efforts to Clean Up after the 'Dirty War,'" *Christian Science Monitor*, 4 December 1997, p. 7; see also "Ceremonia por el beneficio a los fusilados del '56: El Presidente habló de hipocresia," at http://www.fcapital. com.ar/fcapital/odiesea/OdiseaSL/.../miles_de_personas_marcharon_en_e.ht (20 June 1999), in which the survivors of civilians and members of the military killed on 9 June 1956 also became eligible for reparations under Law 24.411.

59. Hebe de Bonafini, "Discurso en la Facultad de Derecho de la Universidad de Buenos Aires, 23 de Marzo de 1995," in *Discursos de Hebe de Bonafini en los actos de repudio al golpe de estado 24/3/1976–24/3/1995* (Buenos Aires: Asociación Madres de Plaza de Mayo, 1995), p. 8.

60. María Elisa Lenci was a member of the local historical commission that created the plaques at the university and at the National High School. Personal interview, La Plata, Argentina, 27 June 2000.

61. Disputes about monuments cut to the core of the problem of historical memory. Debates have ensued over the Vietnam memorial and the World War II memorials in Washington, D.C., over how and what to memorialize about the Nazi concentration camps, and about how and whether to honor those who died in the Warsaw Ghetto uprising. For a cross-section of studies dealing with these issues, see James E. Young, *The Texture of Memory: Holocaust Memorials and Meaning* (New Haven, Conn.: Yale University Press, 1993); and Claudia Koonz, "Between Memory and Oblivion: Concentration Camps in German Memory," *Commemorations: The Politics of National Identity*, ed. John R. Gillis (Princeton, N.J.: Princeton University Press, 1994), pp. 258–80. Robert G. Moeller's *War Stories: The Search for a Usable Past* (Berkeley: University of California Press, 2001) explores the way popular films contributed to how the past was remembered and how guilt was assigned.

The debates about memorialization in Latin America have just begun. In Chile, for example, the Agrupación de Familiares de Detenidos Desaparecidos (Association of Families of the Detained and Disappeared) spearheaded the campaign to build a monument in the municipal cemetery of Santiago and a House of Memory in one of the former detention centers. The Ex-presos Políticos and the Sobrevivientes de Villa Grimaldi (Ex-political Prisoners, Survivors of the Villa Grimaldi) succeeded in saving the land but not the main buildings of the Villa Grimaldi, which they turned into a Park of Peace in 1997. See *Parque por la Paz Villa Grimaldi: Una deuda con nosotros mismos*, ed. Rodrigo de Arteagabeitía, María Angélica Illanes, and Pedro Matta (Santiago, Chile: Ministerio de Vivienda y Urbanismo, 1997).

In Argentina, attempts to memorialize the disappeared meet with the wrath of Hebe de Bonafini and the Asociación de Madres. As arbitrary as their views sometimes appear, their uncompromising positions make them a force to reckon with in arguments about the Dirty War.

62. A discussion about the dedication and the counterdemonstration that followed can be found in "Monumento por las víctimas del terrorismo de estado: Hay heridas que no pueden cerrarse," *Miles de personas marcharon en el*

23 *aniversario del golpe militar,* at http://www.fcapital.com.ar/fcapital/odiesea/ OdiseaSL/.../miles_de_personas_marcharon_en_e.ht (20 June 1999).

63. Ibid.

64. Asociación Madres de Plaza de Mayo, "Parir un hijo, parir miles de hijos," flyer (April 1995).

65. My summary and translation of her recollection in Matilde Mellibovksy, *Circulo de amor* (Buenos Aires: Ediciones del Pensamiento Nacional, 1990), p. 16.

66. Quoted in Fisher, *Mothers of the Disappeared,* p. 125.

67. Quoted in Agosín, *The Mothers of the Plaza de Mayo,* p. 72.

CHAPTER 6

1. The title of the central panel of the Monument to the Detained and Disappeared in the General Cemetery in Santiago, Chile, reads: "In a country of disappearances, all the rest of us are survivors."

2. Pedro Alejandro Matta, "Acción, Verdad y Justicia (HIJOS, Chile)," personal e-mail communication (17 August 2000).

3. Margaret Feitlowitz, *A Lexicon of Terror: Argentina and the Legacies of Torture* (New York: Oxford University Press, 1998), p 179. A truly engaging and courageous book, *A Lexicon* provides a complete description of the origin of HIJOS. Diana Taylor, one of the first scholars to write about HIJOS, analyzes them in relationship to the Madres de Plaza de Mayo in " 'You are Here': The DNA of Performance," *TDR (The Drama Review)* 46, no. 1 (spring 2002): 149–69.

4. "Nosotros sobre nosotros," an internet release describing the origins of HIJOS, available at http://www.hijos.org/espanol/nosotros/html (23 November 1990).

5. Patricia, "Contradicciones, postergaciones," in *Ni el flaco perdón de Dios: Hijos de desaparecidos,* ed. Juan Gelman and Mara La Madrid (Buenos Aires: Planeta Espejo de la Argentina, 1997), pp. 184–85.

6. "Encuentro nacional de HIJOS," available at http://www.derechos.org/ ddhh/hijos/encuentro.txt (28 July 2000).

7. Patricia, "Contradicciones, postergaciones," p. 185.

8. "Voces," in *Ni el flaco perdón,* ed. Gelman and La Madrid, pp. 169–70; "Comunicado de Prensa" 19 October 1995, available at http://www.derechos. org/ddhh/hijos/encuentro.txt (28 July 2000).

9. Adriana Calvo, "Nudos," in *Ni el flaco perdón,* ed. Gelman and La Madrid, p. 267.

10. Gabriela Fried, a doctoral candidate in sociology at UCLA, has considered the Hijos in Uruguay in comparison with those in Argentina. See "On Remembering and Silencing the Past: The Adult Children of the Disappeared of Argentina and Uruguay in Comparative Perspective," paper presented at the Latin American Studies Association meeting, Miami, 16–18 March 2000.

11. For an account of how Naval Captain Adolfo Scilingo's confession influenced the development of HIJOS, see "Nosotros sobre nosotros."

12. Ariel Dorfman, *Widows* (New York: Aventura/Vintage, 1984).

13. From the statement given by Gladys Nélida Díaz, 30 May 1995, to the San Miguel Criminal Court for the indictment of Osvaldo Romo Mena. See *Presupuestos*, Fundación de Documentación y Archivo de la Vicaría de la Solidaridad, Arzobispado de Santiago. The archive requests that their classification numbers be omitted. Please request the documents by category and description.

14. The English edition appears in Horacio Verbitsky, *The Flight: Confessions of an Argentine Dirty Warrior*, trans. Esther Allen (New York: New Press, 1996). A rich account of the episode can be found in Feitlowitz, *A Lexicon of Terror*, pp. 193–206.

15. For some of the reactions outside Argentina to Scilingo's revelations, see David Schrieberg, "I Can't Erase This," *Newsweek*, 27 March 1995, p. 38; Paul Gray and Carl Honore, "Waves from the Past," *Time*, 27 March 1995, p. 47; "The Sea Gives Up Its Dead," *The Economist*, 25 March 1995, p. 45; "The Past Raises Its Ugly Head," *The Economist*, 1 July 1995, p. 31; Mario Benedetti, "The Triumph of Memory," *NACLA: Report on the Americas* 29, no.3 (November–December 1995): 10–12; "Jack Epstein, "Argentina's 'Dirty War' Laundry May Get a Public Airing," *Christian Science Monitor*, 4 December 1997, p. 7.

16. See the recollections of Mario Cesar Villani, a noted physicist who survived four years in Argentinian concentration camps, in Feitlowitz,. *A Lexicon of Terror*, pp. 72–74.

17. *Informe Rettig: Informe de la Comisión Nacional de Verdad y Reconciliación*, 2 vols. (Santiago, Chile: Government of Chile, 1991); translated as *Report of the Chilean National Commission on Truth and Reconciliation*, ed. José Zalaquett, trans. Phillip E. Berryman, 2 vols. (Notre Dame, Ind.: Notre Dame Press, 1993).

18. Gabriela Cerruti, *Herederos del silencio* (Buenos Aires: Planeta Espejo de la Argentina, 1997).

19. Victoria Álvarez, "El encierro en los campos de concentración," in *Historia de las mujeres en la Argentina*, ed. Fernanda Gil Lozano, Valeria Silvina Pita, and María Gabriela Ini (Buenos Aires: Taurus, 2000), 2: 78. Álvarez, like many other historians of the concentration camps, tries not to be judgmental about which of the women were collaborators and which were virtual slaves. Survivors of ESMA embrace the group called "the staff," which consisted of prisoners, primarily from the Montoneros, whom Admiral Emilio Eduardo Massera thought were "redeemable." They each had some quirk or quality that distinguished them from other prisoners and may have helped save their life. Though they did clerical work, they did not go with the so-called work groups into the streets to identify other political activists. The staff members agreed that once all of them were out or known dead, they would try to go abroad to give testimony against their torturers. For accounts by five former women staff prisoners, see Munú Actis, Cristina Aldini/Liliana Gardella, Miriam Lewin, and Elisa Tokar, *Ese infierno: Conversaciones de cinco mujeres sobrevivientes de la ESMA* (Buenos Aires: Editorial Sudamericana, 2001). Another group of prisoners, known as "the mini-staff," seems to have consisted of prisoners who actively collaborated: they rejected their former friends in prison and betrayed them by willingly identifying them to authorities.

In Chile too, some people actively collaborated with the secret police and became implicated in the capture and execution of former comrades. The most notable of these were Marcia Merino, known as "La Flaca Alejandra" (Skinny Alejandra), and Luz Arce. Both became Catholic converts after years of working for the Chilean secret police; both have written confessions. For a thoughtful examination of the confessional literature of the collaborators, see Leigh A. Payne, "Confessions of the Torturers: Reflections from Argentina," paper presented at the History Workshop and the Centre for the Study of Violence and Reconciliation conference, "The TRC: Commissioning the Past," University of the Witwatersrand, 11–14 June 1999. See also her "Confessions of Chilean Collaborators," paper presented at the Latin American Studies Association meeting, Miami, Florida, 16–19 March 2000.

20. Cerruti, *Herederos del Silencio,* pp. 99–100.

21. Sergio Molina responding to a set of e-mails about the origin of the word *escrache,* available at http://majordomo.eunet.es/listserv/apuntes/2000–06/1102: html (28 July 2000).

22. Ibid.

23. The following description comes from "Escrache: El regreso," HIJOS 5, no. 6 (March 2000): 12–13.

24. I am grateful to Ana Julia Ramírez and Enrique Garguin for this information about Aldo Rico. Personal interview, New York, 9 January 2002.

25. "Escrache: El regreso," p. 13.

26. Ibid., p. 15.

27. CORREPI-BOLETIN, no. 29 (19–26 June 1999), available at http://www.derechos.org/correpi/boletin/29.html (16 October 1999).

28. Bulletin of HIJOS prepared by HIJOS Venezuela, available at http://www.hijos.org/espanol/denuncias/bussi.html (28 July 2000). See also Amo La Vida, Derechos Humanos HyperNet, available at http://www.mercosur digital.com/amolavida/dehumanos.htm (28 July 2000).

29. Quotation from Omar Eduardo Torres, file no. 6667 to the National Commission on the Disappeared, cited in *Nunca Más: The Report of the Argentine National Commission on the Disappeared,* intro. Ronald Dworkin (New York: Farrar Straus Giroux, 1986), p. 202.

30. "Notas," in *Ni el flaco perdón,* ed. Gelman and La Madrid, p. 402.

31. "Escrache: El regreso," p. 15.

32. Ibid.

33. See Guy Debord, *Society of the Spectacle* (Detroit: Red and Black, 1977).

34. Arrosagaray, *Biografía de Azucena Villaflor,* p. 271.

35. The most penetrating portrait of Astiz up to 1988 comes from Tina Rosenberg, *Children of Cain: Violence and the Violent in Latin America* (New York: Penguin Books, 1991), pp. 79–141; for his career advancement, see pp. 81–82.

36. The incident was recounted in Miguel Bonasso, "El cuervo no cena tranquilo," *Página/12,* 30 May 1997, p. 36. This was not the first time that Astiz faced public hostility. On his way to a ski lift, a former prisoner at El Vesubio concentration camp recognized Astiz and punched him. Another time

two young men, whom Astiz had cut off in traffic and then taunted, beat him up. According to Marguerite Feitlowitz, the father of the boys, though not proud of what they had done, commented that "this is what happens after you're obliged to tell your children that justice here doesn't function as it should. " See Feitlowitz, *A Lexicon of Terror*, p. 246.

37. "Derechos humanos: Proceso por 'Apologia del Delito: Sorprenden al ex marino Astiz con un escrache en Tribunales,' " *Clarín* (Buenos Aires), 26 February 2000; see also the assessment of Inés Izaguirre, "Recapturing the Memory of Politics," *NACLA Report on the Americas* 31, no. 6 (May–June 1998): 28.

38. *Clarín* (Buenos Aires), 16 May 1998; *Página/12* (Buenos Aires), 9 March 2000.

39. Victoria Ginzberg, "El ex-marino Alfredo Astiz debio presentarse en tribunales por 'Apologia del Delito,' " *Página/12* (Buenos Aires), 26 February 2000.

40. Ibid.

41. Personal interview with Alejandra López, Santiago, Chile, 23 June 2000.

42. Ibid.

43. Pedro Alejandro Matta, "Acción, Verdad y Justicia (HIJOS, Chile)," personal e-mail communication (17 August 2000).

44. Pedro Alejandro Matta, "Coming to Terms with the Past in Chile," a lecture at the New School for Social Research, 21 April 2000.

45. Personal interview with Alejandra López, Santiago, Chile, 23 June 2000.

46. Xavier Febres, "Brusselles l'ombra de Pinochet amenaça Europa," *Aviu* (Barcelona), 11 November 1976, p. 20. This article underscores the way Pinochet defined his enemies: "All those who participated in the Popular Unity government (of Salvador Allende); all those in favor of the international condemnation of the Chilean regime; [and] all those who propose political alternatives for Chile." See also Hugh O'Shaughnessy, *Pinochet: The Politics of Torture* (New York: New York University Press, 2000).

47. "Funa del 2 de Junio (2000)," available at http://www.fpmr.org/chi4. htm (28 July 2000).

48. Ibid.

49. Groups in Brazil, Paraguay, and Bolivia, which had also suffered from Operation Condor, agreed to join the demonstrations, as did supporters in France, Switzerland, and Sweden. The notice of the unified *escrache/funa* appeared in *Boletin Semanal de contr@informacion de Barcelona* 3, no. 114 (31 May–6 June 2000), available at http://www.squat.net/infosquat/msg00024. html (28 July 2000). Originating in Barcelona, the site focuses on news about human rights and labor struggles in Latin America and Spain. Their general web site is http://www.sindominio.net/usurpa.

50. Personal interview with Margarita Romano, Santiago, Chile, 18 June 2000. I am grateful to Margarita Romano for providing me with the two-sided flyer distributed at the *funa* and for her tour of the Peace Park established on the site of the Villa Grimaldi.

51. "Reflexiones sobre una nueva modalidad de lucha: Si no hay justicia hay escrache," HIJOS 5, no. 6 (March 2000): 13.

52. Ibid., p. 14.

53. Personal interview with Margarita Merbilhaá, La Plata, Argentina, 28 June 2000. Along with Miguel Dalmaroni, she has written her own analysis of HIJOS in "Memoria sociale impunidad: Los limites de la democracia," *Punta de vista* (Buenos Aires) 21, no. 63, pp. 1–8.

54. Quoted in "Reflexiones sobre una nueva modalidad de lucha: Si no hay justicia hay escrache," p. 14.

55. Ibid.

56. The Hijos of Malmoe, Sweden called themselves an antiracist, antisexist organization that believes that each group should define its own goals. When asked to reject terrorism, they responded that although they can work in Sweden using nonviolent methods, they know that others in Sweden and Latin America cannot, and they continue to support them. See "El Terrorismo en la Argentina: Para que la violencia no regrese nunca más," available at http://www.geocities. com/CapitolHill/Lobby/31–41/cocinar.htm, and "Bases ideológicas de HIJOS Malmoe," available at http://www.hijos.org/malmoe/bases.html (28 July 2000).

57. María Virginia, "La pulguita en la oreja," in *Ni el flaco perdón,* ed. Gelman and La Madrid, p. 277.

58. "Comunicado de prensa," *Abuelas de Plaza de Mayo,* 27 October 2000. I am grateful to an anonymous reader for providing this information.

59. One of the most notorious of the torturers at ESMA was Julio Simón, known as Julián the Turk. On 18 October 2000, the past caught up with Julián the Turk. Along with Juan Antonio del Cerro, called Colores, Julio Simón was arrested and charged with kidnapping an eight-month-old child, Claudia Victoria Poblete, along with her parents, Gertrudis Hlaczik and José Poblete, on 28 November 1978. The mother, who was tortured in El Garaje Olimpo before she and her husband disappeared, told other prisoners that Julián the Turk and Colores had captured her. Like many other torturers, Julián was arrested for trafficking in babies. Notice of the arrest of Julio Simón appeared in RECOSUR, no. 226, p. 7, available at http://espanol.groups.yahoo.com/group/politicaconosur (18 October 2002).

60. For coverage of the attacks on those making *escraches* and *funas* in Argentina and Chile, see "Massera querella a HIJOS," available at http://www. derechos.org/correpi/boletin/29.html (28 July 2000); and Pedro Alejandro Matta, "Querella criminal—Acción urgente," personal communication by e-mail (20 August 2000). A full report about the attack on the Funas as an illicit organization appeared in *La Nación* (Santiago), 24 August 2000, available at http://espanol. groups.yahoo.com/group/politicaconosur (30 August 2000). See also Margot Olvarría, "Human Rights Activists under Attack in Chile and Argentina," *NACLA: Report on the Americas* 34, no. 2 (September–October 2000): 2, 4, 49–50.

61. Antjie Krog, *Country of My Skull* (Johannesburg: Random House, 1998), p. 99.

62. Personal interview with Mariano Tealdi, Buenos Aires, 29 June 2000.

CHAPTER 7

1. Tina Rosenberg, *The Haunted Land: Facing Europe's Ghosts after Communism* (New York: Vintage, 1996) offers an especially poignant assessment of

how the archives of the secret police came to define people's conduct under the Soviet regime, and how information about the past taken out of context can entirely distort one's identity.

2. Sebastian Balfour, *Dictatorship, Workers, and the City: Labor in Greater Barcelona since 1939* (Oxford: Clarendon Press, 1989), p. vii.

3. Paloma Aguilar Fernández, *Memoria y olvido de la Guerra Civil española* (Madrid: Alianza Editorial, 1996), p. 22.

4. Martha Ackelsberg, *Free Women of Spain: Anarchism and the Struggle for the Emancipation of Women* (Bloomington: Indiana University Press, 1991); Carmen Alcalde, *La mujer en la guerra civil española* (Madrid: Editorial Cambio 16, 1976); Rosa María Capel, *El sufragio femenino en la Segunda República* (Granada: University of Granada, 1975); Temma Kaplan, "Spanish Anarchism and Women's Liberation," *Journal of Contemporary History* 6, no. 2 (1971): 101–10; Mary Nash, *"Mujeres Libres" España, 1936–39* (Barcelona: Tusquets Editor, 1975), and *Defying Male Civilization: Women in the Spanish Civil War* (Denver, Colo.: Arden Press, 1995).

5. Shirley Mangini, *Memories of Resistance: Women's Voices from the Spanish Civil War* (New Haven, Conn.: Yale University Press, 1995), pp. 141–42. See also Fernanda Romeu Alfaro, *El silencio roto...Mujeres contra el franquismo* (n.p.: J. C. Producción, 1994).

6. Introduction to Giuliana Di Febo, *Resistencia y movimiento de mujeres en España 1936–1976* (Barcelona: Icaria, 1979), p. 7. A series of oral histories with women militants done in the seventies, the book is itself a historical document. It reflects on the entire Franco period from the perspective of hopes for the future after Franco's death.

7. Views of the process of democratization are quite skewed by discipline. Nicos Poulantzas, *The Crisis of the Dictatorships: Portugal, Spain, Greece,* trans. David Fernbach (London and Atlantic Highlands: New Left Books and Humanities Press, 1976), was the first to consider how social movements forced authorities to negotiate with the opposition.

A short cross-section of the studies that consider the social dimension of the democratization process in Spain include Aguilar Fernández, *Memoria y olvido de la Guerra Civil española;* Balfour, *Dictatorship, Workers, and the City;* Raymond Carr and Juan Pablo Fusi, *Spain: Dictatorship to Democracy* (London: St Martin's Press, 1979); Robert M. Fishman, *Working-Class Organization and the Return to Democracy in Spain* (Ithaca, N.Y.: Cornell University Press, 1990); José María Maravall, *Dictatorship and Political Dissent: Workers and Students in Franco's Spain* (New York: St. Martin's, 1978), and *The Transition to Democracy in Spain* (London: Croom Helm, 1982); and Victor Pérez Díaz, *Clase obrera, orden social y conciencia de clase* (Madrid: Taurus,1979).

Studies of women during the period of democratization in Spain began to appear in large numbers in the 1990s. Some of the best discussions of the emergence of feminist thought during the transition in Spain can be found in Lola G. Luna, "La representatividad del sujeto mujer en el feminismo de la Transición," and Mabel Pérez Serrano, "La transición con nombres de mujer," in *1898–1998: Un siglo avanzando hacia la igualdad de las mujeres,* ed. Concha Fagoaga (Madrid: Dirección General de la Mujer, Consejería de Sanidad y Ser-

vicios Sociales, Comunidad de Madrid, 1999), pp. 235–50 and 251–74; Asociación 'Mujeres en la Transición Democrática,' *Españolas en la Transición: De
excluidas a protagonistas (1973–1982)* (Madrid: Biblioteca Nueva, 1999); and
Pamela Beth Radcliff, "Imagining Female Citizens in the 'New Spain': Gendering the Democratic Transition, 1975–1978," in *Gender, Citizenships, and Sub-
jectivities,* ed. Kathleen Canning and Sonya O. Rose (Oxford: Blackwell, 2002),
pp. 72–97.

Two classic studies of women in the transitions in Latin America can be
found in Jane S. Jaquette, ed., *The Women's Movement in Latin America: Feminism and the Transition to Democracy* (Boston: Unwin Hyman, 1989); and
Sonia Álvarez, *Engendering Democracy in Brazil: Women's Movements in Transition Politics* (Princeton, N.J.: Princeton University Press, 1989). For another
intelligent and readable discussion of the ways women have helped shape the
process of democratization outside of Spain, see Elisabeth J. Friedman,
*Unfinished Transitions: Women and the Gendered Development of Democracy
in Venezuela, 1936–1996* (University Park: Pennsylvania State University Press,
2000).

Two assessments of the political processes by which constitutional governments replaced authoritarian structures in Spain can be found in Ronald H.
Chilcote, Stylianos Hadjiyannis, Fred A. López III, Daniel Nataf, and Elizabeth
Sammis, eds., *Transitions from Dictatorship to Democracy: Comparative Studies of Spain, Portugal, and Greece* (New York: Taylor and Francis, 1990); and
Juan J. Linz and Alfred Stepan, *Problems of Democratic Transition and Consolidation: Southern Europe, South America, and Post-Communist Europe* (Baltimore, Md.: John Hopkins University Press, 1996).

8. Di Febo, *Resistencia y movimiento de mujeres en España,* p. 155 n. 50.

9. *No pasarán: The Story of La Pasionaria, Dolores Ibárruri* (New York: International Publishers, 1977).

10. I wrote about them in "Spanish Anarchism and Women's Liberation,"
Journal of Contemporary History 6, no. 2 (1971): 101–10. Mary Nash, *"Mujeres Libres" España 1936–1939,* provides a broad selection from the journal
and an analysis of their goals. Martha A. Ackelsberg has studied them in the
broader context of women's social movement theory in *Free Women of Spain.*

11. Consider her reflections on how B. Guidetti Serra's book on women
who fought against Mussolini and Hitler influenced her own work. See Giuliana Di Febo, "Memoria de mujeres en la resistencia antifanquista: Contexto,
identidad, autorepresentación," *Arenal: Revista de historia de las mujeres*
(Madrid) 4, no. 2 (July–December 1997): 243.

12. Daniel James has written poignantly about his dialogues with a politi-
cally militant Peronist meat packer in Argentina, in his groundbreaking work
Doña María's Story: Life History, Memory, and Political Identity (Durham,
N.C.: Duke University Press, 2000). Forged in a social movement, Doña María
Roldán assumed a collective identity similar to those Giuliana Di Febo discov-
ered in the Spanish women she interviewed.

13. Di Febo, "Memoria de mujeres en la resistencia antifranquista," pp.
239–54.

14. Manolita del Arco told her story of work in the underground to Fernanda Romeu Alfaro in *El silencio roto,* pp. 149–50.

15. Even before the controversy over whether *I, Rigoberta Menchú, an Indian Woman in Guatemala* (London: Verso, 1984) was true or not, critics such as Doris Sommer and John Beverly tried to highlight the degree to which testimonials were intended to speak for groups—in fact, whole movements—rather than for individual people. See Doris Sommer, "'Not Just a Personal Story': Women's *Testimonios* and the Plural Self," in *Life/Lines: Theorizing Women's Autobiography,* ed. Bella Brodzki and Celeste Schenck (Ithaca, N.Y.: Cornell University Press, 1988); and John Beverley, "The Margin at the Center of *Testimonio* (Testimonial Narrative)," in *De/Colonizing the Subject: The Politics of Gender in Women's Autobiography,* ed. Sidonie Smith and Julia Watson (Minneapolis: University of Minnesota Press, 1992).

John Beverly sought to explain again why Rigoberta Menchú, like many of the politically engaged people about whom Di Febo wrote, would not distinguish between the individual and the community of which she was a part. See John Beverley's "Our Rigoberta? I, Rigoberta Menchú, Cultural Authority and the Problem of Subaltern Agency," *Subalternity and Representation: Arguments in Cultural Theory* (Durham, N.C.: Duke University Press, 1999).

16. See the discussion in Lidia Falcón, "Especial: El feminismo ha venido, y se ha ido, nadie sabe como ha sido," *Vindicación feminista,* nos. 26–27 (September 1978): 29–42, esp. 38.

17. Historian Sebastian Balfour contends that the strikes of women textile workers between 1946 and 1947 reflected the difficulties Spanish women had feeding their families. *Dictatorship, Workers, and the City,* pp. 10–11.

18. During the long textile strike in Lawrence, Massachusetts, the young women strikers, led by Elisabeth Gurley Flynn, called for Bread and Roses. See Ardis Cameron, *Radicals of the Worst Sort: Laboring Women in Lawrence, Massachusetts* (Urbana: University of Illinois Press, 1993).

19. Conversations with Enric Fuster, Barcelona, April 1968.

20. Balfour, *Dictatorship, Workers, and the City,* p. 20.

21. Ibid., p. 22.

22. An article in *Diario de Barcelona* on 3 March 1951, p. 5, makes reference to "the increased cost of living," which "keeps getting worse in Barcelona."

23. Sam Pope Brewer, "Franco Penalizes Barcelona Labor," *New York Times,* 15 March 1951.

24. Di Febo, *Resistencia y movimiento de mujeres,* pp. 68–69 n. 83.

25. Quoted from an interview between Giuliana Di Febo and Isabel Vicente, January 1976, in Di Febo, *Resistencia y movimiento de mujeres,* p. 169.

26. Llibertat Ferri Jordi Muixí, "Barcelona1951: Del boicot als tramvies a la vega general," *Canigo* (Barcelona), 13 March 1976, pp. 26–27; J. Fabre and J.M. Huertas Clavria, *Tots Els Barris de Barcelona 5 (Dos Eixamples, Sant Antoni, La Sagrada Família, Els Barris de La Barcelona Vella)* (Barcelona: Edicions 62, 1977), p. 81; Hilari Raguer, *El quadern de Montjuïc: Records de la vaga de tramvies* (Barcelona: Claret, 2001); *El Noticiero Universal,* March 1, 1976; *Diario de Barcelona,* February–March 1951; *La Vanguardia,* February–March

1951. The newspapers maintained a complete news blackout, except for a small notice of the price reductions on March 6.

27. *La Vanguardia,* 13 March 1951, p. 11.

28. For consumer rebellions in twentieth-century Spain, see Temma Kaplan, "Female Consciousness and Collective Action: The Case of Barcelona, 1910–1918," and "Women's Communal Strikes in the Crisis of 1917–22" (in Russia, Italy, Spain, and Veracruz, Mexico), in *Becoming Visible: Women in European History,* ed. Renate Bridenthal, Claudia Koonz, Susan Mosher Stuard, 2d ed. (Boston: Houghton Mifflin, 1987), pp. 429–49; Pamela Beth Radcliff, "Women's Politics: Consumer Riots in Twentieth-Century Spain," in *Constructing Spanish Womanhood,* ed. Victoria Lorée Enders and Pamela Beth Radcliff (Albany: State University of New York Press, 1999), pp. 301–24; and María Dolores Ramos, "Crisis de subsistencias y conflictividad social en Málaga: Los sucesos de enero de 1918," *Baetica: Estudios de Arte, Geografía, e Historia* 6 (1983), pp. 441–66.

29. Quotation from Sam Pope Brewer, "Franco Replaces Barcelona Chief," *New York Times,* 17 March 1951. Two days earlier, in "Franco Penalizes Barcelona Labor," *New York Times,* 15 March 1951, he dismissed government charges of Communist infiltration as "nonsense," saying that "the letters were the only evidence that there was an organization behind the strike, and observers here consider that [the strike] was not political in character."

30. Temma Kaplan, "Turmoil in Spain: The Communist Party and the Mass Movement," *Radical America* 11, no. 2 (March–April 1977): 53–72. Even women who worked in factories had to attend classes two hours a day for six months. See Di Febo, *Resistencia y movimiento de mujeres,* p. 141.

31. Di Febo, *Resistencia y movimiento de mujeres,* p. 141

32. For contemporary feminist historical analyses of the Sección Femenina, see Inmaculada Blasco Herranz, *Armas Femeninas para la Contrarrevolución: La Sección Femenina en Aragón (1936–1950)* (Málaga: Servicio de Publicaciones de la Universidad de Málaga, 1999), esp. pp. 121–31 for the social service section. An effort to fit the study of the Women's Division of the Falange with the history of women's social service agencies and a notion of women's rights can be found in Victoria Lorée Enders, "Problematic Portraits: The Ambiguous Historical Role of the *Sección Feminina* of the Falange," in *Constructing Spanish Womanhood,* ed. Enders and Radcliff, pp. 375–97.

33. Blasco Herranz, *Armas Femeninas,* pp. 118–20.

34. Manuel Castells, *The City and the Grassroots: A Cross-Cultural Theory of Urban Social Movements* (Berkeley: University of California Press,1983), pp. 218–19.

35. Di Febo, *Resistencia y movimiento de mujeres,* p. 161.

36. Di Febo, "La lucha de las mujeres en los barrios en los últimos años del franquismo: Un ejemplo de utilización de la 'Historia de género,'" in *La oposición al régimen de Franco: Estado de la cuestión y metodología de la investigación,* ed. Javier Tusell, Alicia Alted, and Abdón Mateos (Madrid: Editorial de la U.N.E.D., 1990), 2: 251–60; Mabel Pérez Serrano, "La transición con nombres de mujer," in *1898–1998: Un siglo avanzando hacia la igualdad de las mujeres,* p. 259. The *New York Times* covered some of these boycotts. On 21 February 1975,

p. 2, they reported that "homemakers participate in boycott of markets and food shops in demonstrations called by clandestine organizations against rising food prices." Two days later, on 23 February, on p. 3, they explained that "thousands of Madrid homemakers joined illegal boycott of Madrid's food shops to protest rising prices and political repression." On 3 March, the demonstrations continued, and on 9 March, the *New York Times* claimed that 2,200 strikes had swept the country the year before, and that inflation had reached 18 percent.

37. Balfour, *Dictatorship, Workers, and the City*, pp. 69–109.

38. Regina Bayo Falcón and M. Encarna Sanahuja, "Mujeres del Mundo," *Vindicación feminista*, no. 19 (January 1978): 62.

39. See my account of discussions with women in one group of Asociaciones de Vecinos in "Turmoil in Spain," pp. 57–59.

40. Amparo Moreno, *Mujeres en lucha: El movimiento feminista en España* (Barcelona: Editorial Anagrama, 1977), p. 29; Mary Salas and Merche Comabella, "Asociaciones de mujeres y movimiento feminista," in *Españolas en la Transición: De excluidas a protagonistas (1973–1982)*, p. 30; Di Febo, *Resistencia y movimiento de mujeres*, p. 158.

41. Lola G. Luna, "La representatividad del sujeto mujer en el feminismo de la Transición," p. 241; Romeu Alfaro, *El silencio roto*, p. 346. Di Febo argues that the MDM also attracted women from the Women's Division of the Falange and from Catholic organizations. *Resistencia y movimiento de mujeres*, p. 158.

42. Marisa Castro in Romeu Alfaro, *El silencio roto*, p. 252.

43. Informal conversation with Esperanza Martínez and Maruja Cazcarra, Zaragoza, Spain, 26 April 2001.

44. Lucía González in Romeu Alfaro, *El silencio roto*, p. 253.

45. Moreno, *Mujeres en lucha*, p. 30; Di Febo, *Resistencia y movimiento de mujeres*, p. 159.

46. Moreno, *Mujeres en lucha*, p. 30.

47. Salas and Comabella, "Asociaciones de mujeres y movimiento feminista," p. 30.

48. "He was said by persons with first-hand experience to have taken an active interest in the forceful and painful interrogations of Basque nationalists suspected of crimes. His interest was said to be especially marked when the suspect was a woman." Richard Eder, "Court-Martial of Fifteen Basques Today Troubling Spain," *New York Times*, 3 December 1970, p. 6. In March 2001, Pope John Paul II named as martyrs Melitón and other people believed to have been assassinated by the ETA.

49. Romeu Alfaro, *El silencio roto*, p. 351.

50. Richard Eder, "Court-Martial of Fifteen Basques Today Troubling Spain." The reporter says that of the fifteen, two are priests and two are women, one of whom is married to one of the other accused. According to the police reports, her husband "has separatist ideology but had not been active." He is said to belong "to [the] Young Catholic Workers [organization], often tak[ing] part in organizing Basque festivities."

51. Salas and Comabella, "Asociaciones de mujeres y movimiento feminista," p. 31.

52. Marisa Castro in Romeu Alfraro, *El silencio roto*, p. 251.

53. "Programa del Movimiento Democrático de Mujeres, extraído del Documento General de la III Reunión de Movimientos Democráticos de Mujeres (octubre 1971)," in Moreno, *Mujeres en lucha*, p. 106.

54. Moreno, *Mujeres en lucha*, p. 54. The question of women's rights emerged in many twentieth-century reformist and revolutionary struggles, but solutions were usually relegated to some time in the future, since differences within the core group were viewed as divisive. One of the best analyses of this phenomenon can be found in Maxine Molyneux, "Mobilization Without Emancipation? Women's Interests, the State, and Revolution in Nicaragua," *Feminist Studies* 11, no. 2 (summer 1985): 227–53.

55. Representative articles in the debate about what principles should govern the feminist movement can be found in Christina Crosby, "Dealing with Differences," 130–43; Drucilla L. Cornell, "Gender, Sex, and Equivalent Rights," 280–96 in *Feminists Theorize the Political*, ed. Judith Butler and Joan W. Scott (New York: Routledge, 1992); and Joan W. Scott, "Deconstructing Equality-Versus-Difference, Or, the Uses of Poststructuralist Theory for Feminism," *Feminist Studies* 14 (1988): 38–47. To elaborate on her earlier position, Joan W. Scott wrote "Feminist Reverberations," *Differences* 13, no. 3 (February 2003), arguing that groups like Women in Black, which began in Jerusalem in 1988, have been able to engage in collective action while recognizing that many differences divide them.

56. The best discussion of the struggles to establish a female subject within the battles for democracy in Spain can be found in Luna, "La representatividad del sujeto mujer en el feminismo de la Transición," pp. 242–44.

57. Moreno, *Mujeres en lucha*, p. 56.

58. "Otro juicio por adulterio: Rueda de prensa del Movimiento Democrático de Mujeres," *El Noticiero Universal* (Barcelona), 12 October 1976, p. 11. MDM leaders who had assembled for a meeting in Valencia gave a press conference, reasserting their commitment to the liberation of women. Many feminists, however, accused the MDM of being concerned only with undifferentiated social change and not with issues directly related to women. But the MDM denied these allegations. They admitted that the left was riddled with chauvinism and refused to permit men to be members of their organization, but they continued to oppose what they considered to be separatism.

59. Teresa Pàmies, *Maig de les dones: Crònica d'unes jornades* (Barcelona: Editorial Laia, 1976), p. 91.

60. Personal interview with Gloria Labarta, Zaragoza, Spain, 26 April 2001.

61. Personal interview with María Inmaculada Benito, Barcelona, Spain, 2 May 2001. The charges and depositions appear in Regulación General 2180, 2093. I am grateful to Gloria Labarta for providing these documents.

62. "El juicio por supuesto adulterio, a puerta cerrada," *Aragón Exprés* (Zaragoza), 6 October 1976; "El caso de la querella por adulterio: La acusación no piensa recurrir contra la absolución," *Aragón Exprés*, 15 October 1976. James M. Markham, "Adultery Law, Favoring Men, Issue in Spain," *New York Times*, October 17, 1976, p. 15; "Compañero de viaje," *Cambio 16* (Madrid),

18 October 1976; Stanley Meisler, "One Case Shocks Many: Spotlight on Spanish Adultery Laws," *Los Angeles Times,* 22 October 1976, p. 16.

63. Personal interview with María Inmaculada Benito, Barcelona, 2 May 2001.

64. Meisler, *Los Angeles Times,* 22 October 1976.

65. Gloria Labarta believes that Caneiro's family felt dishonored and wanted to punish Benito for having shamed them. Personal interview with Gloria Labarta, Zaragoza, Spain, 26 April 2001. For an analysis of the place honor continued to play in Spanish law and gender relations in the early twentieth century, see Nerea Aresti, "Changes in Gender Expectations in Spain (1900–1936)," Ph.D. diss., State University of New York, Stony Brook, 2000. See also her *Médicos, donjuanes y mujeres modernas: Los ideales de feminidad y masculinidad en el primer tercio del siglo XX* (Bilbao: Universidad del País Vasco, 2001).

66. Personal interview with Gloria Labarta, Zaragoza, Spain, 26 April 2001.

67. OSCAR, "Asociación de Mujeres Democráticas Aragonesas 'No a la discriminación,'" *Aragón Exprés,* 7 October 1976.

68. "Esta mañana en la Audiencia: El juicio por supuesto adulterio, a puerta cerrada," *Aragón Exprés,* 6 October 1976; "Juicio por presunto adulterio," *Heraldo de Aragón,* 7 October 1976. The best analysis of the ADMA can be found in Amparo Bella, "La ADMA, la AAM y las radicales del color morado: Organizaciones de mujeres en Zaragoza en los primeros años de la transición," in *Mujeres, regulación de conflictos sociales y cultura de la paz,* ed. Ana Aguado (Valencia: Universidad de Valencia, 1999), pp. 157–76.

69. A. Z., "Ante el próximo Congreso de Mujeres Juristas: La delegación de Zaragoza presentará un estudio sobre las discriminaciones en las leyes penales," *Heraldo de Aragón,* 21 October 1976.

70. R. Vazquez-Prada, "Representantes Aragonesas en el próximo Congreso de Mujeres Juristas," *Heraldo de Aragón,* 28 October 1976.

71. Montserrat Costa Villamayor, "La mujer adultera en España," *Heraldo de Aragón,* 12 October 1976; Marcuello, "A las puertas del año 2000: Querella por adulterio," *Andalán,* 15 October 1976.

72. "Juicio por adulterio en la Audiencia de Madrid: Doce mil firmas de mujeres solicitaron la supresión del delito," *Heraldo de Aragón,* 17 November 1976.

73. For the history of María Angeles Muñoz, see T. Rubio, "Trabajo: Mujer de la limpieza," *Diario de Barcelona,* 10 November 1976, p. 5; "Apoyo de Asociaciones de Vecinos: Sigue la solidardad con María Angeles Muñoz," *Diario de Barcelona,* 12 November 1976, p. 5; Teresa Rubio, "María Angeles Muñoz no llevó su hija al juzgado para entregarla a sus abuelos," *Diario de Barcelona,* 13 November 1976, pp. 7, 18; "Campaña feminista para actualizar la ley," *El País,* 13 November 1976, p. 19; Teresa Rubio, "Cuando los agentes fueron a buscarla a su domicilio, María Angeles Muñoz no entregó Yolanda a la policia," *Diario de Barcelona,* 14 November 1976, pp. 1, 5, 16, 17; "Crece la solidaridad con María Angeles," *Diario de Barcelona,* 17 November 1976, p. 5; "María Angeles Muñoz citada judicialmente," *Diario de Barcelona,* 18 No-

vember 1976, p. 5; "Manifestación por los derechos de la mujer," *Diario de Barcelona,* 19 November 1976, p. 5; "Los abogados de M. A. Muñoz piden un cambio de legislación," *Diario de Barcelona,* 20 November 1976, p. 5; M. F., "Una altra dona procesada per adulteri," *Avui,* 11 November 1976, p. 5; "Contra las discriminaciones legales: Encierro y manifestación de Mujeres en El Besós," *Hoja de Lunes,* 22 November 1976, p. 9; M. Pessarrodona, "Leyes machistas contra María Angeles Muñoz," *Vindicación feminista,* no. 7 (January 1977): 20.

74. News about the struggle against the adultery law permeated the foreign press. In addition to the articles that appeared in the United States, see José-Antonio Novais, "Les manifestations contre les condamnations pour adultère se multiplient," *Le Monde,* 26 November 1976, p. 3.

75. James Markham, "Spain Turns Back Old Adultery Law," *New York Times,* 4 June 1978; Oranich, "Cuestiones de urgencia: Anticonceptivos, divorcio, adulterio, amancebamiento," *Vindicación feminista,* no. 19 (January 1978): 19; Angelina Hurios, "La Mujer y el Derecho," in *Jornadas: Los años de lucha del movimiento feminista* (Barcelona: Icaria, 1985), p. 85; and Lola G. Luna, "La representatividad del sujeto mujer en el feminismo de la Transición," p. 245.

76. Lisa Baldez, *Why Women Protest: Women's Movements in Chile* (New York: Cambridge University Press, 2002), p. 131.

77. Antjie Krog, *Country of My Skull* (Johannesburg: Random House, 1998), p. 16.

EPILOGUE

1. Asociación de Madres de Plaza de Mayo, *Ni un paso atrás: Madres de Plaza de Mayo* (Bilbao: Txalaparta, 1997), p. 12.

2. Jürgen Habermas, *The Structural Transformation of the Public Sphere: An Inquiry into a Category of Bourgeois Society,* trans. Thomas Burger and Frederick Lawrence (Cambridge, Mass.: MIT Press, 1989). A sampling of feminist critiques of Habermas can be found in Johanna Meehan, ed., *Feminists Read Habermas: Gendering the Subject of Discourse* (New York: Routledge, 1995); and Belinda Davis, "Reconsidering Habermas, Gender, and the Public Sphere: The Case of Wilhelmine Germany," in *Society, Culture, and the State in Germany, 1870–1930,* ed. Geoff Eley (Ann Arbor: University of Michigan Press, 1994), pp. 397–426.

3. See esp. Joan B. Landes, *Women and the Public Sphere in the Age of the French Revolution* (Ithaca, N.Y.: Cornell University Press, 1988).

4. Elsa Barkley Brown, "Negotiating and Transforming the Public Sphere: African American Political Life in the Transition from Slavery to Freedom," *Public Culture* 7 (1994): 107–46.

5. Mary P. Ryan, *Women in Public* (Baltimore, Md.: The Johns Hopkins University Press, 1990); and her "Gender and Public Access: Women's Politics in Nineteenth-Century America," in *Habermas and the Public Sphere,* ed. Craig Calhoun (Cambridge, Mass.: MIT Press, 1999), pp. 259–88.

6. Nancy A. Hewitt, *Southern Discomfort: Women's Activism in Tampa, Florida, 1880s–1920s* (Urbana: University of Illinois Press, 2001).

7. Nancy Fraser, "Rethinking the Public Sphere: A Contribution to the Critique of Actually Existing Democracy," in *Habermas and the Public Sphere*, ed. Calhoun, p. 113.

8. Rosa Luxemburg, *The Mass Strike, the Political Party and the Trade Unions and the Junius Pamphlet* (New York: Harper Torchbooks, 1971). For a thoughtful consideration of her analysis of the mass strike, see Norman Geras, *The Legacy of Rosa Luxemburg* (London: New Left Books, 1976), pp. 111–31. Although Luxemburg presumed that the working class constituted the masses, she was concerned with the kind of collective political action in which people organized by community rather than around the point of production.

9. Sometimes protracted struggles and periods of intense violence preceded the transitions, as in South Africa. But the literature on transitions to democracy generally focuses on the high politics of the change, seldom taking into account how authoritarian governments cease to be viable. Significant works include . Juan J. Linz and Alfred Stefan, eds., *Problems of Democratic Transition and Consolidation: Southern Europe, South America, and Post-Communist Europe* (Baltimore, Md.: The Johns Hopkins University Press, 1996); and Guillermo O'Donnell, Philippe C. Schmitter, and Laurence Whitehead, eds., *Transitions from Authoritarian Rule: Latin America* (Baltimore, Md.: The Johns Hopkins University Press, 1986).

There is also a sizeable literature that talks about democratization as a process that includes the social movements of women. See Sonia Álvarez, *Engendering Democracy in Brazil: Women's Movements in Transition Politics* (Princeton, N.J.: Princeton University Press, 1989); and Elisabeth J. Friedman, *Unfinished Transitions: Women and the Gendered Development of Democracy in Venezuela, 1936–1996* (University Park: Pennsylvania State University Press, 2000).

10. Nicos Poulantzas, *The Crisis of the Dictatorships: Portugal, Spain, Greece*, trans. David Fernbach (London and Atlantic Highlands: New Left Books and Humanities Press, 1976), was one of the first to discuss the process by which seemingly invulnerable military dictatorships seem to implode, and he was also one of the few to see the importance of social movements to weakening authoritarian governments.

11. Fundación de Documentación y Archivo de la Vicaría de Solidaridad, Arzobispado de Santiago, "Casols de muertes explicadas como 'enfrentamientos,' denominados genericamente 'Operación Albania'"; "Ministro Juica procesa a alto oficial de Carabineros por caso Albania," *La Tercera* (Santiago), 12 December 2000, available at http://www.tercera.cl/diario/2000/12/12/extras/t-12.11.3a.EXT.ALBANIA.html (12 December 2000).

12. According to Fred A. López III, Poulantzas thought that "popular struggles were the 'determining factor.'" See "Bourgeois State and the Rise of Social Democracy in Spain," in *Transitions from Dictatorship to Democracy: Comparative Studies of Spain, Portugal, and Greece*, ed. Ronald H. Chilcote, Stylianos Hadjiyannis, Fred A. López III, Daniel Nataf, and Elizabeth Sammis (New York: Tailor and Francis Group, 1990), p. 35.

13. Elsa M. Chaney, *Supermadre: Women in Politics in Latin America* (Austin: University of Texas, 1979).

14. Jane S. Jaquette and Sharon L. Wolchik, eds., *Women and Democracy: Latin America and Eastern Europe* (Baltimore, Md.: The Johns Hopkins University Press, 1991); and Jane S. Jaquette, "Women's Movements and Democracy in Latin America: Some Unresolved Tensions," in *Women and the Transition to Democracy: The Impact of Political and Economic Reform in Latin America,* Latin American Program Working Papers, no. 211 (Washington, D.C.: Woodrow Wilson International Center for Scholars, 1994), pp. 1–11.

15. My translation of Elizabeth Jelin, "Los movimientos sociales en la Argentina contemporánea: Una introducción a su estudio," en *Los nuevos movimientos sociales/1* (Buenos Aires: Centro Editor de América Latina, 1985), p. 18.

16. Manuel Antonio Garretón, "Es posible la transición democrática en Chile?" speech delivered in Barcelona, 6–9 April 1988, published as *El plebiscito de 1988 y la transición a la democracia* (Santiago, Chile: FLACSO, 1988).

17. Demobilization of women is only part of the argument Maxine Molyneux raises in "Mobilization without Emancipation? Women's Interests, the State, and Revolution in Nicaragua," *Feminist Studies* 11, no. 2 (summer 1985): 227–53.

18. John Berger, "The Nature of Mass Demonstrations," *New Society* 23 (May 1968): 754–55.

Index

Compositor:	Impressions Book and Journal Services, Inc.
Text:	10/13 Sabon
Display:	Sabon
Printer and Binder:	Maple-Vail Manufacturing Group
Index:	Victoria Baker